PITTSBURGH THEOLOGICAL MONOGRAPHS

New Series

Dikran Y. Hadidian

General Editor

8

FREEDOM OR ORDER?

The Eucharistic Liturgy
in English Congregationalism 1645-1980

FREEDOM OR ORDER?

The Eucharistic Liturgy in English Congregationalism

1645-1980

By

Bryan D. Spinks

PICKWICK PUBLICATIONS
Allison Park, Pennsylvania
1984

4137 Timberlane Drive, Allison Park, PA 15101

Printed in the United States of America

The Companion volume to **Freedom or Order?** is **From the Lord and "the best Reformed Churches".** A study of the eucharistic liturgy in the English Puritan and Separatist traditions, 1550-1633. Edizione Liturgiche (Bibliotheca "Ephemerides Liturgicae" Subsidia), Rome, 1984.

Library of Congress Cataloging in Publication Data

Spinks, Bryan D.

Freedom or order?

(Pittsburgh theological monographs. New series; 8)
Bibliography: p.
Includes index.
1. Congregational Churches—Liturgy—History.
2. Liturgics—History. 3. Lord's Supper (Liturgy): History. I. Title. II. Series.
BX 7237.S65 1984 264'.058036 84-4248
ISBN 0-915138-60-3

Printed and Bound by Publishers Choice Book Mfg. Co.
Mars, Pennsylvania 16046

IN MEMORY OF MY MOTHER

JACQUELINE MARY SPINKS

CONTENTS

FORWORD

The subject of this study has so far received little serious attention from liturgical scholars, and it is high time that the omission was remedied. As the Roman Catholic and Anglican churches move towards a greater degree of flexibility and even freedom from set forms, it becomes more and more important to study the experience of those churches which have had a long tradition of "conceived prayer". It is also interesting to see how far the Free Churches have wished to borrow from set forms of worship.

This study is derived from a thesis for which Mr. Spinks was awarded the degree of Bachelor of Divinity by the University of Durham. He is a liturgical scholar of wide-ranging interests, and has published articles and edited texts in the patristic field as well as in Reformation and post-Reformation liturgy. He is, for example, the only English scholar to have written on Luther's reformed services for many years. I am very glad to commend this authoritative study by one of the most promising of our younger liturgists.

Oxford, October 1982 **Geoffrey Cuming**

PREFACE

This study is concerned to trace the changing structure and content of the Eucharistic liturgy within the English Independent, or Congregationalist, tradition. Any such study is undertaken with obvious limitations. A complete and comprehensive study would necessitate a consideration of every Congregational Church in England from its foundation until the present. Clearly such a study is not possible. What has been undertaken here is a study of the Eucharistic liturgy as far as it can be ascertained from the liturgical texts which the denomination has produced, supplemented by contemporary accounts. Of necessity it is selective, but probably no less representative of the trends in the denomination than, for example, are assessments of Eucharistic liturgy of the pre-fifth century Church.

I am greatly indebted to the following who have given me information, advice and encouragement in my researches: Mr. B. Honess, former librarian of the Congregational Memorial Hall Library; Rev. J. Phillips, Chairman and surviving member of the committee responsible for the 1936 **A Manual for Ministers;** Rev. J. M. Todd, who was responsible for the drafting of many of the more recent Congregational liturgies; Rev. Caryl Micklem, Rev. S. Gibbons, Rev. Dr. J. K. Gregory, Rev. Dr. G. Robinson, Rev. Wynford Evans; Bishop L. S. Hunter for the loan of a copy of the fifth edition of his father's **Devotional Services;** Mr. R. H. Bond, Assistant Archivist in the Essex Record Office; Rev. P. N. Williams; Rev. Dr. Erik Routley, former Chairman of the United Reformed Church Committee for Worship and Doctrine; the Clever Trust and the Brand Charitable Trust for grants toward the initial research; the Very Rev. R. C. D. Jasper who kindly read the draft; and Canon A. H. Couratin who first taught me to look at liturgical texts.

I would also like to thank my wife Linda for her patience while the work was being prepared for publication, and for keeping my daughter Rachel away from the manuscript.

January 1983

Bryan D. Spinks
Churchill College
Cambridge

ABBREVIATIONS

AC	Alcuin Club
BQR	British Quarterly Review
CHST	Congregational Historical Society Transactions
CQ	Congregational Quarterly
CQR	Church Quarterly Review
CYB	Congregational Year Book
ET	English Translation
JEH	Journal of Ecclesiastical History
JTS	Journal of Theological Studies
LR	Liturgical Review
MAL	C. O. Buchanan, **Modern Anglican Liturgies 1958-1968**, Oxford 1968
n.d.	no date of publication
n.p.	no place of publication
N.S.	New Series
SL	Studia Liturgica

Underlining in quotations represents italics in the original text.

Chapter One

INTRODUCTION

Independency, Puritans and Separatists

While it is generally agreed among historians that the English Independent, or Congregational tradition did not emerge as a distinct ecclesiastical movement until the tumultuous years of the 1640's, it has long been a matter of controversy as to the movement's precise origin. [1] Although many precursors have been suggested, [2] it is doubtful whether the emergence of Independency can be narrowly defined in terms of a specific date, a congregation, or a collection of writings; nor can the Independents be located in one particular social class or geographical place. The Independents of the 1640's were a diverse group of men and women. As Dr. G. F. Nuttall has pointed out, among their ministers, some were learned Fellows of Oxford and Cambridge, while others were men of very little learning; many had been in exile in the Netherlands and New England, while many others had not. Some Independent churches took their place as constituent parts of the Cromwellian establishment; others were loosely related to it; still others existed in separation. [3] Men such as John Bunyan and Vavasor Powell were at the same time Independents and Baptists.

There are hints from the leading Independents of the seventeenth century that a wider background for their origins is to be sought. Thomas Goodwin in a speech made when presenting Richard Cromwell with a copy of the **Savoy Declaration of Faith and Order** (14th October, 1658) explained:

> We (desired) in the first place to clear ourselves of that scandal, which not onely some persons at home, but of forein parts, have affixed upon us, viz. That Independentism (as they call it) is the sink of all Heresies and Schisms. We have therefore declared what hath been our constant Faith and Order, to be published to the World.

> And to shew our harmony with the most Orthodox at home and abroad, we have expressed our assent to that Confession of Faith which is the latest and the best; the sum of the Confession of all Reformed Churches, to which also the Churches of Scotland and New England have given their assent; namely, the Articles of Religion approved and passed by both Houses of Parliament after advice had with the Assembly of Divines, to which Confession for the substance of it, we have unanimously and through the Grace of Christ, without the least contradiction, assented and agreed.
>
> We have also with the same unanimity declared in matter of Order (that is, in Church-constitution and Government) and have set forth the main of our Principles and Practice; in which what we differ from our Brethren, will appear. We have also laid some foundations of Agreement with them, which we have from our hearts desired and endeavoured. [**4**]

Goodwin asserted that in matters of faith, the Independents were at one with "all Reformed Churches", that is, those Churches which followed the traditions of Calvin and Beza of Geneva, and to a lesser extent, Zwingli and Bullinger of Zurich; where they differed from their Reformed brethren was in matters of church constitution and government.

Another clue to the wider background of the origin of the Independents was given by five "Dissenting Brethren" in the **Apologeticall Narration**, 1643:

> And wee did then (i.e. in Holland), and doe here publiquely professe, we beleeve the truth to lye and consist in a middle way betwixt that which is falsely charged to us, Brownisme; and that which is the contention of these times, the authoritative Presbyteriall Government in all the subordinations and proceedings of it. [5]

Goodwin's appeal to the Reformed tradition, and the "Dissenting Brethren's" advocacy of a middle way between Presbyterianism and Brownism, point to the wider background of the sixteenth century Puritan and Separatist movements.

The terms "pure", "purify" and "purity" were in common use among the German and Swiss reformers, for it refuted the charge that they were innovators. It was the aim of the reformers to restore the church to its pristine state, and for their authority they appealed to Scripture. However, as to the extent of the purification demanded by Scripture, the reformers were sharply divided. In England the word "Puritan" came to be applied to those who followed the Swiss school of thought, represented by Donne's "Crantz", who

> . . . loves her onely, who at Geneva is call'd
> Religion, plaine, simple, sullen, yong,
> Contemptuous, yet unhansome; As among
> Lecherous humors, there is one that judges
> No wenches wholsome, but coarse country drudges. [6]

The Puritan believed that the sole authority and criterion for the Church was the literal text of the Bible:

> . . . the Word is a rule of faith, a canon to direct our lives. The Word is the judge of controversies, the rock of infallibility. That only is to be received for truth which agrees with Scripture, as the transcript with the original. All maxims in divinity are to be brought to the touchstone of Scripture, as all measures are brought to the standard. [7]

Since the Elizabethan Church retained many pre-reformation elements, and unscriptural names and offices, the Puritan believed that the English Reformation remained incomplete. The Elizabethan Church thus became a target for Puritan criticism, particularly from those who had spent some time in exile during Mary's reign. [8] Peter Toon writes:

> The origin of Elizabethan Puritanism is thus to be sought in the critical attitude of convinced Protestants to the Settlement of Religion. For their biblically-enlightened consciences the essential rock of offence was the large measure of continuity with the Roman Catholic past which persisted in the ministry and government of the Church as well as in its liturgy and church furnishings. Abroad they had seen the Reformed Churches of the Rhineland and Switzerland. They had become Bible Christians - that is they interpreted the Bible in the way that men like Calvin, Beza and Bullinger did. [9]

It has been pointed out, however, that Calvin had believed that the conjunction of Word and Spirit made the Scripture normative through the way in which they created and nourished faith; for many Puritans the efficacy of Scripture rested upon the identification of the text and the Spirit, through a conception of the Bible as verbally inspired and inerrant. In this conception, the English Puritan went beyond Calvin. [10]

Already by 1566 a number of clergymen had been suspended for "nonconformity" in matters of vesture. However, during the 1570's a more radical Puritanism emerged, its leaders including Thomas Cartwright, William Fulke, John Field and Thomas Wilcox. This radical Puritanism urged the establishment of a Presbyterian Church government, and some Puritan ministers organized themselves independently of the Established Church, forming a Presbyterian Classis system, and holding "Prophesyings" - a semi-public discussion of biblical passages.

In Cartwright's lectures on the Acts of the Apostles, the seeds of Separatism can already be seen. [11] If the Church of England refused to conform its ministry and discipline to that laid down in the New Testament, could it in fact be regarded as a Church at all? If it was not a true Church, then argued the Separatists, the faithful should withdraw. Whereas the Puritans strove for a Reformed National Church, the Separatists sought to establish local churches that were independent of the State, restricted to the godly in membership and autonomous in polity. They rejected the idea of a regional Church, Episcopal or Presbyterian; a Church was a gathered community of believers who covenanted together. From their members they elected the officers of Pastor (bishop), teachers, elders and deacons. Each congregation of believers was a complete manifestation of the catholic Church, and though fellowship with other such congregations was important, each congregation was autonomous. This doctrine, similar to that which was to become the hallmark of the Independents, and the point which separated them from their Reformed brethren, is usually associated with the names of Robert Browne, and Henry Barrow, John Greenwood and John Penry, though the latter three disassociated themselves from the writings of the former. [12] For their attack on the Queen's supremacy in the Church, Barrow and his colleagues, Greenwood and Penry, were executed for sedition. Their congregation was taken over by Francis Johnson, a Puritan minister converted by Barrow's writings.

Both Puritanism and Separatism were seedbeds for Independency. But another source were those whom Champlin Burrage called Independent Puritans, such as Henry Jacob, William Bradshaw and the leader of those who were later to become the Pilgrim Fathers, John Robinson. [13] These Puritans, while organizing themselves in covenanting communities similar to the Separatists, still recognized the Established Church as a true Church, and wished to remain in communion with it.

A precedent for such Churches was the existence of the "Stranger Churches" of London. In 1550 a congregation under the reformer John a Lasco had been given permission to organize itself independently of the English Church. In the Royal Charter of 1550 which established a Lasco's Church, the Superintendent and Ministers were granted the right "to practise, enjoy, use and exercise their own rites and ceremonies and their own peculiar ecclesiastical discipline, notwithstanding that they do not conform with the rites and ceremonies in our Kingdom". [14] A Lasco prepared his own order of Service and Discipline. Another similar congregation was to be found in Edward's reign at Glastonbury under Valerand Poullain. In Elizabeth's reign both the Dutch and

French Churches were permitted to worship freely according to their own customs; indeed, the Dutch Church in London was rumoured to be a hot-bed of Puritanism.

The Plumbers Hall congregation of 1567 seem to have considered themselves in the same category as these "Stranger Churches", [**15**] as did that of Henry Jacob in 1605. [**16**] It would seem that John Cotton, minister at Boston, Lincolnshire, who emigrated to New England in 1633 should also be placed in this group. Cotton had become convinced that the visible Church consisted in "visible Saints"; that its form was "a mutuall Covenant, whether an explicite or implicite Profession of Faith, and subjection to the Gospel of Christ in the society of the Church, or Presbytery thereof"; and that the "power of the keyes" belonged to each visible congregation. Cotton insisted that the Congregational Churches of New England were not Separatist Churches; they had indeed separated, but from the world, not the Church of England. [**17**] On the eve of his departure for New England, Cotton had converted Thomas Goodwin, Philip Nye and John Davenport to his views, and through reading his work **Of the Keyes of the Kingdom of Heaven,** 1644, John Owen came to accept "the Congregational way". Cotton claimed to have learned his views from three Puritans, Robert Parker, Paul Baynes and Dr. William Ames. [**18**]

During the 1630's many Puritans and Separatists fled from Archbishop Laud's attacks to the safety of Holland, where on account of the tolerance shown to religious exiles by the Dutch States General, they were able to put into practice some of their ideals. The English Merchant Adventurers in Holland had from time to time enjoyed the ministry of the Puritan Thomas Cartwright, the Separatist Robert Browne, and the Independent Puritan, Henry Jacob. Francis Johnson and the Barrowist congregation went to Middleburg, and then to Amsterdam; John Robinson's congregation settled in Leiden. There was also an English Reformed Church. This latter seems to have been English congregations organized into covenanting communities, but as Independent Puritan Churches, on good terms with the Dutch Reformed Church and being closely related to it, yet still retaining communion with the Church of England. It is thus that we find the scholar, Dr. Ames, and Henry Jacob at Leiden; John Paget at Amsterdam; Hugh Peters at Rotterdam; and the five "Dissenting Brethren"--Philip Nye, Thomas Goodwin, William Bridge, Jeremiah Burroughs and Sidrach Simpson--were connected with a gathered Church at Arnhem, which was in association with the English Reformed Church at Rotterdam. [**19**]

In the events of the 1640's many Puritans returned from exile to take part in the struggle against prelacy. Those who favored Independency were in a minority, and co-operated of necessity with the more numerous Presbyterians, for both wished to be rid of episcopacy. Where the Independents parted company with the rest of the Westminster Assembly of Divines was on ecclesiology, not faith. Indeed, when in 1658 the Independents, or "Congregational men" met at the Savoy to draw up their declaration of faith and order, the confession of faith was based directly upon the Westminster Confession. The changes have been summarized by Peter Toon, and while there was some doctrinal shift, the changes did not significantly alter the High Calvinism of the Westminster Confession. [20] The Declaration of Order certainly stated the Congregational polity of the Independents, but even this may be classified as "Decentralized Calvinism". [21] Rather than to attempt a precise account of the rise of Independency, it would seem that a broader origin is to be considered:

(1) In matters of faith, the Independents were Reformed Churchmen of the Puritan tradition, as is witnessed by their use of the "High Calvinist" Westminster Confession. Their theological origin is the Puritan movement. Hugh Peters, one of Cromwell's chaplains, and who was considered too dangerous to be pardoned after the Restoration, bequeathed his daughter **A Dying Father's Last Legacy to an Onely Child**, (1660), in which he advised her to gather "a little English Library" of Puritan authors--John Dod, Richard Sibbes, John Preston, William Gouge, Thomas Hooker, Thomas Goodwin and Richard Baxter among them. [22] These men included conformist and nonconformist Puritans, some Independent in conviction and some Presbyterian.

(2) In matters of ecclesiology, the Independent position was similar to that of the Separatists, and it was this factor which marked them out from other Puritans. However, as Peter Toon has pointed out, few of the leading Congregationalists of the 1650's wanted to trace their ancestry to the Separatists; they preferred to look to the influence of such men as John Cotton, Hugh Peters, William Bridge, Jeremiah Burroughs, Thomas Goodwin, Sidrach Simpson and Philip Nye. [23] Certainly in more recent times, Congregationalists have been willing to claim both Puritanism and Separatism as their matrix. [24]

The Puritan and Separatist Eucharistic Liturgies

The Independent tradition which emerged during the 1640's inherited not only the theology of Puritanism and Separatism, but also the liturgical traditions of both.

The Puritan liturgical tradition falls into two distinct groups: (a) Adaptations of the **Book of Common Prayer:** (b) The use of rites derived from other Reformed Churches.

(a) Adaptations of the **Book of Common Prayer**

The Puritan protest against the **Book of Common Prayer** was primarily concerned with the criteria for liturgical revision. The Prayer Book had been compiled using the old Latin rites as a basis, and these had been made scriptural as far as the Royal authority deemed it expedient. It may be expressed thus:

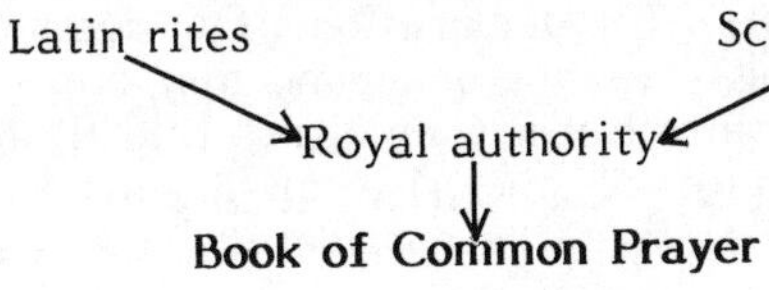

Since such things as vestments and the cross in Baptism were retained--for they were not actually forbidden by Scripture--the English reformation resembled a Lutheran approach to the authority of Scripture rather than a Calvinist approach. This approach was unacceptable to the Puritans, who looked to Geneva for their inspiration. In liturgical matters, as in all others, the Puritan's sole authority and criterion was the written word of God. William Bradshawe, giving a summary of Puritan beliefs, affirmed:

> IMPRIMIS, They hould and mainetaine that the word of God contained in the writings of the Prophets and Apostles, is of absolute perfection, given by Christ the head of the Churche, to bee unto the same, the sole Canon and rule of all matters of Religion, and the worship and service of God whatsoever. And that whatsoever done in the same service and worship cannot bee iustified by the said word, is unlawfull. [25]

Professor Horton Davies, in his study of the worship of the English Puritans, [26] has demonstrated that this attitude derives ultimately from two doctrines of Calvinism: the utter depravity of man, and the all-sufficiency of Scripture for salvation. The result was that the Puritans viewed the literal text of the Bible as a sufficient source for all matters liturgical, and diligently searched it to substantiate their belief. Professor Davies continues:

> The Scriptural citations warranting their main thesis are derived from both Testaments. Thus II Peter i 19-21 and II Timothy iii 15-17 urge the perfection of the Scriptures; while Matthew xv 9, 13, and Rev. xxii 19 are taken to forbid any man-made additons to the worship of God. Even more relevant and stronger proof-texts are found in the Old Testament. Exodus xx 4-6 (the Second Commandment), Joshua i 7, Deut. iv 2, xii 32, and Proverbs xxx

6 assert that God will not tolerate any additions to his worship since he is a "jealous God". [27]

As early as 1555 an English congregation in exile at Frankfurt had adapted the **Book of Common Prayer** to bring it into greater conformity to the Continental Reformed rites. [28] From 1578 onwards there appeared a series of printed Prayer Books bound with the Genevan Bible, but differing in some details from the enacted Prayer Book. The precise nature and implications of these books are disputed, [29] though A. E. Peaston has argued strongly that these books were Puritan abridgements, representing subtle attempts to alter the Prayer Book by minor changes which might go undetected. [30] Apart from these, it is fairly clear that many Puritan ministers made their own ad hoc alterations and omissions. Since individual Puritans differed as to their precise criticisms of the Prayer Book, different oral versions of the services must have flourished.

For the adaptation of the eucharist, we have the evidence of the 1555 **Liturgy of Compromise.** This adaptation omitted everything connected with the liturgical calendar. Thus the collect, Epistle and Gospel were replaced by "A Prayer for the Time, and the whole state of Christ's Church"; after the comfortable words, the sursum corda, preface, proper preface and sanctus disappeared. While the printed books which appeared after 1578 contain no alterations of significance in the eucharist, we know from the complaints in the Ecclesiastical Courts, together with the Puritans' own criticism, that similar ad hoc omissions continued to be made. [31]

(b) The use of rites derived from other Reformed Churches.

Of much more significance is the use the Puritans made of other Reformed rites. Already in 1550 an English translation of Calvin's rite had appeared, and prior to the exiles at Frankfurt adopting the adaptation of the Prayer Book called the **Liturgy of Compromise**, a liturgy had been compiled for their use by John Knox, William Whittingham, Anthony Gilby and John Fox, which was based upon the English edition of Calvin. [32] It proved to be too Reformed for many of the Anglicans, and when the **Liturgy of Compromise** was drawn up, Knox and his followers were expelled, and withdrew to Geneva. It was there that they reissued their liturgy, **The Forme of Prayers**, 1556, though it is more popularly known as Knox's Genevan Service Book. It was later adopted as **The Book of Common Order** in Scotland. However, we know that it was in use in the Plumber's Hall congregation in 1567, and revised editions with borrowing from the Dutch rite, were published in 1584 **(The Waldegrave Book)** and 1586, 87 and 1602 **(The Middleburg Book).** While there are important differences between Calvin,

The Forme of Prayers 1556, and the later editions, the general pattern of the eucharistic rites was as follows:

The Sunday Morning Service

A Confession of our synnes, framed to our tyme, out of the 9. chap. of Daniel.
or An other Confession, for all states and tymes.
Psalm.
Prayer for illumination.
(Lection and)
Sermon.
A Prayer for the whole estate of Christes Churche.
Lord's Prayer.
Creed
Psalm.
Aaronic Blessing and the Grace.

The Maner of the Lordes Supper

(after the Creed and psalm).
Institution Narrative.
Exhortation with excommunication.
Eucharistic Prayer.
Fraction and delivery; reading of Scripture during delivery.
Thanksgiving.
Psalm 103 or a similar psalm.
Blessing (from the Morning Service).

The basis of this rite was Calvin's Genevan liturgy, which in turn was based on the Strasbourg rite of Martin Bucer, and the Genevan rite of Farel. The former can be traced back through various reforms to the medieval mass, [33] whereas that of Farel was influenced by the medieval vernacular service called Prone. [34] H. O. Old, however, would maintain that Calvin's rite represents the quintessence of all continental Reformed rites:

> Like all liturgies, it has passed through many hands: Surgant, Zwingli, Marot, Luther, Oecolampadius, Schwarz, Farel, Geiler, Blarer, Capito, and Zwick. Like all true liturgies it has passed through just as many cities: Bern, Memmingen, Aigle, Neuchâtel, Ulm, Augsburg, Paris and Strasbourg. In each hand and in each city it has picked up a bit more polish and has joined itself a bit more closely to history. It is in a very real sense the liturgy not of Calvin, not of Geneva, but the liturgy of the Reformed Church. [35]

Already Calvin's rites had discarded many features which had become traditional in the eucharistic liturgy--Gloria in excelsis, salutations, Preface and sanctus, Agnus Dei, and the variable collect, Epistle and Gospel reflecting the liturgical calendar. The first part of the rite centered upon confession, preaching and intercession, while the eucharist itself was dominated by a lengthy exhortation, prefaced by the institution narrative read as a warrant for the rite. Furthermore, although "Word" and "Sacrament" were intended to belong together, the eucharist was celebrated only quarterly at Geneva, thus giving the impression that Word and Sacrament were separate elements.

A significant alteration by Knox and his group was the inclusion of a Eucharistic Prayer. This may well have been the work of Knox himself, as the first part of the prayer was adapted from Knox's own liturgy for Berwick on Tweed, 1550. [**36**] A feature of the later Waldegrave and Middleburg editions was the elaboration of the fraction.

Another Reformed rite used by some Puritans was that of the "Stranger Churches". That of Valerand Poullain's French congregation at Glastonbury was essentially Calvin's Strasbourg rite. [**37**] However, the London "Stranger Churches" under John a Lasco used a liturgy drawn up by a Lasco and Maarten Micron. [**38**] It seems to have been dependent upon Poullain's rite and a Lasco's knowledge of the rite of East Friesland. [**39**] The rite as published in a Lasco's **Forma ac Ratio**, 1555, was as follows:

Exhortation to Prayer.
Prayer before the Sermon.
Lord's Prayer.
Psalm.
Bible Lection.
Sermon.
Prayer after the Sermon, that the word may be inscribed in our Hearts.
Decalogue (Exodus 20).
Admonition to confession.
Confession.
Absolution.
Apostles' Creed.
General Prayer for the Church and World.
Lord's Prayer.
Psalm.
Commendation of the Poor and Aaronic Blessing.

The Lord's Supper followed the General Prayer:

Public reminder of those who are excluded.
Prayer.

Words of Institution.
Exhortation.
1 Cor. 5:7-8.
Fraction and delivery.
During the administration one of the ministers may read John 6, or 13, 14, or 15.
Words of Assurance.
Exhortation on the fruits of communion.
Thanksgiving.
Admonition.
Psalm.
Blessing.

Lastly, it is also clear that during the 1620's and 30's some Puritans in Holland used an English translation of the Dutch Reformed rite of Petrus Datheen. [40] This latter originated in 1566, being written for the Dutch congregation in the city of Frankenthal in the Palatinate, and in turn being based upon the Pfalz Liturgy of 1563. Datheen's provisions for a morning service are meagre--two prayers--but it seems fairly clear that this was provided as a directory rather than as a fixed rite. [41] The Eucharist itself was almost a word for word translation of that of the 1563 Pfalz liturgy.

Whereas the Puritans objected to a particular imposed liturgy, the Prayer Book, and not to printed liturgies as such, the Separatists objected to all set forms of prayer. The Separatists believed that prayer was a gift of the Spirit, and set forms of prayer quenched the Spirit. This concept of worship was closely connected with their ecclesiology. The true Church was founded upon the Word of God, and established by him, and filled with his Spirit. Where a Church was ordered according to God's Word, there true liturgy could be found. According to John Greenwood:

> The worde leitourgia signifieth publicum munus, ergon laon, the worck of, or for the people: that is the very execution of the ministeriall actions in the church, according to the worde of all the officers thereof, that is the practise of those ministeriall duties prescribed by Christ, we may every where reade. . . . Nowe, to make other leiturgia, is to lay an other foundation, and to make an other gospell, not that ther is an other gospell, but that ther are some willing to pervert the gospell of Christ. [42]

Liturgy in the narrower sense of prayer was the gift of the Holy Spirit, given to those called to exercise this gift. Even the Lord's Prayer was only an example, and not a prayer to be recited by heart. [43] It was a sin to attempt to quench the Spirit by using set forms of prayer.

While the Separatists, quite naturally, have left no texts of the prayers uttered in the Spirit, there are brief references in the writings of their leaders, and some descriptions found in depositions made before Ecclesiastical Courts.

According to Robert Browne, the morning worship included prayer, thanksgiving, reading of scripture, exhortation and edifying, with provision for discussion on subjects which were "doubtful & hard". [44] For the eucharist, there must be preparation and exhortation, and there were separate blessings over the bread and the wine. The service concluded with thanksgiving. [45]

The Barrowists seem to have spent a great deal of time expounding the Bible in their worship, and praying. [46] The eucharist seems to have been based upon the reading in 1 Cor. 11:23ff. As with the Brownists, there was a separate blessing over the bread and the wine.

Later Independency

Because of Independent opposition, it proved impossible for a strong Presbyterian government to be implemented, and thus during the Commonwealth each minister in his parish was virtually a law unto himself. Some ministers did organize themselves into voluntary Presbyterian church government, and Hexter has shown that some Independents co-operated in this. [47] But there was no central authority, and many sects of an unorthodox nature came into being--Quakers, Fifth Monarchy men, Muggletonians and Ranters among them. The Presbyterians blamed the Independents for these sects, and it was this charge that the **Savoy Declaration of Faith and Order** sought to rebuff.

After the Restoration in 1660, and the Great Ejectment of 1662, the Independents and the Presbyterians, together with the Baptists, shared the same lot, becoming Protestant Dissenters and harassed by harsh laws. It proved impossible in such circumstances for Presbyterians to set up a Presbyterian church government, and there was in fact little to distinguish Independents and Presbyterians. The main difference was that whereas the Presbyterian minister was ordained and placed over a congregation by other ministers, the Independent was ordained by the congregation; but this difference tended to disappear, Presbyterian Churches having Independent ministers and vice versa.

Aware that they shared the same faith, and that their differences and divisions were a poor testimony to their nonconformist position, attempts were made to bring the two bodies together, first by efforts on the part of Richard Baxter and John Owen, and later, more successfully, in the joint establishment of the

Merchant's Lecture at Pinners-Hall, founded in 1672, the establishment of the "Common Fund", 1690, and a theological rapprochment, the "Heads of Agreement" resulting in the "Happy Union" of 1691. But this unity was short lived; there were in fact serious theological differences growing between the two parties. The influence of Arminianism, Federal Theology and Amyraldism produced a moderate Calvinism, and in turn led to the Antinomianism and Neonomianism debates; Presbyterians such as Daniel Williams, as representatives of moderate Calvinism, found themselves in dispute with "High Calvinists" such as Richard Davis of Rothwell, Isaac Chauncy and Thomas Cole, on issues such as the Law of God, the satisfaction of Christ's death, and justification. Many moderate Calvinists among the Presbyterians also became influenced by Socinian and Arian ideas, and drifted into Unitarianism. On the other hand, as a reaction to moderate Calvinism, some Independents adopted what has been called "Hyper-Calvinism". [**48**] The two denominations tended to drift apart. On the whole, among Independents in the eighteenth century, those ministers who had been trained at an English Academy or a Scottish University, such as Isaac Watts and Philip Doddridge, were moderate Calvinists, while those self-taught theologians such as Joseph Hussey and Lewis Wayman tended to be "Hyper-Calvinists". [**49**]

Although these theological controversies ruled out union between the two denominations, the Independents realized the need for close co-operation amongst themselves in their opposition to the Established Church. In 1695, the Independents withdrew from the "Common Fund" and established their own "Congregational Fund". The London Board of Congregational Ministers was formed in 1727, "to take cognisance of everything affecting the interests of that Denomination, and of religion in general", and three years later the "Monthly Exercises of Congregational Ministers and Churches in the Metropolis" was started; in the eighteenth century various County Associations were also formed. [**50**] In 1831 many of the Independent Churches covenanted together to form the Congregational Union of England and Wales.

During the eighteenth century the ranks of the Independents were swelled by the Calvinist Methodists of George Whitefield and the Countess of Huntingdon's Connexion; these new congregations, which "subsided into Independent Churches", [**51**] were the product of the Methodist Evangelical Revival, and their Calvinism was far less rigid. It is of little surprise, therefore, that the **Declaration of Faith** of the Congregational Union of 1833 was rather different in its theological stance from that of the **Savoy Declaration**: that of 1833 has been described as "diluted Calvinism". [**52**]

Towards the end of the nineteenth century the denomination's Calvinism was further weakened by the impact of Biblical

Higher Criticism; as a direct result of this, many Congregationalists in the early decades of the present century became leading exponents of Liberal Theology or Modernism. [53] However, since the 1940's, the denomination has been influenced by the Neo-orthodox movement, or "Barthianism", which has led both to an emphasis on orthodox belief, and a re-emphasis of the Reformed origins of the denomination. It is this re-emphasis which underlies the new **Declaration of Faith** issued in 1967, [54] and also the reconstitution of the Congregational Union in 1966 to become the Congregational Church in England and Wales; as John Huxtable has said, by 1966 "Union" no longer adequately described them:

> Their awareness of mutual interdependence was so clear that they recognized in it sufficient similarities to the life of a local church to call it by the same name; and since in a local church all the members covenant with one another in the fellowship of the Church, the churches formed themselves into a Church by covenanting together. [55]

In the use of the Westminster Confession in the Savoy Declaration, the seventeenth century Independents affirmed that in matters of faith they were in agreement with their Presbyterian brethren, though subsequently union proved to be impossible. However, since 1933 Congregationalists had worked very closely with the Presbyterian Church of England (being the remnants of the seventeenth century Presbyterian congregations who did not become Unitarian, together with congregations of Scottish families who settled in England), in the hope that union might eventually be possible. By 1972 both Churches felt that union was possible, and by an Act of Parliament taking effect on the 5th October, 1972, the United Reformed Church came into being, comprised of a union between the Presbyterian Church of England, and most of the Covenanted Churches of the Congregational Church in England and Wales. Some congregations of Congregationalists felt that they could not surrender their principles of church polity to the new Church, and have continued as Independent Churches in the Congregational Federation. However, since the large majority of Congregational Churches have entered the United Reformed Church, this Church has a legitimate claim to be the successor of the Congregational men of the 1658 Savoy conference.

Independency and Liturgical Forms 1645 - 1800

Just as the Independent Puritans steered a middle way between Presbyterianism and Separatism in ecclesiology, so they steered a middle course in matters liturgical. Writers such as William Ames, John Robinson and John Cotton defended the gift of free prayer, and attacked the imposition of set forms. However, they did allow that in some circumstances set forms were justifiable. [56]

During the early debates of the Westminster Assembly, it became clear that the Independents would not agree to the imposition of a set liturgy, Reformed or otherwise. However, they were willing to assist in drawing up a directory for worship, following the general pattern of Reformed liturgy, and the result was the **Westminster Directory**, April 1645. The fact that set forms were permissable in some circumstances led to **A Supply of Prayer for Ships**, in which some of the Directory forms were turned into set prayer. [57]

Despite the promises of the Declaration of Breda of "a liberty to tender consciences, and that no man shall be disquieted or called in question for differences of opinion in matter of religion, which do not disturb the peace of the Kingdom", [58] the **Book of Common Prayer**, only slightly revised, was reintroduced with an Act of Uniformity in 1662. Those who could not conform were expelled, and hindered by the Conventicle Acts, the Five Mile Act and the Test Act. Although at the Savoy Conference 1661 an attempt had been made to accommodate moderate Presbyterian Puritans, the Savoy men of 1658 had no part in it, and simply waited for the naively optimistic Presbyterians to join them in their nonconformity. In a situation of persecution, sometimes with heavy fines and imprisonment, [59] it is not difficult to understand why the Independents rejected one of the major causes of their harassment, namely, prescribed liturgy. Philip Nye, John Bunyan and Vavasor Powell all rejected the imposition of set forms of prayer, and defended free prayer. [60] The Independent argument was systematically and forcibly set out by Dr. John Owen in his **A Discourse Concerning Liturgies and their Imposition**, 1661. Owen began with the Old Testament ordinances for worship; Scripture frequently declares:

> That the rites and ordinances of the worship in the Church (i.e. Jews) observed, were from the original in their nature carnal, and for the number many, on both accounts burdensome and grevious to the worshippers. . . [61]

The teachers and rulers of Israel increased these institutions. Jesus attacked these human practices:

> He freed them, by his teaching, from the bondage of Pharisaical, arbitrary impositions, delivering their consciences from subjection to any thing in the worship of God but his own immediate authority. [62]

The obligations of the Mosaical institutions, so Owen argued, were dissolved and taken away by Christ at his death; from that day all his disciples were made free from obligations in worship other than God's own institutions and commands. Many Jewish converts still adhered to the old institutions, "Partly for want of clear light and understanding in the doctrine of the person and office of the Messiah; partly through the power of those unspeakable prejudices which influenced their minds. . . " [63] The disciples and apostles also continued to observe these ceremonies until the time of the destruction of the Temple, "until the appointed season". [64] Some attempted to force the Gentiles to observe these ceremonies, but Paul defended the Gentiles, and he taught the full implications of the Liberty of Christ; Christ had abolished these man-made ceremonies. However, in succeeding ages an ignorance of the righteousness of God had resulted in the re-introduction of ceremonies in worship.

Owen next turned to consider what rules Christ himself gave for matters of worship. For the preaching of the Word and the administration of the Sacraments, he has given special gifts to some christians--grace and spiritual gifts from heaven. [65] Worship is spiritual. But he gave

> allowance unto, the framing of a stinted form of prayers and praises, to be read and used by the administrators of his ordinances in their administration of them? [66]

In Chapters 3-6 Owen considered this latter question. the Lord's Prayer, he conceded, was given to the apostles by Christ as a prayer. But it was given before the glorification of the Savior, at a time when he was "minister of the Circumcision". [67] Since then, the Church had received the Spirit. Furthermore, the Lord gave the prayer for private devotion; this is quite distinct from men giving long written forms for public worship. According to Owen, the argument from the Lord's Prayer to imposed written liturgy was an invalid one.

Owen then proceeded to examine the antiquity and authenticity of the classical liturgies. Several texts were known by this time. A Latin and Greek version of St. Basil and St. John Chrysostom was printed in Venice in 1528; [68] a Greek version of St. James was printed in 1560, and a Latin version in the **Bibliotheca patrum** in 1575. [69] Three Anaphoras of the Ethiopic Rite were published in 1548, [70] and Apostolic Constitutions was well known. [71] Furthermore, **Bibliotheca patrum** also contained a version of St. Mark's Liturgy, and a Romanized Byzantine rite called the Liturgy of St. Peter. [72]

Owen's consideration of the first three centuries led him to conclude:

> It doth not, then, appear, for aught as I can yet discover, that there was any attempt to invent, frame, and compose any liturgies or prescribed forms of administering the ordinances of the gospel, exclusive to the discharge of that duty by virtue of spiritual gifts received from Jesus Christ, much less for an imposition of any such forms on the consciences and practice of all the ministers of the churches within the time mentioned. [73]

The Apostles did not compose liturgies; and Justin Martyr was quoted with approval:

> This was, it seems the liturgy of the church in the days of Justin Martyr; they called upon God with prayer and thanksgivings, according to the abilities they had received. [74]

"Pourth out of his ability" (hose dunamis auto anapempei) Owen took to mean that prescribed forms of worship were unknown to Justin. [75] Owen was not impressed by the selection of the classical texts available in **Bibliotheca patrum**:

> It is not worth our stay to consider what is pretended concerning the antiquities of liturgies, from some yet extant that bear the names of the apostles or evangelists. There is one that is called by the name of James, printed in Greek and Latin; another ascribed unto Peter, published by Lindanus; one also to Matthew, called the Ethiopic; another to Mark; which are in the Bible P.P. (**Bibliotheca patrum**) . . . They must be strangers to the spirit, doctrine and writings of the apostles, who can impose such trash upon them as these liturgies are stuffed withal. [76]

In particular Owen considered the Liturgy of St. James. He readily acknowledged that "some passages and expressions of it are used by Cyril of Jerusalem in his Mystagog V. [77] Like most modern scholars, Owen rejected the idea that the liturgy was composed by the apostle James; however, whereas most scholars accept that Cyril knew a rite similar to that of St. James, Owen argued in another vein; a liturgy such as St. James could not have existed in the time of Cyril, and the use of the words homoousios and theotokos proved it to be post-nicene. He concluded:

> Yea, it is most probable, that whosoever was the composer of that forged liturgy, he took those passages out of those reputed writings of Cyril, which were known in the church long before the name of the other was heard of. [78]

His final judgment on these texts was quite unequivocal:

> We need not any longer stay to remove this rubbish out of our way. [**79**]

In the West, explained Owen, the Roman rite came to prevail. At the Reformation when God's light again shone, reforms were made, and the **Book of Common Prayer** was made as an interim device.

However, having established that forms of written liturgy are late, Owen did not for this reason attack the **Book of Common Prayer**, nor on account of its Roman origin; rather, having established the liberty of Christ, he objected to the imposition of set forms, including penalties attached for non-use. [**80**] In the remainder of the treatise, Owen was concerned to demonstrate that although someone may use a set liturgy if his conscience allows him, it is against the liberty and authority of Christ to impose set forms upon others; with an Act of Uniformity, the King and Parliament were placed above the authority of Christ. [**81**] On the imposition of set forms he concluded:

> It hath no institution or appointment by Jesus Christ, it is wholly of men; there is nothing antecedent unto its imposition that should make it necessary to be imposed; a necessity of its observation is induced upon and by its imposition, which is directly destructive to our liberty in Jesus Christ. [**82**]

With the penalties of the Act of Uniformity, together with other repressive Acts, it is hardly surprising that the Independents adopted a militant anti-liturgical attitude. In the years immediately after "Black Bartholomew", Independency and liturgy were incompatible concepts. The post-Restoration Independents were not, therefore, like the later non-juring divines, fascinated by the classical liturgies; [**83**] likewise, the abortive attempt at Comprehension by a revision of the Prayer Book in 1689, had no appeal to them; [**84**] nor did the many Unitarian and Semi-Arian revisions of the Prayer Book by Dissenters in the eighteenth century interest them. [**85**] It was with considerable naivety that the writer of the Preface of **A New Form of Common Prayer**, 1753, believed that a revision of the Prayer Book would bring back the Independents to the Church of England. [**86**]

Nevertheless, in the eighteenth century there was a mellowing of attitudes. Independents such as Isaac Watts and Philip Doddridge could approach the subject with less bitterness, for they had been born into dissent, and with the accession of the House of Hanover, enjoyed some relief from the Law. Thus, for example, in his **A Guide to Prayer**, 1716, Watts attempted to steer a middle course between what he regarded as two extremes. Considering the neglect among Dissenters on the art of prayer, Watts stated:

> I am persuaded that one reason of this neglect has been the angry zeal for parties among us, which has discouraged men of sober and moderate principles from attempting much on this subject, while the zealots have been betrayed into two extremes. Some contend earnestly for precomposed set forms of prayer, and will worship God no other way. These have little need of any other instructions but to be taught to read well, since the words, matter, and method of their prayers are already appointed. Other violent men, in extreme opposition to them, have indulged the irregular wanderings of thought and expression, lest by a confinement to rules they would seem to restrain the Spirit, and return to carnal ordinances. [87]

While allowing that set forms of prayer were sometimes necessary for some people, Watts felt that such forms do quench the Spirit. [88] Nevertheless, Watts was equally critical of spontaneous prayer, addressed to God without thought or preparation. His preference was for "Conceived or free prayer" which was thoughtfully worked out beforehand. His treatise offered guides under the headings Invocation, Adoration, Confession, Petition, Pleading, Profession or Self-Dedication, Thanksgiving, Blessing, and "Amen", with examples. The key note was preparation.

A moderate approach is also to be found in Philip Doddridge. [89] While assisting in the Chapel of Lady Huntingdon at Ashby-de - la - Zouch, Doddridge even used the Prayer Book. [90]

Prejudice against set forms was also further eroded by three distinct factors. First, the gradual introduction of hymns into Independency--however scriptural--meant that set forms of worship were now being used. If written hymns could be used, why not prayers? Second, there was an awareness that some Puritans in the past had used set liturgies. A reprint of the Genevan Service Book appeared in **The Phenix** in 1708, and of much greater significance, Dr. Daniel Neal, Pastor at Aldersgate Street, London, published **The History of the Puritans**, volume three of which (1736) gave the **Westminster Directory** in its entirety. Independents who were interested in their historical origin were thus reminded by Neal of the liturgical tradition which was rightly theirs. [91] Third, some Calvinist Methodist congregations, founded by Whitefield and Lady Huntingdon, became Independent Churches, and brought with them to the denomination the **Book of Common Prayer**. [92]

The Liturgical Revival 1800 - 1975

The nineteenth century saw a Liturgical revival in Independency. In contrast to the previous 150 years, nineteenth century Congregationalists (as they were now known) not only produced books, pamphlets and essays on the subject of liturgical worship, but a number of printed liturgies appeared for use within the denomination.

Two important publications in the former category were **A New Directory**, 1812, and Thomas Binney's edition of Charles Baird's **Eutaxia** under the title of **A Chapter on Liturgies: Historical Sketches**, 1856. The first, as the Preface acknowledged, had been suggested by Neal's reprint of the **Westminster Directory**, and was concerned to offer suggestions to improve the general presentation of worship. The second work was more concerned with the historical liturgies of the Calvinist tradition. Baird's work had been addressed to American Presbyterians, but Binney addressed the work to his fellow Congregationalists. In his Preface Binney wrote:

> I can imagine there will be many who will learn from it with surprise the views entertained respecting the use of Liturgical forms by those of the Reformers where followers in this country have long repudiated everything of the sort. The sections on CALVIN and KNOX will to some be especially interesting; . . . There are those who will be surprised to find that Calvin not only approved of forms of prayer, but that he lamented the lengths to which some had gone in rejecting altogether certain ecclesiastical rites and customs; [93]

He also noted:

> some of the English Puritans and Separatists used the prepared Continental forms in their secret meetings; and that latter Nonconformists had no objection to a Liturgy <u>as such</u>, but only wished some changes to be made in that which was in use,--that it should not be <u>exclusively</u> enforced, that there should be the means of giving variety to the services, and the opportunity afforded for free prayer. [94]

The implications of this work formed the title of an Appendix by Binney, "Are Dissenters to have a Liturgy?", a title which put very succinctly one of the questions with which many nineteenth century Congregationalists were concerned. Over the next decades the issue was frequently debated. A Congregational Union Tract, **Conduct of Public Worship**, 1845 had been adamant that liturgical services were pernicious; [95] J. S. Pearsall was against their use, [96] and the eminent minister of Carr's Lane, Birmingham, R. W. Dale, while admitting that there was nothing inconsistant between Congregationalism and a liturgy, expressed the opinion that the use of the latter was out of harmony with the genius of the denomination. [97] But equally, Christopher Newman Hall was far from being alone in urging the use of liturgies. [98] One of the reasons seems to have been a dissatisfaction with the type of free prayer being offered by ministers in the denomination, and the need to improve and make more acceptable Congregational worship; to render it fitting, devout, edifying; to make it attractive, fuller, richer, more impressive, deeper; to give it comeliness and decorum. [99] There was need for "beauty" in worship, and a higher aesthetic standard. [100]

Despite the view of R. W. Dale, several liturgies appeared for use by Congregationalists. Some of these were "Biblical Liturgies"--services composed purely from scriptural verses; others were liturgies which were clearly based upon the **Book of Common Prayer**; a few were worthy independent compositions. The following list, which does not claim to be exhaustive, gives some indication of this liturgical revival:

1847	**The Congregational Service Book. A Form of Public Worship designed for the use of the Independent and other Nonconformist Bodies in Great Britain.**
1855 ff.	**A Biblical Liturgy,** by David Thomas. Several editions
nd.	**A Biblical Service for Prayer for the House of the Lord.**
1864	**The Book of Common Prayer Adapted for the Use of the Congregational Church, Finchley Common.**
1867	**Free Church Service Book.**
1867	**The Book of Common Prayer and Administration of Baptism and the Lord's Supper, with other services prepared for use in the Evangelical Churches by ministers and members of the Established and Nonconformist Churches.**
1869	**A Form of Morning and Evening Service, for the Use of Free Churches.**
1870	**Forms submitted for the use of Nonconformist Churches.**
1874	**The Liturgy of the Church of England** (Abridged), by David Thomas.
1879	**Liturgies for Divine Worship.**
1880 ff.	**Devotional Services for Public Worship.** John Hunter. Several editions.
1891	**Manual of Congregational Worship.** J. L. Pearse.
1895	**Devotional Services for use in Mill Hill School Chapel.**
1896	**Intercessory Services for aid in Public Worship,** P. T. Forsyth.
1897	**Let us Pray.** ed. C. S. Horne and T. H. Darlow, 2nd edition.
1897	**The Free Church Prayer Book,** J. Mountain.

Of these, the liturgy by John Hunter was by far the most original, and the most influential in the denomination.

The Liturgical revival of the nineteenth century has continued into the twentieth century. Liturgical forms have continued to be issued by individuals, such as C. H. Davis, **Orders of Service for the Solemnization of Matrimony, The Baptism of Infants, The Burial of the Dead and the Ordinance of the Lord's Supper**, Isle of Wight 1909, and G. H. Russell's **Intercession Services for Congregational Use in Public Worship,** 1923. By far the most famous individual enterprise was the **Divine Service** of Dr. W. E. Orchard, 1919 and 1926, which was based on Catholic liturgical forms, and used by Orchard at the King's Weigh House, Mayfair with Catholic ceremonial. However, the Congregational Union itself also produced forms--**Book of Congregational Worship**, 1920 and **A Manual for Ministers**, 1936.

These latter two books were marked by a dependence upon the **Book of Common Prayer**, and the influence of Liberal Theology. However, both the Ecumenical and the Liturgical Movements began to make some impact on the denomination. In the same year that **A Manual for Ministers** appeared, a collection of essays edited by Nathaniel Micklem was published under the title **Christian Worship.** As well as the philosophy of worship, the Old Testament and Jewish backgrounds, and the New Testament data, the collection contained a sympathetic appraisal of the early texts of the Didache, Justin Martyr, Hippolytus' **Apostolic Tradition** and Ambrose, and of the Roman Catholic Tridentine Mass and the Orthodox Liturgy. The essays also included a consideration of the liturgical work of some of the Reformers, pointing out particularly the Calvinist background of the Puritans and their Free Church successors.

A far richer compilation, drawing upon Classical and Reformation liturgical sources, was published by John Huxtable, John Marsh, Romily Micklem and James M. Todd, entitled **A Book of Public Worship,** 1948. A companion volume, **Prayers and Services for Christian Festivals,** by James M. Todd appeared in 1951. The influence of these two books was such that in 1959 the Congregational Union issued for the denomination **A Book of Services and Prayers,** which abandoned the ethos of **A Manual for Ministers,** and followed closely that of the 1948 and 1951 publications.

Congregationalists had taken an active part in the Faith and Order discussions of the World Council of Churches, and have contributed to the discussions of worship and liturgy. The denomination was also represented on the Joint Liturgical Group, an English ecumenical liturgical group which first met in 1963, and which produced essays (1965), a Calendar and Lectionary (1967), a Daily Office (1968), Services for Holy Week (1971) and a statement on the structure of Christian Initiation and the Eucharist (1972). The denomination itself formed a Liturgical Group in 1964, subsequently to become the Liturgical Committee, 1966 and the Worship Committee, 1967. The Committee produced a Eucharistic liturgy which was published in 1970. Amongst individual ventures was **Contemporary Prayers for Public Worship**, 1967, being the collective work of Anthony Coates, John Gregory, Caryl Micklem, William Sewell, David Stapleton, Roger Tomes and Brian Wren. These prayers were in modern English, abandoning the "Thee" form of address.

With the formation of the United Reformed Church in 1972, some Congregationalists refused to enter this union, and formed the Congregational Federation. By 1974 the Federation had taken no steps to produce any new liturgical compilations. The United Reformed Church, on the contrary, has produced liturgical forms, the first being a Eucharistic liturgy under the title **Book of Order for Worship**, 1974. However, the General Assembly of the United Reformed Church had expressed a desire for services for congregational use, [**101**] while the 1974 Order was for the ministers' guidance. The desire for a service for congregational use was partly met by **New Church Praise** 1975, a hymn book supplement at the back of which was printed the new communion service. It could be argued that with **New Church Praise** the early Puritan desire was fulfilled: the people are provided with "common prayer", allowing variations and extemporary prayer, and without an Act of Uniformity. A complete book of worship, **A Book of Services**, was published in 1980.

It is the purpose of this study to trace in detail the shape of the Eucharistic liturgy--Word and Sacrament--from the 1645 Westminster Directory, to the first Eucharistic order produced by the United Reformed Church.

NOTES

1. G. F. Nuttall, **Visible Saints**, Oxford 1957; G. Yule, **The Independents in the English Civil War**, Cambridge 1958; R. Tudur Jones, **Congregationalism in England 1662-1962**, London 1962.

2. F. J. Powicke, **Robert Browne Pioneer of Modern Congregationalism**, London 1910; C. Burrage, **The Early English Dissenters**, 2 vols., Cambridge 1912; A. Peel, **The First Congregational Churches**, Cambridge 1920; E. Troeltsch, **Protestantisches Christentum und Kirche in der Neuzeit** Die Kultur der Gegenwart,

1: IV, 1,2., Halfte 1922, 590; C. Hill and E. Dell, **The Good Old Cause: The English Revolution of 1640-60: Its causes, course and consequence,** Oxford 1950; B. Gustafsson, **The Five Dissenting Brethren,** Lund 1955; R. P. Stearns, **Congregationalism in the Dutch Netherlands,** Chicago 1940.

3. G. F. Nuttall, op.cit., 8; see also the discussion in G. Yule, op.cit.

4. Quoted in A. G. Matthews, **The Savoy Declaration of Faith and Order,** London 1959, 12-13.

5. Thomas Goodwin, Philip Nye, William Bridge, Jeremiah Burroughes and Sidrach Simpson, **An Apologeticall Narration,** London 1643, 24; called "Dissenting Brethren" on account of their dissent from the proposed Presbyterian form of church government.

6. John Donne, "Satyre on Religion".

7. Thomas Watson, **A Body of Divinity,** 1692, Banner of Truth Trust edition, London 1970, 30.

8. See **Puritan Manifestoes,** ed. W. H. Frere and C. E. Douglas, London 1907.

9. P. Toon, **Puritans and Calvinism,** Swengel, Pennsylvania 1973, 12.

10. P. Toon, **Hyper-Calvinism,** London 1967, 16.

11. See P. Collinson, **The Elizabethan Puritan Movement,** London 1967; Cf. B. R. White, **The English Separatist Tradition from the Marian Martyrs to the Pilgrim Fathers,** Oxford 1971.

12. C. Burrage, **The True Story of Robert Browne,** Oxford 1906; B. R. White, op.cit.; ed. L. H. Carlson, **The Writings of Henry Barrow 1587-1590,** London 1962.

13. C. Burrage, **The Early English Dissenters,** vol. 1, 281ff.

14. The Charter is given in J. Lindeboom, **Austin Friars. History of the Dutch Reformed Church in London 1550-1950.** The Hague 1950.

15. **The Remains of Edmund Grindal,** Parker Society, London 1843, 203-4; C. Burrage, op.cit., vol. 2, 13.

16. C. Burrage, op.cit., vol. 1 286.

17. J. Cotton, **The Way of Congregational Churches Cleared,** 1648. Cited in C. Burrage, op.cit., vol. 1, 361-2.

18. Ibid.

19. B. Gustafsson, op.cit., 19-28.

20. P. Toon, **Puritans and Calvinism**, 52-84.

21. G. Yule, op.cit., 11.

22. Quoted in G. S. Wakefield, **Puritan Devotion. Its Place in the Development of Christian Piety**, London 1957, 3.

23. P. Toon, op.cit., 72.

24. R. Tudur Jones, op.cit.; ed. N. Micklem, **Christian Worship**, Oxford 1936.

25. W. Bradshawe, **English Puritanism. Containing the main opinions of the rigidist sort of those that are called Puritans in the realme of England**, London 1605.

26. H. Davies, **The Worship of the English Puritans**, Oxford 1948.

27. Ibid., 50.

28. H. J. Wotherspoon and G. W. Sprott, **The Liturgy of Compromise used in the English Congregtion at Frankfurt**, Edinburgh 1905.

29. J. F. Gerrard, **Notable Editions of the Prayer Book**, Wigan 1949, 13-15; P. Collinson, op.cit., 365.

30. A. E. Peaston, **The Prayer Book Tradition in the Free Churches**, London 1964, 16-32.

31. Ronald Marchant, **The Puritans and the Church Courts in the Diocese of York 1560-1642**, London 1960; **A Parte of a Register**, Middleburg 1593; The Seconde Parte of a Register, Morrice Collection A,B,C, Dr. William's Library, London.

32. W. D. Maxwell, **The Liturgical Portions of the Genevan Service Book**, Edinburgh 1931, London 1965.

33. L. Büchsenschütz, **Histoire des Liturgies en Langue Allemande dans l'Eglise de Strasbourg au XVIe siècle**, Cahors 1900; W. D. Maxwell, op.cit.

34. For Farel, see ET in Bard Thompson, **Liturgies of the Western Church**, New York 1962; from Prone, see F. Schmidt-Clausing, **Zwingli als Liturgiker**, Göttingen 1952.

35. H. O. Old, **The Patristic Roots of Reformed Worship**, Zurich 1975, 96.

36. P. Lorimer, **John Knox and the Church of England**, London 1875, 290-2.

37. A. C. Honders, **Valerandus Pollanus Liturgia Sacra (1551-1555),** Kerkhistorische Bijdragen 1, Leiden 1970.

38. Ed. A. Kuyper, **Joannis a Lasco Opera,** 2 vols., Amsterdam 1866, vol. 2,; W. F. Dankbaar, Marten Micron, **De Christlicke Ordinancien der Nederlantscher Ghemeinten te Londen (1554),** Kerkhistorische Studien Deel VII. 's-Gravenhage 1956.

39. A Sprengler-Ruppenthal, **Mysterium und Riten nach der Londoner Kirchenordnung der Niederlander**, Köln 1967.

40. C. Burrage, op.cit., vol. 2; King Charles to Sir Henry Vane, November 1629, State Papers 16, vol. 152, fol. 74.

41. **Forme om het heylighe Avendtmael te houden;** H. Hageman, "The Liturgical Origins of the Reformed Church", in, ed. J. H. Bratt, **The Heritage of John Calvin,** Grand Rapids, Michigan 1973; J. M. Maxwell, **Worship and Reformed Theology.** The Liturgical Lessons of Mercersburg, Pittsburgh, Pennsylvania 1976, 53-54.

42. John Greenwood, **An Answere to George Gifford's Pretended Defence,** in, ed. Leland H. Carlson, **The Writings of John Greenwood 1587-1590,** London 1962, 73-74.

43. Ibid., 44-45.

44. Robert Browne, **A True and Short Declaration,** in, ed. L. H. Carlson and A. Peel, **The Writings of Robert Harrison and Robert Browne,** London 1953, 422.

45. Ibid., 280-284.

46. Ed. L. H. Carlson, **The Writings of John Greenwood 1587-1590,** 294-299; **The Writings of John Greenwood and Henry Barrow 1591-1593,** 319; **The Writings of Henry Barrow 1587-1590,** London 1962, 383.

47. J. H. Hexter, "The Problem of the Presbyterian Independents", in **Reappraisals in History,** London 1961.

48. For the use of this term and a discussion on the complicated labyrinth of theological data, see P. Toon, **Hyper-Calvinism.**

49. Ibid, 147-148.

50. A. Peel, **These Hundred Years.** A History of the Congregational Union of England and Wales 1831-1931. London 1931, 6.

51. Walter Wilson, cited by Peel, in ibid., 22.

52. Ibid, 75.

53. W. B. Glover, **Evangelical Nonconformists and Higher Criticism in the Nineteenth Century,** London 1954; J. W. Grant, **Free Churchmanship in England 1870–1940,** London n.d.

54. Text in **Christian Confidence.** Theological Collections 14. S.P.C.K., London 1970.

55. J. Huxtable, "God's Sovereignty over the Church", in ibid., 121–139, 134.

56. William Ames, "Of Instituted Worship", in **The Marrow of Sacred Divinity,** London 1642, 271; John Robinson, "Of Written Liturgies", in A Just and Necessary Apology, 1625, in **Works,** ed. R. Ashton, London 1851, vol. 3; J. Cotton, **A Modest and Cleare Answer to Mr. Balls Discourse of Set Formes of Prayer,** London 1642.

57. Bryan D. Spinks, "The Supply of Prayer for Ships: A Forgotten Puritan Liturgy", in, The Journal, United Reformed Church History Society, 1:5 (1975), 139–148.

58. Gee and Hardy, **Documents Illustrative of English Church History,** London 1896, 585-588, 587.

59. Tudur Jones, op.cit., 76ff.

60. P. Nye, **Beames of Former Light,** London 1660; John Bunyan, **A Discourse Touching Prayer,** London 1662; Vavasor Powell, **Common-Prayer-Book. No Divine Service,** London, 2nd. ed. 1661.

61. J. Owen, A Discourse Concerning Liturgies and their Imposition, 1661, in **The Works of John Owen,** ed. W. H. Goold, vol. 15, Banner of Truth Trust edition 1966, Chap. 1, p. 3.

62. Ibid., 4.

63. Ibid., 5.

64. Ibid., 6.

65. Chap. 2, ibid., 11.

66. Ibid., 12.

67. Chap. 3, ibid., 14.

68. F. E. Brightman, **Liturgies Eastern and Western,** vol. 1 Eastern Liturgies, Oxford 1896, lxxxiii–lxxxvi.

69. Ibid., xlviii.

70. J. M. Harden, **The Anaphoras of the Ethiopic Liturgy**, London 1928, 13.

71. Brightman, op.cit. xviii.

72. Ibid., lxiii, xci.

73. Owen, op.cit., Chap. 5, ibid., 21.

74. Ibid., 23.

75. Ibid., 24.

76. Ibid., 20.

77. Ibid., 22; Mystogogical Catechesis 5.

78. Ibid.

79. Ibid., 20.

80. Chap. 7, ibid., 33-34.

81. Chap. 8, ibid., 44.

82. Chap. 10, ibid., 55.

83. W. Jardine Grisbrooke, **Anglican Liturgies of the Seventeenth and Eighteenth Centuries**, AC, London 1958.

84. T. J. Fawcett, **The Liturgy of Comprehension, 1689**, AC Southend-on-Sea 1973.

85. A. Elliott Peaston, **The Prayer Book Reform Movement in the XVIII th. Century**, Oxford 1940.

86. Ibid., 43.

87. I. Watts, **A Guide to Prayer**, in **The Works of the Rev. Isaac Watts, D.D.**, 7 vols., Leeds 1800, vol. IV, 111.

88. Ibid., 190.

89. P. Doddridge, **Lectures on Divinity**, in **The Works of the Rev. P. Doddridge D.D.**. 5 vols., Leeds 1804, vol. 5, Lecture cvciv.

90. **The Life and Times of Selina Countess of Huntingdon**, by a member of the Houses of Shirley and Hastings, 2 vols. 1839, vol. 1, 153, 171.

91. D. Neal, **A History of the Puritans**, 4 vols., London 1732-38.

92. C. E. Watson, "Whitefield and Congregationalism", in CHST 8 (1920-1923), 171-180, 237-245; Edwin Welch, **Two Calvinist Methodist Chapels 1743-1811,** London Record Society, Leicester 1975.

93. C. W. Baird, **A Chapter on Liturgies: Historical Sketches,** with an Introduction and Appendix by Thomas Binney, London 1856, ix.

94. Ibid., ix-x.

95. **Conduct of Public Worship,** Congregational Union Tract, No. XIV, 1845.

96. J. S. Pearsall, **Public Worship,** London 1867.

97. R. W. Dale, **A Manual of Congregational Principles,** London 1884, 164.

98. CYB, 1853, 58.

99. Binney, **A Chapter on Liturgies,** xxiv; **Conduct of Public Worship,** 1; J. S. Pearsall, **Public Worship,** 3; W. H. Willans, "Attendance at Public Worship", CYB 1874, 59; G. S. Barrett, "Congregational Worship", CYB, 1897, 86; **The Congregational Service Book.** A Form of Public Worship designed for the use of the Independent and other Nonconformist Bodies in Great Britain, 1847, Preface; Cf. Dale, **A Manual of Congregational Principles,** 163.

100. Anon, **Public Prayer** by an Independent Minister, 1869, 9; G. W. Conder, **Intelligent and True Worship: A Sermon Preached in the Congregational Church, Cheetham Hill, August 22nd, 1869 Preparatory to the Introduction of a Liturgical Service,** Manchester 1869, 13; J. G. Rogers, "Liturgical Forms", CYB, 1871, 112; H. Allon, "The Worship of the Church", in **Ecclesia,** London 1870, 450ff.; E. G. Herbert, "The Congregational Character", in **Religious Republics,** London 1867, 106.

101. The United Reformed Church, General Assembly 1973, **Reports to Assembly,** 25.

Chapter Two

THE INDEPENDENTS AND THE WESTMINSTER DIRECTORY

> Mr. Ney objected, That our Directory about the communion is larger than any Directory which ever he hath seen, and much larger than the Rubricks.*

In an order of the House of Commons of 18th September 1643, which was finally passed as an ordinance of both Houses on the 12th October 1643, Parliament empowered the recently convened Westminster Assembly of Divines to debate and propound concerning a Directory of Worship which would replace the **Book of Common Prayer.** [1] Reform of the Church of England had been high on the agenda of the Long Parliament when it met in 1640, though at this date reform had meant nothing more than the curbing of ceremonial excesses and subordinating Canon Law to parliamentary jurisdiction. But the moderate demands of 1640 had been escalated by the events of civil war, and part of the price the parliamentary side had had to pay for Scottish assistance was acceptance of the Solemn League and Covenant which called for reformation of religion--in doctrine, worship, discipline and government--"according to the Word of God" and the example of the best reformed churches. [2] The Puritan Assembly of Divines had been appointed to effect this reformation. It was within the debates of the Assembly that the differences between Presbyterians and Independents clearly emerged.

Robert Baillie, one of the Presbyterian Scottish Commissioners attached to the Assembly, recorded that the Divines turned their attention to reforming worship in the belief that there was unanimity on this question, thus deferring the inevitable disagreement on church polity until later. [3] However, this plan was not a success, for the compilation of the **Westminster Directory**

---

* George Gillespie, **Notes of Debates and Proceedings of the Assembly of Divines and other Commissioners at Westminster. February 1644 to January 1645**, ed. D. Meek, Edinburgh 1846.

represented a watershed in Independent liturgy. Until this point the Independents shared the general Puritan heritage in liturgy. Now, just as they steered a middle course between Presbyterianism and Brownism in matters of church government, so they steered the same course in liturgy. They accepted the general pattern of reformed worship, but refused to be bound by either Calvin or the **Genevan Service Book.** Baillie, referring to the stubbornness of the Independents over the form of the **Directory**, admitted, "We must dispute every inch of our ground". [4]

The compilation of the **Directory** for worship was placed in the hands of a subcommittee, consisting of four Scottish Commissioners--Robert Baillie, George Gillespie, Samuel Rutherford and Alexander Henderson, four English Presbyterians--Stephen Marshall (Chairman), Thomas Young, Herbert Palmer and Charles Herle, the latter often siding with the Independent viewpoint, and an Independent--Thomas Goodwin, who, much to Baillie's indignation, took it upon himself to co-opt another Independent, Philip Nye, on to the subcommittee. [5] The whole **Directory**, with the exception of the Preface, was finished on the 12th November 1644, though it was not until the 17th April 1645 that the Commons enforced it and abolished the **Book of Common Prayer;** penalties for the neglect of the former and the use of the latter were also imposed. [6]

In the Preface to the **Directory**, the compilers appealed to the Word of God, both for authority for the laying aside of the **Book of Common Prayer**, and for the compilation of the new **Directory** which gave only "the general heads, the sense and scope of the Prayers". But this appeal to the Word of God neatly disguises four distinct liturgical factors which determined the shape and content of the **Directory.**

1. Reaction to "Laudian" liturgical trends.

The great wish of the "Laudian" school was to bring the Prayer Book communion service more into line with those of the classical rites, and that of the Prayer Book of 1549, and to clothe it with dignified ceremonial. The influence of the "Laudian" school on the **Directory** was, as might be expected, a negative one. The Puritan compilers paid respect to the original compilers of the **Book of Common Prayer**, but stated that because of abuses it had become a source of offence. There would be no possibility of reforming it or altering it; it was simply abolished. [7]

2. The Scottish Presbyterians and the Radical Party of the Kirk.

The idea for a **Directory** of worship for both England and Scotland had originally come from the Scots, for the Solemn

League and Covenant had originated amidst a liturgical storm. The 1637 Liturgy for Scotland had been a revision of the **Book of Common Prayer** with concessions to Scottish Calvinism. In the Eucharistic liturgy, however, the revisers had sought to reintroduce features of the 1549 **Book of Common Prayer,** including an offertory of bread and wine, an invocation for the sanctification of the elements, and an anamnesis. None of these features was in absolute contradiction to Scottish usage, but the liturgy was interpreted as "popery". W. Jardine Grisbrooke points out that for the Scots it was not so much what it was as whose it was; 1637 was the prelate's liturgy. [8]

The Scottish Kirk, in taking first the National Covenant, and then the Solemn League and Covenant, sought to restore the original reformed discipline of John Knox's day, which included the reformed worship of the **Book of Common Prayer (Genevan Service Book).** Thus in 1644 the **Settled Order,** an adaptation of the **Book of Common Order,** was presented to Parliament for its consideration. [9]

However, it would be wrong to assume that all members of the Kirk felt that a return to reformed standards implied the restoration of the **Genevan Service Book.** There existed a radical party within the Kirk which questioned certain practices in public worship, including the recitation of the Creed, set prayers, and the singing of doxologies. Samuel Rutherford and George Gillespie, both Scottish members of the subcommittee compiling the **Directory,** seem to have been associated with this party. [10]

3. The Presbyterian Puritans.

The English Puritans inherited both the earlier Puritan criticisms of the **Book of Common Prayer,** and the proposed alternatives--the various editions of the **Genevan Service Book.** In 1641 and again in 1643 **The Service and Discipline,** an abridgement of 1556, was presented to Parliament for consideration. In common with some of the Independents, some Presbyterian members of the Westminster Assembly had been exiled in Holland, and had experienced the freedom of the directory-type of liturgy of the Dutch Reformed Church. However, with the abolition of the Prayer Book, and the compilation of a new order, the Presbyterian Puritans were able for the first time to give liturgical expression to their Eucharistic theology, a factor which should not be overlooked.

4. The Independents.

It is the Independent contribution to the **Directory** with which we are mainly concerned here. Although sharing the same heritage as the Presbyterians, and differing primarily only on matters of church polity, there does appear to have been a growing prejudice amongst the leading Independents in favor of free prayer. In their **Apologeticall Narration** the "Dissenting Brethren" described their practice in the Netherlands, being at pains to establish their conformity with the Reformed Churches:

> Our publique worship was made up of no other parts than the worship of all other reformed Churches doth consist of. As, publique and solemne prayers for kings and all in authority, &c, the reading the Scriptures of the Old and New Testament; Exposition of them as occasion was; and constant preaching of the word; the administration of the two Sacraments, Baptisme to infants, and the Lord's Supper, singing of Psalms; collections for the poor, &c every Lords day. [**11**]

But at the same time there was a firm assertion of the right to use free prayer:

> Againe, concerning the great ordinance of Publique Prayer and the Lyturgie of the Church, whereas there is this great controversie upon it about the lawfulnesse of set formes prescribed; we practiced (without condemning others) what all sides doe allow, and themselves does practice also, that the publique Prayers in our Assemblies should be framed by the meditations and study of our own Ministers, out of their own gifts, (the fruits of Christs Ascension) as well as their Sermons use to be. [**12**]

The English Independents held the New England Independent, John Cotton, in high esteem. Cotton furnishes us with a full description of Independent worship in New England, and at least with regard to the Eucharist itself, Baillie confirms that such was also the usage of the English Independents. [**13**]

> First then when wee come together in the Church according to the Apostles direction, 1 Tim 2:1, wee make prayers and intercessions and thanksgivings for our selves and for all men, not in any prescribed forme of prayer, or studied Liturgie, but in such a manner, as the Spirit of grace and of prayer (who teacheth all the people of God, what and how to pray, Rom 8:26, 27) helpeth our infirmities, wee having respect therein to the necessities of the people, the estate of the times, and the works of Christ in our hands.
>
> After prayer, either the Pastor or Teacher, readeth a Chapter in the Bible, and expoundeth it, giving the sense, to cause the people to understand the reading,

according to Neh 8:8. And in sundry Churches the other (whether Pastor or Teacher) who expoundeth not, he preacheth the Word, and in the afternoone the other who preached in the morning doth usually (if there be time) reade and preach, and he that expounded in the morning preacheth after him.

Before Sermon, and many times after, wee sing a Psalme, and because the former translation of the Psalmes, doth in many things very from the originall, and many times paraphraseth rather than translateth; besides divers other defects (which we cover in silence) wee have endeavoured a new translation of the Psalmes into English meetre, as neere the originall as we could expresse it in our English tongue, so farre as for the present the Lord hath been pleased to helpe us, and those Psalmes wee sing, both in our publick Churches, and in private.

The Seales of the Covenant (to wit, the Sacrament of Baptisme and the Lords Supper) are administered, either by the Pastor or by the Teacher; . . . Both the Sacraments we dispense. . .

. . . The Lords Supper to such as neither want knowledge nor grace to examine and judge themselves before the Lord. Such as lie under any offence publickly known, doe first remove the offence, before they present themselves to the Lords Table; according to Mat 5:23, 24. The members of any Church, if any be present, who bring Letters testimoniall with them to our Churches, wee admit them to the Lords Table with us, . . . The prayers wee use at the administration of the seales, are not any set formes prescribed to us, but conceived by the Minister, according to the present occasion, and the nature of the dutie in hand. . . . The Lords Supper we administer for the time, once a moneth at least, and for the gesture, to the people sitting; according as Christ administered it to his Disciples sitting, (Mat 26:20, 26) who also made a Symbolicall use of it, to teach the Church their majoritie over their Ministers in some cases, and their judiciall authoritie, as cosessors with him at the last Judgement, (Luk 22:27 to 30) which maketh us to looke at kneeling at the Lords Supper, not only as an adoration devised by man, but also as a violation by man of the institution of Christ, diminishing part of the Counsell of God, and of the honour and comfort of the Church held forth in it.

In time of solemnization of the Supper, the Minister having taken, blessed, and broken the bread, and commanded all the people to take and eate it, as the body of Christ broken for them, he taketh it himselfe, and giveth it to all that sit at Table with him, and from the Table it

> is reached by the Deacons to the people sitting in the next seats about them, the Minister sitting in his place at the Table.
>
> After they have all partaked in the bread, he taketh the cup in like manner, and giveth thanks a new, (blesseth it) according to the example of Christ in the Evangelist, who describes the institution Mat 26:27. Mark 14:23. Luk 22:17. All of them in such a way as setteth forth the Elements, not blessed together, but either of them apart; the bread first by it selfe, and afterwards the wine by it selfe; for what reason the Lord himselfe best knoweth, and wee cannot be ignorant, that a received solemne blessing, expresly performed by himselfe, doth apparently call upon the whole assembly to looke againe for a supernaturall and special blessing in the same Element also as well as in the former; for which the Lord will be againe sought to doe it for us.
>
> After the celebration of the Supper, a Psalme of thanksgiving is sung, (according to Mat 26:30) and the Church dismissed with a blessing. [**14**]

Some things here are of special note. The "fencing of the Table" was carefully adhered to, the Independents being particularly careful as to who was admitted to the Supper. As in the description given by the separatist Robert Browne, two blessings or Eucharistic Prayers were used relating to the bread and the wine, in strict interpretation of the biblical accounts. The communicants were seated, not kneeling. However, unlike the Church of Scotland, a Lasco and the Dutch Church, the Independents remained in their pews, and did not sit in succession at the table. This proved to be a point of great controversy between the Independents and the Scottish Commissioners in the compilation of the **Directory.**

These four factors colored the Assembly's interpretation of "the Word of God".

The **Directory** for worship eventually emerged from the subcommittee after, to use its Chairman's words, "many serious & sad debates about the prayers & difficultyes on both sides". [**15**] We have little information regarding the debates and decisions of the subcommittee: two pages of notes from George Gillespie, and sporadic information from Baillie's letters--both Scottish members of the subcommittee. More information is available concerning its passage through the Assembly: the Journal of John Lightfoot, and the manuscript minutes of the Assembly in Dr. William's Library, London.

As with Calvin's, the Puritan, and other Reformed liturgies, the Eucharistic liturgy of the **Directory** may be considered as two distinct parts: the Morning Worship, and the Eucharist proper.

The pages of the **Directory** which provided an order for Morning worship consisted of three separate sections: the matter of public prayer, which seems to have been completed by the whole committee; Of Public Reading of the Holy Scriptures, which was given to Thomas Young; [16] and Of Preaching of the Word, being the work of Steven Marshall, the Chairman. [17] A letter of Robert Baillie reveals that at least to begin with, Goodwin, the elected Independent member of the subcommittee, was in disagreement over the precise sequence of the prayers, and even the whole idea of a **Directory:**

> We were next settling on the manner of the prayer, If it were good to have two prayers, as we use, before sermon, or but one, as they use: If in that first prayer it were meet to take in the King, Church and Sick, as they doe, or leave these to the last prayer, as we. While we are sweetlie debaiting on these things, in came Mr. Goodwin, who incontinent assayed to turn all upside downe, to reason against all directories, and our verie first grounds, also that all prefaceing was unlawfull; that according to 1 Tim ii. 1, it was necessare to begin with prayer, and that in the first prayer we behooved to pray for the King. [18]

Goodwin's argument concerning the first prayer corresponds with the order given by Cotton. However, Goodwin was reconciled, [19] and the order finally recommended was as follows:

Call to worship (Prefacing).
Prayer of approach.
Psalm reading.
Old Testament chapter.
New Testament chapter.
Psalm, sung.
Prayer before the sermon (some petitions may be deferred until after the Sermon).
Sermon.
General prayer (some petitions may be used before the sermon).
Lord's Prayer
Psalm, sung.
Blessing.

The service itself allows some flexibility, not only in what could actually be said in the prayers, but also in the recommended sequence; according to preference, the thanksgiving and intercessions may come before or after the sermon. This flexibility is further illustrated by **A Supply of Prayers for Ships** where the **Directory** sequence has been rearranged: [20]

Prayer of Approach.
Lord's Prayer.
Psalm reading.
Old Testament chapter.
New Testament chapter.
Psalm, sung.
Prayer of Confession.
Prayer for the Church.
Psalm, sung.
General prayer.
Blessing.

Such flexibility allowed the Independents to adopt a sequence of prayers in accordance with their own preferences.

The call to worship seems to have been an extension of the Votum of Calvin, "Our help is in the name of the Lord", and Goodwin took exception to it. The prayer of approach echoes the theme of the confession of Calvin and 1556, though it asked in addition for pardon, assistance, and acceptance in the whole service, and a blessing on the particular portion of the Word to be read, thus also combining the prayer of illumination of previous Calvinist/Puritan rites. However, it is interesting to note that similar themes are also combined in one opening prayer in the Dutch liturgy of Datheen.

The directions for the reading of Scripture carefully excluded the Apocrypha. However, dispute arose in the Assembly as to exactly who was to read the lections. The Independents' practice was to limit reading to the Pastor and Teacher, and this was supported by Palmer and Herle; but on Thursday the 13th of June, 1644, the Assembly agreed to extend the privilege to those who intended ordination. [21]

The position of the prayer before the sermon seems to have been a compromise; it was not the opening prayer, as the Independent Goodwin demanded (Cf. Cotton), but neither was it after the sermon as was the corresponding prayer in Calvin and 1556. Some of the petitions could be deferred until after the sermon, allowing the pattern of Calvin and 1556. The prayer itself fulfils the function of the Long Prayer and the "Prayer for the Whole Estate of Christes Churche" in these two liturgies, but in both of these, the intercessory prayer presupposed an opening confession. The Prayer of the **Directory** is a confession and intercession. Its structure and themes are close to the third alternative prayer found in **Waldegrave** and **Middleburg**, being a shortened version of Datheen's "Prayer after the Sermon" in the Dutch liturgy. That of the **Directory** seems nearer to the original Dutch version of the prayer than the shortened version of Waldegrave and Middleburg. [22] Although there is no positive evidence, it may be the case that the compilers, consciously or unconsciously, based the prayer upon that of the Dutch liturgy.

The **Directory** provided a comprehensive guide for the preacher to prepare the sermon, laying down careful rules for its structure and content. It would appear to be the only liturgy ever to take the sermon seriously as an integral part of the service, giving it rather more attention than a mere indication of where it was to come in the service. The original text which came from the subcommittee contained a direction to "abstain in the pulpit from speaking Latin, Greek and Hebrew", which was debated by the Assembly. [23] Philip Nye had no objection to the use of foreign languages, "but denied the use of human learning, as poets, &c as too pedantical". [24] The final text recommended abstention from the "unprofitable use of unknown tongues".

The prayer after the sermon repeated some of the themes of the prayer before the sermon; in **A Supply of Prayers for Ships**, the same prayer was entitled a "Thanksgiving".

The Lord's Prayer was only recommended since the Independents regarded it as an example of prayer, and not something which was required to be used.

The order was to end with a "Solemn Blessing". No text was provided in the **Directory**, but **A Supply of Prayer for Ships** has a multiple blessing (Aaronic, 1 Thess. 2:5, and the Grace):

> The Lord blesse us, and keep us; the Lord make his face to shine upon us, and be gracious unto us; the Lord lift up his countenance upon us, and give us his Peace; And the very God of Peace, sanctifie us wholly, that our whole spirit, soul and body, may be preserved blamelesse unto the coming of our Lord Jesus Christ; And the grace of our Lord Jesus Christ, and the love of God the Father, and the Communion of the Holy Ghost be with us all, Amen.

When the Eucharist was to follow, the blessing might be used at this point in the service, and/or at the end of the Eucharist. [25]

The absence of the Creed and the Decalogue is explained by the Minutes of the Sessions of the Assembly:

> December 16, 1644 ordered: That Dr. Burges inform the Honble Houses of Parliament that the reason why the Assembly have sent up nothing in the Directory concerning the Creed and the Ten Commandments, is because they reserve it for the Directory for catechizing, where they conceive it will be most proper. [26]

The compilation of the Eucharistic liturgy proper, entitled "Of the Celebration of the Communion, or Sacrament of the Lord's Supper". was in the hands of the Scottish Commissioners. [27] and it is only to be expected therefore that behind the **Directory** the **Genevan Service Book** in its version in the **Book of Common Order** can be clearly seen. However, it would be quite wrong to assume that the Scots had entirely their own way in the matter; the Independents' Eucharistic rite, as represented by Cotton, was considerably shorter in structure, and they were not anxious to abandon their way of celebration. Baillie complained:

> The unhappie Independents would mangle that sacrament. No catechising nor preparation before; no thanksgiving after, no sacramentall doctrine or chapters, in the day of celebration; no coming up to any table; but a carrying of the element to all in their seats athort the church: yet all this, with God's help, we have carryed over their bellies to our practise. [28]

From the evidence that is extant, there appears to have been little discussion on the actual texts of the prayers, but quite heated debates on the rubrics. A quaint piece of ceremonial was propounded by Nye:

> Mr. Nye told us his private judgement, that in preaching he thinks the minister should be covered and the people discovered; but in the sacrament, the minister should be discovered, as a servant, and the guests all covered. [29]

Not surprisingly, it remained merely Nye's private judgement.

The main problem which faced the subcommittee was over the position for the reception of the elements. The Scottish practice was to sit at the table, as also the practice of the Dutch Church; the Independents remained in their seats and the elements were brought to them by the deacons.

According to Gillespie, the problem was raised in subcommittee as early as March 4th, 1644:

> Mr. Marshall, Palmer, Herle, and Goodwin too, said it was enough that the elements be blessed on the table, and that some sit at table, but that the elements may be carried about to others in their pews or seats. Against this we alleged, I. Christ's example, making use of a table, Luke xxii. 21, and that for a signification, ibid. ver. 30. 2. The example of the church at Corinth, and the apostles calling it the Lord's table, 1 Cor. x. 21, which is more than partaking of the bread, ver. 17; or the Jews eating of the sacrifices, ver. 18; even an honourable fellowship with Christ opposed to fellowship with devils, ver.

> 20; and chap. viii. 10, we give bread and drink to many whom we admit not into our fellowship, so as to sit down at table with us. 3. The nature of a feast requireth that the guests be set at table, and that all the guests be set about it, for the use of a table is not for some, but for all the guests, else no table is necessary, but a cupboard. [30]

Marshall seems to have been won over, for to the Assembly itself he explained that the intention was that the people should sit down at the table, company after company. [31] But the Independents were not convinced; during the debates in the Assembly in June and July, Nye, Goodwin and Bridge pressed for communicating everyone in their seats without coming up to a table. [32] The final rubric was a compromise, allowing either practice: "the communicants may orderly sit about it, or at it."

Another problem was the fraction and administration, it being debated whether the communicants might distribute the bread one to another, and whether every communicant might break the bread for himself after the minister had broken the loaf. The distributing of the bread and the cup from party to party was granted, but "breaking" the bread, which included cutting it up for distribution, was reserved for the minister. [33]

According to the rubrics, the Eucharist was to be celebrated frequently, though the Assembly left this to the discretion of the minister and officers of the congregation. In some cases, it was rarely celebrated; for example Thomas Palmer of Aston-on-Trent, Derbyshire, and R. Lancaster of Amport, Hampshire, were reputed to have rarely administered communion. [34]

The order finally agreed upon was as follows:

Exhortation: the benefit of the sacrament; Excommunication; encouragement of those who labour under the sense of the burden of their sins to communicate.

Words of Institution. 1 Cor. 11:23-27.

Optional explanation of the words.

Prayer of Thanksgiving, or Blessing of the Bread and Wine.

Fraction and delivery: According to the holy Institution, command, and example of our blessed Saviour Jesus Christ, I take this Bread, and having given thanks, I break it, and give it unto you. Take yee, eat yee; This is the Body of Christ which is broken for you. Do this in remembrance of him.

According to the Institution, command, and example of our Lord Jesus Christ, I take this Cup, and give it unto you. This cup is the New Testament in the

> Blood of Christ, which is shed for the remission of the sins of many; Drink ye all of it.
>
> Exhortation.
>
> Solemn Thanksgiving.
>
> (The Collection for the Poor is so ordered that no part of the worship is hindered).

The opening Exhortation is a familiar characteristic of previous Puritan liturgies, though the **Directory** deviated from Calvin, 1556, à Lasco and Datheen in that the Words of Institution did not preface it, nor formed any part of it. In comparison with the Genevan order and its derivations, an inversion in sequence of themes appears to have been made. Calvin and 1556 considered the danger of unworthy eating, excommunication, invitation and encouragement, with a brief reference to the benefits of the sacrament; the **Directory** commenced with an explanation of the benefits, and ended with the use of the sacrament, with directions which appear to require a brief theological résumé of the Eucharist. In this it came nearer to Datheen's order than to Calvin and 1556.

After the exhortation, the communicants sitting about the table, or at it, the Minister was to begin the action by "sanctifying and blessing" the elements, the term "consecration" being rejected by the Assembly. [35] The rubric defined the means of this setting apart or blessing:

> . . . that those elements now set apart and sanctified to this holy use, by the Word of Institution and Prayer.

This would seem to account for the removal of the Words of Institution from their place in the previous Puritan orders of before the exhortation to now immediately before the Eucharistic Prayer. In Calvin the words were part of the exhortation, for the Word must be preached; [36] in 1556 they were placed before the exhortation, as a warrant; in the **Directory** they still serve both purposes, the Minister being permitted to give a word of explanation, but they were here made an integral part of the setting apart or sanctifying the elements. The words represented the Divine promise or pledge, and reflected Puritan Eucharistic teaching. William Perkins, one of the Elizabethan Cambridge Puritans, maintaining that the minister's actions at the Eucharist was four-fold, explained the second as

> . . . his blessing of it, whereby he, by the recital of the promises, & prayers conceived to that end, doth actually separate the bread and wine received from their common unto an holy use. [37]

Similarly William Ames taught:

> But this word of institution distinctly applied with fit prayers, is called the word of consecration, of blessing, the word of sanctification, and separation. [38]

The same teaching was also propounded by Richard Vines, one of the leading Divines of the Assembly. [39] The rearrangement of the Calvin/1566/à Lasco/Datheen positioning of the Words of Institution would appear to make explicit the Puritan theology of sanctification or consecration.

The Eucharistic Prayer, termed the Thanksgiving, is of some significance, and needs to be considered at some length.

A Eucharistic Prayer occurs in 1556 and its later Puritan editions, and in Datheen's rite. From the account of John Cotton, the Independent practice, like that of Browne, and Barrow, was to have two Eucharistic Prayers, relating to the bread and the wine respectively. This practice they attempted to retain in the **Directory**; the Minutes of the Assembly record Nye's argument:

> I have not conceived it to be indifferent to extend the blessing to them both at once. It is the mind of Christ to hold forth these 2 more distinctly than if they were to be blended together in a meale (?)
> that place in the 1 Cor. 10.
> I believe it is the mind of Jesus Christ to have some kind of distinction in these 2, distinct blessing & distinct receiving by the whole. [40]

William Bridge, another leading Independent Divine, also appears to have argued that this was the practice in Matthew, Mark and 1 Corinthians. [41]

Against a double consecration George Gillespie argued that Matthew and Mark speak of the thanksgiving over the cup in the past tense, implying only one prayer; and

> . . . if ther was a double blessing first at the bread & then at the giving of the cup, then either this was misticall & soe intended, or it was only occasional as the upper chamber was. [42]

If there had been a second blessing, Gillespie suggested, then it might not have been an audible prayer at all, but simply a lifting up of the eyes to heaven; [43] Gillespie seems to have believed that there was only one blessing.

The Minutes also record that a certain Mr. Walker appealed

to Beza's opinion that there was only one prayer used at the Institution, and Walker suggested that that prayer was preserved in John 17. [44]

As the **Directory** shows, the Independents had to give way to the Scottish and English Presbyterians. In a sermon written during the time that the **Directory** was in force, Richard Vines explained:

> And here let me shew you a reason why the Churches now are not bound to consecrate and distribute the Bread before they consecrate the Wine, as it was in Christs Supper, because the Rite was so at that time, and the thing being meerely occasional, is not obligatory, but indifferent: We pronounce the words of signification, This is my Body, This cup is, &c, severally, but we do not distribute the Bread before we bless the Wine; that Christ did occasionally to the Rite. [45]

The fact that Vines bothered to raise the subject in a sermon may suggest that the double consecration was still a live issue, and still practiced by the Independents. [46]

The prayer itself divides into three paragraphs. The first two were based upon that of 1556, some of the phraseology of the latter being incorporated with little change: confession, thanksgiving for redemption in Christ, and for the means of grace, and the confession of the name of Jesus. The first paragraph seems to have been the source of the "General Prayer of Thanksgiving" in the 1662 **Book of Common Prayer**. [47]

The third paragraph of the prayer was a petition for consecration, or sanctification, and needs some explanation.

The first problem which arises here is the nature of this petition. Both W. D. Maxwell and Horton Davies have classified it as an Epiklesis. [48] In so far as "Epiklesis" means an invocation addressed to God, this is correct, but then it is also true of most prayer. However, in comparative liturgy the term Epiklesis is usually understood to refer to the petition for consecration found in the Eastern and some non-Roman Western Anaphoras. There is a variety of terminology used, but the mature Epiklesis requests God to send the Holy Spirit upon the elements of bread and wine, to make them the Body and Blood of Christ. What we have in the **Directory** is rather different; God is asked

> (a) to vouchsafe his gracious presence
> (b) and the effectual working of his Spirit in us
> (c) and so to sanctifie these Elements both of Bread and Wine, and to blesse his own Ordinance, that

> we may receive by Faith the Body and Blood of Jesus Christ.

Here God the Father sanctifies the elements, and the Holy Spirit works in us, so that by Faith we may receive the Body and Blood of Christ. This is certainly not the Epiklesis of the Eastern Anaphoras, and is described more cautiously by E. C. Ratcliff as "two explicit petitions for sanctifying or consecrating the elements". [49]

The second problem concerns the source of the petition. For the doctrine, we need look no further than John Calvin; Calvin taught that by faith and through the Holy Spirit the communicant received the Body and Blood of Christ as the bread and wine were received. [50] But, although Calvin's rite did contain the petition "that we may with a constante and assured fayth, receave bothe hys bodye and bloude, yea, verelye CHRIST hymselfe wholye" (William Huycke's English translation, 1550), it came after the sermon in the Long Prayer, and nowhere near the actual taking of the elements; furthermore, it does not make explicit Calvin's teaching. Nor does anything corresponding to the petition in the **Directory** occur in 1556 and its later editions.

William McMillan [51] and W. D. Maxwell [52] have both adduced evidence for such a petition for consecration being used in Scotland. The 1629 proposed revision of the **Book of Common Order** contained the following petition:

> Mercifull father wee beseech thee that wee receiving these thy creatures of bread and wine, according to thy sonne our Saviour his holy institution, may be made partakers of his most blissed body and blood. Send doune o Lord thy blissing upon this Sacrament that it may be unto us the effectual exhibitive instrument of the Lord Jesus. [53]

And the petition in the proposed liturgy of 1637,

> . . . vouchsafe so to bless and sanctify with thy Word and Holy Spirit these thy gifts and creatures of bread and wine, that they may be unto us the body and blood. . .

would seem to be as much a concession to current Scottish usage as a resurrecting of the 1549 Prayer Book rite. This evidence led E. C. Ratcliff to conclude:

> We may, then, reasonably attribute the introduction of the petition for sanctifying the bread and wine to the Scottish members of the subcommittee. [54]

The evidence offered by McMillan and Maxwell certainly indicates that the Scottish members of the subcommittee would favor an explicit petition for consecration. However, there would appear to be no sound reason for attributing this petition in the **Directory** exclusively to Scottish influence as Ratcliff does. There is ample evidence to show that the petition for sanctification or consecration reflects the thought of the English Puritans, who were only now able to give liturgical expression to their Eucharistic theology. For example, William Fulke wrote:

> These words (as every man may see plainley) make nothing for adoration of the Sacrament, but for spirituall reverence to be given to Christ, of them that come to receive the Sacrament, by which we are assured (if we come worthely) that we are made partakers of the verie body and bloud of Christ, after a spirituall manner, by faith on our behalfe, and by the working of the Holy Ghost, on the behalfe of Christ. [55]

Similarly Dudley Fenner, commenting upon 1 Cor. 10:5 explained the sacrament as

> . . . an instrument whereby truly is communicated by the working of the H. Ghost to our faith, the very bodye and blood of Christ. [56]

The same teaching is to be found in other English Puritan writings, such as those of William Perkins, Richard Greenham and Walter Marshall. [57] Furthermore, the liturgical expression of Calvin's teaching was not limited to Scotland; one Reformed rite in particular--and one known well to some of the members of the Assembly--contained a similar type of petition, namely the Dutch liturgy of Datheen. God the Father was asked that in the Ordinance

> . . . thou wilt be pleased to work in our hearts through the Holy Ghost, that we may give ourselves more and more with true confidence to thy Son Jesus Christ that our broken and burdoned hearts may be fed and comforted through the power of the Holy Spirit with his body and blood.

It could be the case that the knowledge of this petition in the Dutch liturgy encouraged the Assembly in the formulation of the petition in the **Directory**, giving liturgical expression to Calvinist eucharistic doctrine. There is certainly no need to attribute the petition exclusively to Scottish influence.

The fraction, with words of delivery, followed the Prayer, maintaining the heightening of the fraction which, as we have noted, was already developing in the **Waldegrave** and **Middleburg** books. There appears to have been silence during the administration, though an exhortation could follow. On this point the Independents seem to have had their own way; Stephen Marshall proposed that some sentences should be spoken during the administration, since Jesus spoke to his disciples at the Supper (Luke 22:15ff). This idea was steadfastly resisted by Herle and Nye. [58]

Possibly a psalm was sung at this point after the administration, since this was the practice of both the Presbyterians and Independents. There is no rubric to this effect, but it was possibly covered by the psalm before the blessing in the order for Morning worship.

The collection for the poor is mentioned at the end of the service; the only material offering allowed by Reformed theology could take place at any convenient point in the service.

At a number of points attention has been drawn to the similarities that exist between the **Directory** and the Dutch liturgy. Some of the members of the Westminster Assembly knew the Dutch liturgy, and the Ordinance for the introduction of the **Directory** referred to the example of the best Reformed Churches, suggesting a wider source than merely the **Book of Common Order** of Scotland. The members of the Assembly were allowed access to whatever books or texts they liked, and thus there is every possibility that the Dutch liturgy had been examined. [59] Furthermore, the Assembly itself seems to have maintained close contact with the Dutch Reformed Church. [60] It must be admitted, however, that none of the members of the subcommittee who compiled the **Directory**, with the exception of Goodwin, had been exiled in Holland, and there is no direct evidence to suggest that the members deliberately drew upon the Dutch rite. The suggestion that the Dutch liturgy formed the source for certain items in the **Directory** must remain an interesting conjecture.

With the compilation of the **Directory** we have for the first time a liturgy produced by the English Puritan tradition which was quite distinct from the **Book of Common Prayer** and the **Genevan Service Book**. It represents a synthesis between previous Independent Puritan and Separatist practices. Nevertheless, behind this liturgy can be seen that of 1556, and that of Calvin, and in turn therefore, Bucer and the Roman Mass, and Farel and Prone. The pedigree is still just discernible.

The **Directory** also represents an important stage in Independent Eucharistic liturgy. As the Independents emerged clearly as a distinct form of Puritanism, they made their influence felt in the compilation of a written liturgy; after the **Directory**, the Independents turned their backs upon written liturgical texts for almost two hundred years. And not for another three hundred and thirty years would the "Congregational men" co-operate with their Presbyterian brethren in the compilation of a Eucharistic liturgy.

NOTES

1. W. A. Shaw, **A History of the English Church During the Civil Wars and Under the Commonwealth 1640-1660,** vol. 1, 337; J. Lightfoot, The Journal of the Proceedings of the Assembly of Divines, **Works,**, ed. J. A. Pitman, 13 vols., London 1824, vol. 13, 17.

2. The phrase "according to the Word of God" was inserted at the insistance of the Independents Philip Nye and Sir Henry Vane, to escape the necessity of a Presbyterian Church government.

3. R. Baillie, **Letters and Journals,** ed. D. Laing, 3 vols., Edinburgh 1841, vol. 2, p. 117.

4. Ibid., 195.

5. Ibid., 131.

6. A Fine of 40s. for neglect of the **Directory;** for using the **Book of Common Prayer,** a £5 Fine for the first offence, £10 for the second, and for a third, one year in prison. **Acts and Ordinances of the Interregnum. 1642-1660,** ed. C. H. Firth and R. S. Rait, 3 vols., 1911, vol. 1, pp. 755-757.

7. The "Laudian" estimate of the **Directory** was probably best summed up by Henry Hammond when he referred to it as the "No-Liturgy". **A View of the New Directorie,** Oxford 1646, 95.

8. W. Jardine Grisbrooke, **Anglican Liturgies of the Seventeenth and Eighteenth Centuries,** 8.

9. Text in P. Hall, **Reliquiae Liturgicae,** Bath 1847, vol. 1. Appendix.

10. David Stevenson, "The Radical Party in the Kirk 1637-45", in JEH, 25 (1974), 135-165.

11. T. Goodwin, et.al. **An Apologeticall Narration,** p. 8.

12. Ibid., 12.

13. Baillie, op.cit., 148-149.

14. J. Cotton, **The Way of the Churches of Christ in New England,** 66-68; Cf. T. Lechford, **Plaine Dealing,** 1642, 17, quoted in H. M. Dexter, **The Congregationalism of the Last Three Hundred Years,** London 1880, 453.

15. Minutes of the Sessions of the Westminster Assembly of Divines. (Adoniram Byfield). (Dr. William's Library). From a typescript of the Original. vol. 2, fol. 86.

16. Baillie, op.cit., 140.

17. Ibid.

18. Ibid., 123.

19. Ibid.

20. For a fuller discourse see my "A Supply of Prayer for Ships: A Forgotten Puritan Liturgy".

21. John Lightfoot, **The Journal of the Proceedings of the Assembly of Divines,** (January 1643 - December 1644) 284.

22. See appendix.

23. Lightfoot, op.cit., 281. Friday, June 7th, 1644.

24. Ibid., 282. Presumably Nye disapproved of the Areopagus Speech Acts 17:28!

25. Ibid., 285, 325.

26. **Minutes of the Sessions of the Westminster Assembly of Divines. (November 1644 to March 1649),** (vol. 3 of the Ms.), ed. A. F. Mitchell and J. Struthers, Edinburgh & London 1874, 21.

27. Baillie, op.cit., 140.

28. Ibid., 195.

29. Ibid., 149.

30. George Gillespie, **Notes of Debates and Proceedings of the Assembly of Divines and other Commissioners at Westminster. February 1644 to January 1645,** ed. D. Meek, Edinburgh 1846, 101.

31. Lightfoot, op.cit., 286-287.

32. Ibid., 286-296; Baillie, op.cit., 199.

33. Lightfoot, op.cit., 288-289.

34. **Calamy Revised,** ed. A. G. Matthews, Oxford 1934, 380, 313. For further examples, G. F. Nuttall, **The Holy Spirit in Puritan Faith and Experience,** Oxford 1946, 94.

35. Lightfoot, op.cit., 288.

36. **Institutes,** 4.14.4.

37. William Perkins, **Workes,** 3 vols., London 1626-31. Vol. 1, 75.

38. William Ames, **The Marrow of Sacred Divinity,** London 1642, 187.

39. Richard Vines, **A Treatise of the Right Institution, Administration and Receiving of the Sacrament of the Lord's Supper delivered in XX Sermons at St. Lawrence Jewry,** 1657, 91.

40. Minutes of the Sessions, Ms, vol. 2, fol. 104b.

41. Ibid., fol. 103. The full minute is missing.

42. Ibid., fol. 103b.

43. Ibid., fol. 104.

44. Ibid., fol. 104b.

45. Richard Vines, op.cit., 86.

46. See below for later Independent practice.

47. G. J. Cuming, "Two Fragments of a lost liturgy?" in **Studies in Church History,** vol. 3, Leiden 1966, 247-253.

48. W. D. Maxwell, **The Liturgical Portions,** 135; Horton Davies, **The Worship of the English Puritans,** 137.

49. E. C. Ratcliff, "Puritan Alternatives to the Prayer Book", in Ramsey, et.al., **The English Prayer Book 1549 - 1662,** AC, London 1963, 56-81, 69. In note 1, Ratcliff writes, "This type of petition is not to be taken as a form of epiclesis".

50. **Institutes,** 4.17.10.

51. W. McMillan, **The Worship of the Scottish Reformed Church 1550 - 1638,** London 1931, 170ff.

52. W. D. Maxwell, **The Liturgical Portions,** 134-135.

53. Quoted in Maxwell, ibid., 135.

54. E. C. Ratcliff, "Puritan Alternatives to the Prayer Book", 70.

55. William Fulke, **The Text of the New Testament . . . with a confutation,** 526, on 1 Cor. 11:18.

56. Dudley Fenner, **The Whole doctrine of the Sacramentes.** n.p.

57. William Perkins, A Reformed Catholic, in **The Works of William Perkins,** 3 vols., 1626-1631. Vol. 1, 610; Cases of Conscience, vol. 2, 83; Richard Greenham, **Workes,** 1601, 479; Walter Marshall, **The Gospel Mystery of Sanctification,** 1692, 44.

58. Minutes, vol. 2, fol. 110; Lightfoot, op.cit., 290.

59. Lightfoot, op.cit., 29.

60. S. W. Carruthers, **The Everyday Work of the Westminster Assembly,** Philadelphia 1943, 36ff.

Chapter Three

THE SAVOY CONFERENCE 1661

It is with some hesitation that the work of the Savoy Conference of 1661--a conference between the Presbyterians and the restored Episcopalians--has been included within this study. The Independents had no part in this conference; they did not expect comprehension nor was it offered to them. Furthermore, the main spokesman for the Presbyterians, Richard Baxter, preferring the title "mere Catholick" or "mere Nonconformist", [1] consistently attacked separation and Independency; his own liturgical work must be classed as Presbyterian, and not Congregationalist. However, it is impossible to pass over this attempt at liturgical accommodation without comment. Modern Congregationalists have included Richard Baxter within the Puritan tradition which they claim as their own, and the compilers of the 1948 **A Book of Public Worship** saw fit to draw upon Baxter's liturgy as part of their own liturgical heritage. [2] For this reason we consider here the Eucharistic proposals of the Savoy Conference.

In the Declaration to all his loving subjects of the kingdom of England and dominion of Wales, concerning ecclesiastical affairs, Charles II proposed that a number of divines from the Episcopalian and Puritan sides should be appointed to revise the **Book of Common Prayer** and to supply alternative forms in scriptural phrase. The terms of reference of the commission appointed in March 1661 seemed to limit the conference's task to a moderate revision of the Prayer Book. [3] The Puritan party interpreted the terms of reference of the commission by the Declaration, and thus provided a blueprint for a revised **Book of Common Prayer**, and an alternative liturgy. The Savoy Conference provides us, then, with two Eucharistic liturgies: The revised Prayer Book communion, and that of Baxter's **Reformed Liturgy**.

The Revised Prayer Book Communion

The Puritan criticisms of the Prayer Book, entitled **Excep-**

tions against the Book of Common Prayer, were a skillful restatement of the old sixteenth century Puritan complaints. [4] They were divided into General and Particular complaints and detailed suggested amendments, and together they were intended to correct the Prayer Book and make it acceptable to all who held "the substantials of the protestant religion". The **Exceptions** which had any bearing on the Eucharistic liturgy may be summarized as follows:

1. General and Particular complaints.

(a) According to Scripture, the minister is "the mouth of the people to God in prayer" and the people's part is to attend reverently and in silence. Therefore, apart from the "Amen", all responses should be omitted.

(b) The collects of the day were too short, and were not agreeable to scriptural examples, nor suited to the gravity and seriousness of corporate prayer. The various petitions should be put together into one long prayer.

(c) The Prayer Book was defective because it lacked a preparatory prayer for God's assistance, and failed to mention original and actual sin.

(d) The observance of Saints' days and their vigils had no scriptural warrant.

(e) The words "priest" and "Sunday" were to be replaced by "minister" and "Lord's Day" respectively.

(f) There were to be no readings from the Apocrypha.

(g) There was to be no use of the surplice, no kneeling for the communion, and as little movement as possible.

2. Detailed suggested amendments.

(a) The opening rubrics were to be transformed into an examination of faith and excommunication of evil doers, in accordance with the King's Declaration of October 1660.

(b) The Decalogue was to be prefaced by the full scriptural introduction, and the fourth commandment to read as in Exodus 20 and Deuteronomy 5 ("He blessed the Sabbath"). The responses were to be omitted, and the Decalogue to be concluded with a prayer by the minister.

(c) Preaching was to be strictly enjoined.

(d) The collection for the poor might be better made at or a little before the departing of the communicants (Cf. the **Directory**).

(e) The confession said by the minister only.

(f) There were faults in the wording of the proper prefaces for Christmas and Whitsunday.

(g) The "Prayer of Humble Access" was to be altered to read "that our sinful souls and bodies may be cleansed through his precious body and blood".

(h) In the "Prayer of Consecration" a petition for consecration and directions for the fraction were to be added.

(i) The words of administration were to be scriptural.

(j) The "Black" rubric was to be restored.

From these **Exceptions**, together with the pattern of previous Puritan liturgies, it is possible to piece together the structure of the revision of the Eucharist which is envisaged (the number of the **Exceptions** summarized above is given in brackets):

Examination and Excommunication (2.a) cf. **Directory.**
Prayer for God's assistance, including confession of sin (1.c) cf. **Directory.**
The Decalogue and prayer (2.b).
Long prayer for all estates (1.b).
Readings.
Sermon (2.c).
Prayer after the sermon (?). Cf. **Directory**, leading up to the subject of the Lord's Supper. Perhaps examination and excommunication here.
Confession by minister alone (2.e).
Thanksgiving (?). Cf. **Directory**; mentioned in the preface to the **Exceptions.**
Prayer of Humble Access, emended (2.g).
Prayer of consecration, with petition for sanctification of the elements and to bless the ordinance (2.h).
The fraction (2.h).
Words of administration from Scripture (2.i); communicants may sit or stand.
Psalm (?). Prayer of oblation or thanksgiving.
Blessing.
Collection (2.d).

This outline is, of course, only conjectural, and a different outline could be made equally as well as this. However, the other liturgy which we have to consider--Baxter's **Reformed Liturgy**--was to be an alternative form. When this is taken into consideration, it will be apparent that a Prayer Book communion with an order something similar to that outlined above was envisaged, or otherwise Baxter's work would become a replacement rather than an alternative form for the minister. This reform outlined in the **Exceptions** provided an order which would have stood in the tradition of emended Prayer Books reaching back to the **Liturgy of Compromise.**

Richard Baxter's Reformed Liturgy

The second provision of the **Declaration** of 1661--an alternative form of prayers in scriptural phrase--was left to Richard Baxter (1615-1691).

Baxter was without doubt one of the most distinguished Puritan divines of the seventeenth century. After renouncing his chances of a career under Sir Henry Herbert, Master of the Revels, he taught himself theology--Aquinas, Scotus, Durnadus and Ockam being particularly to his taste. He was ordained deacon, and probably priest, in the Church of England. [5] Following a mastership at Dudley school, and several months as assistant at Bridgnorth, he was appointed lecturer at Kidderminster, and after acting as army chaplain to the parliamentarians, he returned to Kidderminster to replace the deprived vicar, George Dance. While at Kidderminster, he was responsible for the organizing of the Worcestershire Association of Ministers, and throughout his ministry he was concerned with church unity and peace. Yet despite this, Baxter had an unfortunate manner, and his writings were the cause of much strife. Furthermore he himself disliked contradiction; when he remarked of Cromwell "what he learned must be from himself", the Protector might have said the same of Baxter with equal truth. [6] It was on account of his unpopularity in some quarters that Baxter at first declined the invitation to serve as a commissioner for the Puritan side at the Savoy Conference. Not only did he change his mind on this matter, but he became their chief spokesman.

Baxter himself recorded that he composed his **Reformed Liturgy** in a fortnight:

> My leisure was too short for the doing of it with Accurateness, (which a Business of that Nature doth require) or for the consulting with Men or Authors. I could not have time to make use of any Book, save the Bible and my Concordance (comparing all with the Assemblies Directory, and the Book of Common Prayer

> with Hamon L'Estrange). And at the Fortnight's end I brought it to the other Commissioners. [7]

However, it would be wrong to suppose that the **Reformed Liturgy** was the result of a fortnight's work from scratch; F. J. Powicke was surely correct:

> I think we may account for the swiftness and preparedness with which he afterwards wrote out a whole liturgy of his own in a fortnight, by the fact that he was but writing out and supplementing what he had practised at Kidderminster. [8]

It would be even more accurate to say that the **Reformed Liturgy** was the embodiment of Baxter's beliefs and practices reaching back to his mastership at Dudley school.

During his early ministry until the civil war, Baxter was acquainted with and used the **Book of Common Prayer.** But while at Dudley he became convinced by the objections to the Prayer Book of Dr. William Ames and Dr. Burgess.

> The result was as follows: Kneeling he "thought lawful"; the surplice he "more doubted of" and purposed not to wear it unless compelled; the Ring in Marriage he made no scruple about; the cross in Baptism he resolved never to use; the Prayer Book he "judged to have much disorder and defectiveness in it but nothing which should make the use of it, in the Ordinary Publick Worship, to be unlawful to them that have not liberty to do better". [9]

During the Commonwealth he had used the **Directory,** and it was this liturgy which stood firmly behind his own **Reformed Liturgy.** Baxter had also written on the subject of liturgy in his **Five Disputations of Church Government and Worship,** 1659, which reveals that he was not entirely ignorant of the classical rites. In the fourth disputation, Baxter examined the word Leitourgia, the worship of God. God has, so Baxter argued, made it our duty to assemble for worship, but the form of liturgy is left to us in a similar way as is the text for the sermon. [10] It is lawful to pray to God in the set words that we find in Scripture; to pray thus is to use a form, and therefore a form is lawful. [11] Jesus used a psalm at the passover or Eucharist, and forms were used in Africa, Asia, and in the Reformed Churches in France, Holland and Geneva; furthermore, some forms were necessary, such as the use of the Words of Institution. [12] But other forms were optional:

> Forms were at first introduced in Variety, and not as necessary for the Churches Unity to Agree in one: And they were left to the Pastor's Liberty, and none were forced to any forms of other mens composing. When Basil set up his new forms of Psalmodie and other Worship, which the Church of Neocaesarea were so offended at, he did not for all that impose it on them, but was content to use it in his church at Caesarea. [13]

Some ministers, Baxter maintained, can do well without a form, and some are better if they use a form; but it is a sin for magistrates and prelates to impose a set form. [14] The safest way of composing a "stinted" liturgy is to take it all, or as much as possible--words as well as matter--from scripture; in appealing to ancient venerable forms, there is nothing more ancient and venerable than Scripture itself. [15] It was this latter principle--the use of scriptural words and matter--that Baxter carefully followed in the **Reformed Liturgy.**

In the **Reformed Liturgy** [16] Baxter retained the familiar Puritan separation of the liturgy of Word and Sacrament. The usual Sunday Morning service was entitled "The Ordinary Public Worship on the Lord's Day"; the following order was proposed:

A prayer for God's assistance, with a shorter alternative.
The Apostles' or Nicene Creed; sometimes the "Athanasian" Creed.
The Decalogue.
Sentences of Scripture moving the people to penitence.
Confession of sin and prayer for pardon, with Lord's Prayer, with a shorter alternative.
Some sentences of Scripture strengthening faith, and for raising the penitent, similar to the "comfortable words".
Psalm 95, 100, or 84.
Psalms of the day.
Chapter of the Old Testament.
A psalm, sung, or Te Deum, said.
Chapter of the New Testament.
Prayer for the King and Magistrates.
Psalm 67, or 98, or some other psalm, or Benedictus or Magnificat.
Prayer for the Church, extemporized by the minister in the pulpit.
Sermon.
Prayer, including a blessing on the word of instruction and exhortation.
Hymn (optional).
Blessing.

Professor Ratcliff observed that this service was composed of elements of the Prayer Book Morning Prayer, Litany and Ante-communion without the repetitions, redundancies, and other "un-meet" liturgicalia of the Prayer Book. [17] Nevertheless, behind this order, that of the **Directory** is clearly discernible--the prayer for God's assistance, the chapter of both Testaments, and the Long Prayer before or after the sermon.

Baxter's Eucharistic liturgy was entitled "The Order of Celebrating the Sacrament of the Body and Blood of Christ", and when celebrated, it was to follow the prayer after the sermon at Morning worship, though no directions regarding the frequency of celebration were given. The order was accepted by the other Puritan commissioners with one exception:

> . . . they put out a few Lines in the Administration of the Lord's Supper, where the Word Offering was used: [18]

The structure of Baxter's Eucharistic liturgy was as follows:

Explication of the nature, use, and benefits of this sacrament.
Exhortation.
Confession.
The bread and wine are set upon the table, if not previously placed there.
Eucharistic Prayer(s) and three actions shape:
- Prayer to the Father for sanctification of the elements;
- Words of Institution; ministerial declaration of consecration.
- Prayer to the Son; fraction and libation with appropriate words.
- Prayer to the Spirit for worthy communion; administration.
- (The prayers may be read as one, followed by the three actions. The communicants may stand, sit or kneel.)

Prayer of thanksgiving.
Exhortation, if there is time.
Hymn in metre, or Psalm (such as 23, 116, 103 or 100).
Blessing: Hebrews 13:20.

As was the case of Morning worship, Baxter based his rite on the **Directory**. There are differences, but these are accounted for by the latitude allowed by the **Directory**, and by the fact that the **Reformed Liturgy** was meant to be a compromise with the **Book of Common Prayer**. Allowance must also be made for Baxter's own ideas founded upon experience, and it is useful to bear in mind his own account of his method of celebration at Kidderminster in 1657:

> A long table being spread, I first open the nature and use of the ordinance, and the qualification and present duty of the communicants; and then the deacons (3 or 4 grave, pious men chosen and appointed to that office) do set the bread and wine on the table; and in prayer we beseech the Lord to accept of those his own creatures now dedicated and set apart for his service, as sanctified to represent the body and blood of his Son; and after confession of sin, and thanksgiving for redemption, with commemoration of the sufferings of Christ therein, and ransom thereby, we beg the pardon of sin, and the acceptance of our persons and thanksgivings now offered up to God again, and his grace to help our faith, repentance, love, etc. and renewal of our covenant with him, etc. And so after the words of institution etc. I break the bread and deliver it in Christ's general terms to all present, first partaking myself, and so by the cup: which is moved down to the end of the table by the people and deacons (who fill the cup when it is emptied); and immediately after it, each one layeth down his alms to the poor, and so arise, and the next tableful succeedeth to the last: after which I proceed to some words of exhortation, and then of praise and prayer, and sing a psalm, and so conclude with the blessing. [**19**]

This account serves as a useful bridge between the **Directory** and the **Reformed Liturgy.**

The explication on the nature, use, and benefits of the sacrament was to be given by the minister if "needful". Baxter's model was Puritan verbosity at its best, covering the whole of salvation history: the creation, the fall, the atonement, and the Eucharist, a "continued representation and remembrance of his death". Eight "holy qualifications" for communion were given:

1. True belief in the Trinity and the person of Christ.
2. Sense of sin.
3. Desire for pardon.
4. Thanks for God's love.
5. Exercise of holy love and joy.
6. Love to one another.
7. Self-oblation to God.
8. Hope in the coming of Christ and for glorification.

This is probably Baxter's interpretation of the **Directory** rubric that "Something concerning that ordinance, and the due preparation thereunto, and participation thereof, be taught". The exhortation was characteristic of the "Genevan" family of liturgies. It took the form of an invitation to look upon the sacrificed lamb of God, whose will it is "to be thus frequently crucified before our eyes"; here the Agnus Dei and the idea of sacrifice reappear in the Puritan tradition. Because of judgment, the congregation was exhorted to revive its love for one another and to receive a "crucified Christ here represented".

The confession, said by the minister alone (cf. **Exceptions**) was constructed out of biblical phrases, and represented the logical conclusion of the "Word of God" as being the only criterion for liturgical forms. Some of the phrases echoed the Prayer Book "We do not presume", and this confession corresponded to the Prayer Book communion confession, absolution, comfortable words and "Prayer of Humble Access".

After the confession, Baxter suggested the following rubric:

> Here let the Bread be brought to the Minister, and received by him, and set upon the Table; and then the Wine in like manner: or if they be set there before, however let him bless them, praying in these or the like words.

Baxter's rubric allows an offertory or presentation of the elements before the Eucharistic Prayer, or allows that the elements may be already upon the table, thus recognizing a double practice. One of his sources was Hamon L'Estrange's compilation of the various editions of the Prayer Book, and it may be that this work suggested Baxter's rubric, being a concession to the "Laudian" divines. The 1549 Prayer Book communion contained a rubric before the Sursum corda requiring the minister to take and prepare the bread and the wine, and to set them both upon the altar, this rubric replacing the "Little Canon" of the mass. However, the 1552 and subsequent revisions made no such provision, thereby abolishing and excluding any idea of offering the elements to God. Thus Bishop Cosin could comment upon the Prayer Book:

> And somewhat is also wanting for a direction when & where to sett ye Bread & wine for ye Comn upo yt Table. [**20**]

What appears to have happened was that a double practice arose; some clergy followed the older practice as represented in 1549, while others place the elements upon the table at the beginning of the service. The "Laudian" school of divines, believing that the presentation of the elements was an integral part of the eucharistic action, wished for the restoration of the 1549 rubric. Thus in the 1637 Liturgy for Scotland:

> And the Presbyter shall them (i.e. alms) offer up and place the bread and wine prepared for the Sacrament

> upon the Lord's Table, that it may be ready for that service. [21]

The Durham Book, containing the revisions of the Prayer Book proposed by bishops Cosin and Wren in 1661, had the following rubrics before the "Prayer for the Church Militant":

> i. Add: And if there be a Communion, the Priest shall then offer up, & place ye Bread & Wine in a comly Paten & Chalice upon the Table, that they may be ready for the Sacrament, so much as he shall think sufficient.
> ii. Read: And if there be a Communion, the Priest shall then offer up, & place upon the Table so much Bread & wine as he shall think sufficient. [22]

Baxter's rubric, allowing a two-fold practice, was a genuine compromise; but the permissive use suggests that for Baxter the presentation of the elements was not an integral part of the Eucharistic action, but was purely utilitarian. [23]

It was after this rubric that Baxter's Eucharistic action began; it was a systematic reordering and development of the **Directory** rubric for sanctification "by the word of Institution and Prayer".

In his **Catechising of Families.** [24] on the subject of Christ's sacrificed Body and Blood, Baxter argued that the eucharistic action was three-fold: (1) Consecration; (2) Commemoration; (3) Covenanting and communication. It was around this three action shape that he constructed his Eucharistic Prayer(s).

(1) Consecration.

To the question "What is the consecration?" Baxter wrote:

> It is the separating and sanctifying the bread and wine, to this holy use; by which it ceaseth to be mere common bread and wine, and is made sacramentally, that is, by signification and representation, the sacrificed body and blood of Christ. [25]

To the reply "But some say it is done only by saying these words, 'This is my body', or by blessing it", Baxter explained:

> It is done by all that goeth to a dedication and separation from its holy use; and this is, 1. By declaring that God commandeth and accepteth it, (which is best done by reading his institution,) and that we then accordingly devote it. 2. By praying for his acceptance and blessing. 3. By pronouncing ministerialy that it is now, sacramentally, Christ's body and blood. [26]

Elsewhere he wrote:

> In the consecration, the church doth first offer the creatures of bread and wine, to be accepted of God, to this sacred use. And God accepteth them, and blesseth them to this use; which he signifieth both by the words of his own institution, and by the action of his ministers, and their benediction. They being the agents of God to the people in this accepting and blessing, as they are the agents of the people of God, in offering or dedicating the creatures to this use. [27]

Thus according to Baxter, the prayer, the scriptural warrant and the ministerial declaration were all necessary for consecration.

In the **Reformed Liturgy** the prayer for consecration called upon God the creator who gave his Son to reconcile us to himself, to

> . . . sanctify these thy creatures of bread and wine, which, according to thy institution and command, we set apart to this holy use, that they be sacramentally the body and blood of thy son Jesus Christ. [28]

The Institution Narrative from 1 Cor. 11 was read, and then the minister was to declare that

> "This bread and wine, being set apart, and consecrated to this holy use by God's appointment, are now no common bread and wine, but sacramentally the body and blood of Christ."

(2) Commemoration.

The commemoration or anamnesis, as the Puritan tradition understood it, was here made clear and distinct. In the classical anaphoras the anamnesis was interpreted in terms of offering the consecrated bread and wine in remembrance of the passion, death and resurrection of Christ; "Do this" in remembrance equalled "Offer this" in remembrance. In the 1552 Communion service, Cranmer seems to have interpreted "remembrance" as the actual eating and drinking of the elements; thus "Do this as ofte as ye shal drinke it in remembrance of me" was followed immediately by the administration with the words "Take and eate this in remembrance that Christ died for thee, etc." The Puritan tradition seems to have centered the "remembrance" on the visual breaking of the bread and the pouring of the wine, as already witnessed in the heightening of the fraction in the Waldegrave and Middleburg books, and the **Directory**. Baxter showed the same concern.

> As Christ himself was incarnate and true Christ, before he was sacrificed to God, and was sacrificed to God before that sacrifice be communicated for life and nourishment to souls; so in the sacrament, consecration must first make the creature to be the flesh and blood of Christ representative; and then the sacrificing of that flesh and blood must be represented and commemorated; and then the sacrificed flesh and blood communicated to the receivers for their spiritual life.
>
> The commemoration chiefly (but not only) respecteth God the Son. For he hath ordained, that these consecrated representations should in their manner and measure, supply the room of his bodily presence, while his body is in heaven: and that thus, as it were, in effigy, in representation, he might be still crucified before the church's eyes; and they might be affected, as if they had seen him on the cross. And that by faith and prayer, they might, as it were, offer him up to God; that is, might shew the Father that sacrifice, once made for sin, in which they trust, and for which it is that they expect all the acceptance of their persons with God, and hope for audience when they beg for mercy, and offer up prayer or praises to him. [**29**]

Baxter explained further his understanding of commemoration:

> It containeth the signal representation of the sacrificing of Christ, as the Lamb of God, to take away the sins of the world. Where the signs are, 1. The materials, the bread and wine. 2. The minister's breaking the bread and pouring out the wine. 3. The presenting them to God, as the commemoration of that sacrifice in which we trust; and declaring to the people, that this is done to this commemoration.
>
> The things signified, are, 1. Christ's flesh and blood, when he was on earth. 2. The crucifying of Christ, the piercing of his flesh and shedding his blood. 3. Christ's offering this to God as a sacrifice for man's sins. And this commemoration is a great part of the Sacrament. [**30**]

And regarding the term "sacrifice":

> As the bread is justly called Christ's body, as signifying it, so the action described was of old called a sacrifice, as representing and commemorating it. And it is no more improper than calling our bodies and our alms, and our prayers sacrifices (Rom. xii.1; Eph. v. 2; Phil. ii. 17 and iv. 18; Heb. xiii. 15, 16; 1 Pet. ii. 5f). [**31**]

This explains Baxter's elaborate fraction and libation. The prayer, which "chiefly respecteth God the Son", asked

> . . . by thine intercession with the Father, through the sacrifice of the body and blood, give us the pardon of our sins, and thy quickening Spirit, without which the flesh will profit us nothing. Reconcile us to the Father: nourish us as thy members to everlasting life.

In earlier Puritan liturgies, the fraction had been accompanied by the Words of Institution. Baxter broke with this tradition, using his own formula, and being influenced by the Agnus Dei, the chant associated with the fraction in the Roman Mass:

> The body of Christ was broken for us, and offered once for all to sanctify us: behold the sacrificed Lamb of God, that taketh away the sins of the world.

And the libation:

> We were redeemed with the precious blood of Christ, as of a Lamb without blemish and without spot.

The demand for the fraction to be emphasized was made in the **Exceptions**, and the manual acts required during the words of Institution in the 1662 "Prayer of Consecration" were a minor concession to Puritan wishes.

(3) Covenanting and Communication

The final part of the three action shape of the Eucharist was the administration. According to Baxter,

> It containeth the signs, and the things signified, as communicated. The signs are, 1. The actual delivery of the consecrated bread and wine (first broken and poured out) to the communicants, with the naming what it is that is given them. 2. Bidding them take, eat and drink. 3. Telling them the benefits and blessings given thereby: and all this by a minister of Christ, authorized thus to act in his name, as covenanting, promising, and giving what is offered.
>
> And on the receiver's part the signs are, 1. Freely taking what is offered (the bread and wine). 2. Eating and drinking. 3. Vocal praise and thanksgiving to God, and professed consent to the covenant. [**32**]

Baxter listed the benefits as reconciliation, pardon of sins, everlasting life and strengthening of faith, hope, love, joy, patience and all grace.

As in the case of the Consecration and Commemoration, this third action in the **Reformed Liturgy** was accompanied by prayer and words of warrant and explanation. The prayer, addressed to the Spirit, was an "Epiklesis" as far as the Calvinist tradition understood it:

> . . . illuminate us, that by faith we may see him that is here represented to us. Soften our hearts, and humble us for our sins. Sanctify and quicken us, that we may relish the spiritual food and feed on it to our nourishment and growth in grace.

Thus the Spirit was asked to act upon the communicant, reflecting Calvin's teaching of communion by faith and the Holy Spirit. The words of administration were based upon those of the **Directory.**

Baxter provided a version of the substance of the three prayers as one prayer, but in this alternative his careful trinitarian structuring was obscured, for the three prayers concerned with Consecration, Commemoration, and Covenanting and communication, were addressed to the Father, Son and Holy Spirit respectively. He also allowed for the consecration and administration of the bread before the consecrating and administration of the wine, suggesting that the double consecration was still an issue for some.

A rubric provided for flexibility regarding the place and manner of reception--at the table, or not; in the hand, or handing it to one another; no one was forced to stand, sit or kneel. On this point Baxter was offering comprehension to all consciences. His own preference was for sitting; when at Kidderminster, Sir Ralph Clare, the Lord of the Manor and leader of the parish episcopalians, had asked to receive communion kneeling; Baxter had replied that he was prepared to allow it, but that the example of Christ and his apostles was to receive sitting. [**33**] The place of the collection was also optional.

After the administration, a prayer of thanksgiving was to follow, being mainly concerned with the benefits of communion. The positioning of the Gloria in excelsis in the Prayer Book may have influenced Baxter here, since the Lucan phraseology occurred in the prayer.

If there was time, an exhortation was provided, reminding the worshippers of God's love and pardon. This was followed by a hymn in meter, or a psalm of praise--23, 116, 103 (as in the **Genevan Service Book**) or 100 being suggested. The rite concluded with a blessing from Hebrews 13:20-21; it was very fitting that the Epistle of the Atonement should have been chosen to provide words to conclude a liturgy, much of the language of which dwelt upon the crucifixion.

Baxter's Eucharistic liturgy was an attempt to harmonize the Genevan liturgical family with the **Book of Common Prayer,** and thus its derivation may be traced back to the Latin Mass through two lineages; though, if we may borrow biological language, in Baxter's **Reformed Liturgy** the Genevan genes were dominant. But commenting upon his conception of the liturgical action of the Eucharist, E. C. Ratcliff wrote:

> Certainly Baxter's eucharistic and liturgical ideas approach more closely to the historic western tradition than the ideas expressed or implied in the Communion Service of the contemporary Prayer Book. If Baxter could have digested into an historic western liturgical shape what he believed and wished to express, his rite would have commended itself to John Cosin and other High Church Anglicans of the descent of Andrewes and Overall. In matters of worship, Baxter was divided from High Church Anglicans less in doctrine and spirit than in shape, or liturgical form, and letter. [**34**]

Be that as it may, with the failure of the Savoy Conference this latest branch of the Genevan liturgical family died without issue.

NOTES

1. For the use of these titles, F. J. Powicke, **A Life of the Reverend Richard Baxter**, London 1924, 167; **The Reverend Richard Baxter under the Cross (1662-1691)**, London 1927, 71ff.

2. N. Micklem, ed., **Christian Worship: A Book of Public Worship,** Introduction, xiii.

3. E. C. Ratcliff, "The Savoy Conference", in, ed. G. F. Nuttall and O. Chadwick, **From Uniformity to Unity**, London 1962, 116.

4. Text in E. Cardwell, **A History of Conferences**, 303-363.

5. G. F. Nuttall, **Richard Baxter**, London 1965, 18. For biographical details see also F. J. Powicke, op.cit.

6. G. F. Nuttall, ibid., 80.

7. **Reliquiae Baxterianae**, ed. M. Sylvester, London 1696, I. ii., 306.

8. F. J. Powicke, **A Life**, 95.

9. Ibid., 23. For Baxter's own "Exceptions" to the Prayer Book, **Reliquiae Baxterianae** I. ii, 308-316.

10. Richard Baxter, **Five Disputations of Church Government and Worship**, London 1659, 362.

11. Ibid., 363.

12. Ibid., 364-5.

13. Ibid., 391.

14. Ibid., 373.

15. Ibid., 378.

16. Text in Bard Thompson, **Liturgies of the Western Church;** valuable comments on this liturgy are to be found in E. C. Ratcliff, "The Savoy Conference" in **From Uniformity to Unity 1662-1962**, ed. G. F. Nuttall and O. Chadwick, 1962, and E. C. Ratcliff, "Puritan Alternatives to the Prayer Book" in **The English Prayer Book 1549-1662**, M. Ramsey, et al.

17. "The Savoy Conference", op.cit., 121.

18. **Reliquiae Baxterianae**, I. ii., 334.

19. Baxter Manuscripts (Dr. William's Library) 3:156, a letter of March 1657, quoted in G. F. Nuttall, **Richard Baxter**, 53.

20. Cosin, Particulars, 45 (1660), in **Works**, Vol. 5, cited in ed. G. J. Cuming, **The Durham Book**, Oxford 1961, 145.

21. For the Laudian argument, W. Jardine Grisbrooke, **Liturgies of the Seventeenth and Eighteenth Centuries.**

22. Ed. G. J. Cuming, 146.

23. In the resulting book of 1662 the rubric directed: "And when there is a communion, the priest shall then place upon the Table so much Bread and Wine, as he shall think sufficient". The double practice seems to have continued. Bishop Hicks, the Non-juring bishop of Thetford, complained that the rubric "to the great reproach of the clergy, was almost never since (its restoration) observed in Cathedral or Parochial Churches. I say never, (he adds), because I never knew or heard but of two or three persons, which is a very small number, who observed it; but the bread and wine was still placed upon the Table before the Office of the Communion began, without any solemnity, it may be the clerk or sexton, or any other, perhaps unfitter, person, to the great derogation of the reverence due to the holy Mystery". W. E. Scudamore, **Notittia Eucharistica**, London 1876, 383-384.

24. Ed. W. Orme, **The Practical Works of the Rev. Richard Baxter,** London 1830, Vol. 19.

25. Ibid., 274-275.

26. Ibid., 275.

27. **Christian Economics**, ed. Orme, **The Practical Works,** 4:315.

28. Once again, this is not an epiklesis (W. D. Maxwell and Horton Davies); it resembles more the Quam oblationem of the Canon Missae than the Eastern Epiklesis. See the previous discussion with reference to the **Directory.** It should be noted that it also corresponds to the petition in the **Book of Common Prayer,** but expresses a higher doctrine; it asks for the definite sanctifying of the elements.

29. **Christian Economics,** in op.cit., 316.

30. **Catechizing of Families** in op.cit., 280.

31. Ibid.

32. Ibid., 281.

33. F. J. Powicke, **A Life,** 179ff.

34. E. C. Ratcliff, "Puritan Alternatives to the Prayer Book", in op.cit., 79.

Chapter Four

A PERIOD OF LITURGICAL OBSCURITY: 1658 - 1800

Information about the Eucharistic liturgy among the Independents from the time of the **Savoy Declaration** of 1658 until the end of the eighteenth century is extremely sparse. During this period Independency was synonymous with a refusal to use any set forms of prayer in worship, and thus presents a situation like that of the Elizabethan Separatists.

For the sources of Independent Eucharistic liturgy during this period we have to rely on a few contemporary accounts that are known to exist:

1. An account from a manuscript common-place book of the Reverend Robert Kirk, a Scottish minister who visited London in 1689/90, and who recorded the worship he witnessed in various Churches.

2. An account of the Morning service at Angel Street Chapel, Worcester, and the Eucharist as celebrated at the Rothwell Independent Meeting, Northampton, both dating from the late seventeenth century.

3. An account of the Morning service and the Eucharist in Isaac Watt's Church at Bury Street c. 1723.

These accounts may be supplemented by the outline of the Lord's Supper recommended to his pupils by Philip Doddridge, together with comments of Samuel Cradock, Isaac Chauncy, and some valuable material from Doddridge's diaries relating to his own celebrations of the Supper.

These sources must be used with caution, bearing in mind that they give us only an outline of worship, and not a full text of the prayers used.

It is also useful to refer briefly to the liturgical practice of orthodox Presbyterians and Baptists during this same period. We have previously drawn attention to the fact that after the Ejection, the distinction between Presbyterian and Independent ministers was not always clear; Churches sometimes alternated between Presbyterian and Independent ministers, as for example at Reading, where the Presbyterian Samuel Doolittle was followed by the Independent George Burnet, and he again was followed in 1718 by the Presbyterian Richard Rigby. [1] In the same way, Vavasor Powell and John Bunyan belonged to congregations which were both Independent and Baptist. We may suggest that there may have existed some overlap in liturgical practice.

The clear distinction between Morning service and the Eucharist, already inherent in the Genevan rite, practiced by the Separatists, and encouraged by the **Directory's** lack of direction on frequency of the Eucharist, seems to have been perpetuated in Independency during his period. Whereas the Sunday Morning worship was observed every Sunday, the Eucharist was usually celebrated once a month, [2] and could be held at night, or at noon, during the afternoon or the morning. [3] According to the Bury Street records, it followed after the sermon, while Doddridge presupposed an interval "between the close of the general service and the administration of the ordinance". [4]

Morning Worship

An account of Morning worship as conducted by an Independent minister of the name Cockain [5] was recorded by the Scottish minister Robert Kirk; [6] he also recorded the Morning service of two notable Presbyterian divines, William Bates and, interestingly enough, Richard Baxter. It is valuable to compare the summary of these accounts with the Independent worship of Angel Street, Worcester, and of Bury Street, London. (see page 73)

If Kirk's accounts are reliable, the Presbyterian Bates and the Independent Cockain both followed what appears to have been the minimum order of service--prayer, sermon, prayer. Like the order of Datheen, this appears to have been a basic structure which could be expanded according to taste. [7] We may assume that Cockain opened with prayer.

Baxter's service followed very closely the order suggested by the **Directory**, and not that of his own **Reformed Liturgy** of 1661, suggesting that even he regarded the latter as a dead letter. The same similarity to the **Directory** underlies orders of Angel Street and Bury Street, though, reflecting Independent opinion expressed at the Westminster Assembly, in both cases the Long Prayer came before the sermon (though not at the opening of the service); in Baxter's service it came after the sermon.

BATES	MR. COCKAIN	ANGEL STREET	BURY STREET	BAXTER
		Singing	Psalm	Psalm
		Short Prayer	Short Prayer	Extempore Prayer
				Psalm Reading
		O. T. Lesson	Exposition	O. T. Lesson
		N. T. Lesson		N. T. Lesson
		Hymn	(Psalm or Hymn)	
Prayer	Prayer	Long Prayer	Long Prayer	Prayer
Sermon	Sermon	Sermon	Sermon	Sermon
		Psalm or Hymn	(Psalm or Hymn)	
Prayer	Prayer	Short Prayer	Short Prayer	Long Prayer & Lord's Prayer
		Blessing	Blessing	(Psalm and Blessing?)

From this sparse evidence it would appear that a wide latitude was allowed in the order of Morning service. Kirk distinctly recorded that Dr. Bates omitted to use the Lord's Prayer, whereas Baxter concluded the Long Prayer with it, as in **Waldegrave, Middleburg** and the **Directory**. The Independent accounts have no reference to the Lord's Prayer at all.

John Owen argued that the Lord's Prayer was given at a time when Jesus was a minister of the circumcision; his death and subsequent glorification freed Christians from the obligation of reciting it. [8] It would appear that most Independents endorsed his conclusion. Doddridge, however, rejected the idea that it was for temporary use only, and insisted that it suits Christians in every age; [9] he introduced it into Sunday worship at Kibworth. [10]

Some idea of the type of prayers used may be gained from sections of Isaac Watt's **A Guide to Prayer**. This work, as the title implies, was no more than a guide to prayer in general, and not a complete manual for public worship. Watts considered the various parts of prayer: invocation, adoration, confession, petition, pleading, profession, or self-dedication, thanksgiving and blessing. At certain points he gave examples and summaries, which may well reflect his own usage in worship, and the type of prayer used. For example, in the section on thanksgiving we find the following:

> We praise thee, O Lord, for thine original designs of love to fallen man; that thou shouldest make a distinction between us and the angels that sinned: what is man, that thou art thoughtful about his salvation; and sufferest the angels to perish for ever without remedy: that thou shouldest chuse a certain number of the race of Adam, and give them into the hands of Christ before all worlds, and make a covenant of grace with them in Christ Jesus, that their happiness might be secured, that thou shouldest reveal this mercy in various types and promises to our fathers by the prophets, and that in thine own appointed time thou shouldest send thy Son to take our nature upon him, and to redeem us by his death? We give glory to thy justice and to thy grace for this work of terror and compassion, this work of reconciling sinners to thyself by the punishment of thy Son: we praise thee for the gospel which thou hast published to the world, the gospel of pardon and peace; and that thou hast confirmed it by such abundant testimonies, to raise and establish our faith: we give glory to that power of thine that has guarded thy gospel in all ages, and through ten thousand oppositions of Satan has delivered it down safe to our age, and has proclaimed

> the glad tidings of peace in our nation: we bless thee that thou hast built habitations for thyself amongst us, and that we should be born in such a land of light as this is: it is a distinguishing favour of thine, that among the works of thy creation we should be placed in the rank of rational beings; but it is more distinguishing goodness, that we should be born of religious parents under the general promises of grace. We give thanks unto thy goodness for our preservation from many dangers which we could never foresee, and which we could not ask thee to prevent: how infinitely are we indebted to thee, O Lord, that thou hast not cut us off in a state of nature and sin, and that our portion is not at this time amongst the children of eternal wrath! That our education should be under religious care, and that we should have so many conveniences and comforts of life conferred upon us, as well as the means of grace brought near to us; and all this before we began to know thee, or sought any of the mercies of this life or the other at thine hands! [**11**]

Dealing with this theme of confession, Watts advised his readers to include

> A confession of our sins, both original, which belong to our nature; and actual, that have been found in the course of our lives. [**12**]

This latter seems to be an echo of the wording of the confession in the **Directory** and there is no reason to doubt that Watts was acquainted with the work of the Westminster Assembly. Indeed, a knowledge of the **Directory** would explain why the Bury Street service approximates so closely to it.

In the section concerning petition, Watts outlined a comprehensive description. [**13**] Philip Doddridge also exhorted:

> Forget not the public--but pray for them with seriousness. - Plead for Heathens, Jews, Mahometans, Papists, and persecuted Protestants. - Pray for your own country with cordial love and esteem - Remember that praying for the King is part of the condition on which our toleration is granted. - Forget not magistrates, - and ministers. [**14**]

Allowing for the fact that Christian intercessions will always include certain themes, nevertheless in both the above, these are fair summaries of the corresponding section in the **Directory**. The examples given by Watts seem to correspond to the substance of the Long Prayer as described in the Bury Street records:

> ... the variety of blessings, spiritual and temporal, for the whole congregation, with confession of sins, and thanksgiving for mercies; petitions also are offered up for the whole world, for the Churches of Christ, for the nation in which we dwell, for all our rulers and governors, together with any particular cases which are represented.

Cockain's prayer as recorded by Kirk was of the same themes, though less comprehensive.

In summary we may say that a wide latitude was allowed in Morning worship, the basic pattern being prayer, sermon, prayer, to which could be added more prayers, psalms, lections and a blessing. In some Independent Churches the service was therefore very close to that suggested by the **Directory.**

The Eucharist

For the Eucharistic liturgy proper we are dependent upon two contemporary accounts: that of the Rothwell Church in Northamptonshire, under the pastorate of the Reverend R. Davis, recorded in c. 1700 by an anonymous Anglican; and that of Bury Street in the time of Isaac Watts, 1723. [**15**] We give both accounts in full.

1. Rothwell

> Every member is required to receive the Sacrament as often as it is administered. The Table stands in the midst of the Congregation, near the Pulpit. The Pastor sits in his Chair near the Table, and the Receivers on Forms around about it; the People, as Spectators, at some small distance behind them.
>
> The Pastor prays (all standing) and craves a Blessing on the Bread; then sets it apart in almost the same Words which the Church of England uses; then breaks it into small pieces, and puts them on divers Plates, saying, whilst he is breaking, Thus was our Lord's body torn, mangled, broken, &c. The Bread thus broken is carried in the Plates, by the Deacons, to the several Receivers. The Pastor sits in his Chair Eating with the rest.
>
> As soon as the Bread is Eaten, the Pastor Prays; then pours out the Wine, saying, Behold the Blood of Christ poured out for thee, and for me, and for all of us, &c. Drink ye all of this, drink large draughts of the

Love of Christ, &c. as he thinks most proper to express himself. Then he drinks and gives to the Deacons. When all have drunk the Pastor Prays, an Hymn is Sung, and the Assembly is dismissed.

They forbid all private Prayer at this Ordinance, saying, the Pastors Prayers are sufficient. They esteem it a Memorial only: Examine none before they come, saying, There is no need of any more Preparation at that time than any other. In the absence or sickness of the Pastor, there must be no Sacrament.

2. Bury Street

(The first Lord's day in every month the Lord's Supper is administered just after sermon.)

The Lord's Supper is administered alternately by the two pastors (Dr. Watts and Rev. S. Price) (v13) in the plainest manner, just according to the institution, first the history of the institution of this ordinance is read, either out of Matthew's gospel or the first ep. Corinthians, that it may ever be kept in mind to regulate every part of the practice; and the sermons of that day being equally suited to the design of the Lord's Supper, or a commemoration of the sufferings of Christ 'tis but seldom that any other speech or exhortation is made before the celebration.

The minister, taking hold of the plate in which the bread lies, calls upon the people to join with him in seeking for a blessing on it, which is done in a short prayer of eight or ten minutes. Then the minister says "Having blessed this bread, we break it in remembrance of our Saviour's body, &c." Then the loaves, which are before cut in squares, almost through, are broken by the minister into small pieces, as big as walnuts, or thereabouts, and taking the plate of bread in his hand, he says, "This is the body of Christ, or the emblem or figure of the body of Christ, which was broken for you: take it and eat ye all of it, in remembrance of our Saviour who died for us", or such like words, which are a plain declaration that the bread represents the body of Christ, according to his own appointment: it is then distributed by the pastor to the deacons, and to one or more of the members who are appointed to it, and it is carried by them to the various members of the church. Then, after a short space, an inquiry being made if all have received the bread, and that those who have not received it are desired to stand up and signify it, the pastor proceeds, in like manner, to pour out the wine, at least into one of the cups, then he asks a blessing on the

> cup; and then distributes it, as before, to the members or the deacons, and they to some other members of the church, by whom it is carried round to all the seats. In many churches, the pastor is frequently speaking proper sentences or texts or scripture, to awaken the faith, hope, and joy of Christians, and I cannot but approve of it in the main. But our former pastor, Dr. Chauncey, was so much against it, that it was not practiced among us. But when most of the members, on some particular occasion, met together, the two pastors proposed it to them, whether we should keep up this practice or leave them to their own silent meditations. They seemed generally to approve our silence, and this is the reason we omit it.
>
> After this there is a psalm or hymn sung, suited to the ordinance. Then the plate is sent round to collect for the necessities of the poor. After this, particular cases of the members are represented who desire the public prayers of the church; and then, with a prayer offered on this occasion, together with thanksgiving and the final benediction, this service is concluded.

These two accounts may be supplemented by certain elements from Philip Doddridge's lectures to his theological students, Lecture XX, "On Administering the Lord's Supper", and from his diary in which he recorded meditations and reflections on the sacrament. [16] In the latter Doddridge recorded the Scripture text for meditation, or brief homily, and the substance of his discourse at the breaking of the bread and pouring the wine; he also recorded the substance of "the prayer", which, from its position, would appear to have been the post communion prayer.

(1) Extempore meditations on some select texts of Scripture.
(2) Prayer before receiving the bread, with confession of sin.
(3) Breaking of bread with discourse.
(4) Distribution of bread - in silence. Address a word now and then.
(5) Prayer before the cup.
(6) Pouring out of wine with discourse.
(7) Distribution of wine - in silence.
(8) Singing.
(9) Prayer of Thanksgiving and Intercession.
(10) Collection.

The main elements of these three accounts may be compared as follows:

Rothwell	Bury Street	Doddridge
	Institution Narrative - Matthew or 1 Cor. 11.	
	(Exhortation)	Extempore Meditation
Blessing on bread	Blessing over bread	Prayer with confession & Blessing of bread
Fraction with words	Fraction with words	Fraction with discourse
Distribution	Distribution - in silence though some ministers quote sentences.	Distribution - in silence but with an occasional word
	Pouring out of wine	
Prayer over wine	Prayer over cup	Prayer over wine
Pouring out of wine with words		Pouring out of wine with discourse
Distribution	Distribution	Distribution
Hymn	Psalm of hymn	Singing
	Collection	
	Intercession & thanksgiving	Thanksgiving & intercession
Dismissal	Benediction	Collection

From what is known of orthodox Presbyterianism, the Eucharist was similar in outline, though conforming more to the 1645 **Directory**, with an exhortation and fencing of the table, a single prayer of consecration and an admonition afterwards. [17]

An account of a Baptist celebration in recorded by Thomas Grantham in **Hear the Church: or an Appeal to the Mother of us all**, 1687; the order is somewhat fuller than those of the Independents, with an exhortation, a statement of faith, and an exhortation afterwards. However, like the Independents, there was a "double consecration", the separate consecration of the bread and wine.

The summaries of the three Independent orders show variations, as might be expected in a reconstruction from accounts; but variation should be expected as inherent to Independency. As in the case of the account of Morning service, the Bury Street Eucharist comes very close to that outlined in the **Directory;** but if the **Directory** represents a compromise between Puritanism and Separatism in favor of the **Genevan Service Book,** the Bury Street order shifts the balance back to the Separatists. The Rothwell account--seen through Anglican eyes--is close to the New England celebration as given by John Cotton. All three, however, agree on the double consecration and the deliberate fraction and libation. We may consider these two features further.

(a) The Double Consecration.

The double consecration which the Independents had argued for in the **Directory** seems to have been the normal practice at this period; so Watt's predecessor at Bury Street, Isaac Chauncy carefully noted:

> That each Element be distinctly blessed, and apart by it self, by calling upon God in Christ for a Blessing. [18]

At Bury Street the blessing over the bread is described as "a short prayer of eight or ten minutes". In fact the prayer must have been considerably long by modern standards. [19] Unfortunately we are given no indication of what was in the prayer, other than that a blessing was craved. Samuel Cradock, a leading Independent theologian, writing on the subject of the Lord's Supper, says of Christ:

> He blessed the Bread and the Wine severally (as the Jews manner was) by thanksgiving and prayer to God. Hence this Sacrament is called the Eucharist. And this blessing and praying over the Bread and Wine is called the consecration of the Elements, or setting them apart from a common to a holy use. [20]

The duty of the minister according to Cradock is:

> To praise God for the elements of bread and wine; and setting them apart (according to Christ's institution) from a common to this religious use, to pray to God

> that they be effectual representations, signs and seals of the spiritual blessings they are appointed to signifie, to all those who shall receive them in a right manner. And then to distribute the bread and wine so consecrated to the Communicants. And the duty of the communicants is to take and eat of this bread and drink this wine in a right manner. [21]

There certainly seems to have been a specific "consecration". Doddridge records in his diary, "I forgot to consecrate the bread in prayer, but afterwards set it apart". [22] The manner of consecration was presumably the Words of Institution, the prayers of thanksgiving, and the fraction and libation together. However, there does seem to have been a specific petition for a blessing in the prayers; at least, Doddridge suggests that this was the case:

> May the Holy Spirit in this ordinance take of the things of Christ, and show them unto us, a blessing for which the ancient church used especially to pray at this holy ordinance. [23]

Here Doddridge seems to be appealing to the epiklesis of the classical anaphora, and he was widely enough read for this to be possible. [24] The petition probably was similar to that suggested in the **Directory**. In his consideration of Eucharistic doctrine among the Independents at this time, E. P. Winter found representatives of both Calvinism and Zwinglianism, or subjective memorialism. [25] The **Savoy Declaration** itself, though acknowledging that the sacrament was a memorial only, affirmed the Calvinist doctrine that worthy receivers by faith spiritually receive and feed upon Christ crucified; [26] the efficacy of the sacrament depended upon the work of the Spirit and Word of Institution. [27] Doddridge's remark should probably be interpreted in this sense, namely that the Holy Spirit works in us so that by faith we may receive the Body and Blood of Christ. The same Reformed teaching probably underlies the mention of the Spirit in two hymns of Richard Davis of Rothwell:

> The Lamb i' th' midst o' th' Throne of Grace
> us now hath freely fed;
> And by his Spirit down hath sent
> from Heav'n the living Bread. [28]
>
> The Blood of Christ, that great High-priest
> the Spirit does apply. [29]

(b) The Fraction and Libation.

The significance of the fraction and libation was given by Watts in his **Second Catechism**.

61. Q. What doth the bread signify?
A. The bread when it is broken signifies the body of Christ, which was wounded or broken on the cross for us.
"1 Cor. xi. 23, 24,--He took the bread, and when he had given thanks he brake it, and said, take eat, this is my body which is broken for you."

62. Q. What doth the wine signify?
A. The wine poured out into the cup signifies the blood of Christ, which was poured out in his death to take away our sins. "Mat. xxvi. 27, 28. And he took the cup, that is, the cup of wine, or the fruit of the vine, as verse 29, and gave thanks, and gave it to them, saying, drink ye all of it; for this is my blood of the New Testament, which is shed for many for the remission of sins". [30]

In the same vein Cradock could identify the Eucharist as "a visible representation and commemoration of his death till he come to judgment", [31] and Doddridge in words reminiscent of Baxter could speak of Christ being "crucified and set forth before me". [32] It seems to have been a quite deliberate and careful ceremony (as in John a Lasco's rite): the Quay Meeting at Woodbridge had two silver plates and three large silver cups for the communion. [33] Both Watts and Davis appear to have paraphrased the Words of Institution at this point in the service. [34] Doddridge seems to have used the fraction and libation as an opportunity to extemporize a short meditation or homily, and carefully preserves some summaries in his diary. For example, the Fourth Sacrament, July 5th 1730:

> While breaking the bread, I discoursed of the free love of Christ. What could deserve all this? I appealed to Conscience in pouring out the wine. Had we shed the blood of Jesus, what self-resentment would have attended it! What the guilt of having drawn down such agonies on the Son of God! Let us not increase it by trampling it under foot. When taking the cup I observed: Shall I be ashamed of a public engagement? No. Were the whole world of men and angels assembled, I would glory in it; that I am the disciple of a crucified Jesus; and that I receive this sacred cup in token of my sincere resolution of devoting to him all I am and have, of being his for time, and his for eternity. [35]

And June 19th 1731:

> In breaking the bread. - Christ commands us to do this in remembrance of him. But, alas, how little do we remember him. Strange that we should need a memorial; but how much stranger that we should forget him with

> it! Nay, sometimes, that we should be ready to forget him at his table; or remember him there in a manner little better than forgetfulness: yet he remembers us in heaven itself. Blessed Jesus, may thy kindness to us, as it shames our unkindness and ingratitude to thee, so cure it. In giving the cup. - It is the cup of blessing - the cup of blessings. O, what a variety of blessings! Here is pardon; and strength; and grace; and the foretaste of glory! We bless it. May God bless it. So let us bless God that gives us this cup, and humbly pray that it may be indeed a cup of blessing to us. May the taste of it refresh us! and may the memory of it refresh us too! [36]

Doddridge also recorded the summary of the post-communion prayer. Again we give here two examples to give some idea of the substance of this prayer.

> In the prayer, I considered it as an engagement to live and die to the Lord; and as an encouragement to hope that we shall be the Lord's both in life and in death; declaring our dependence upon God, that he would perform his part of the covenant, and upon his grace that we might perform ours. [37]

> In the prayer I adored God for all his blessings, for Himself, his Son, his Spirit, and Heaven, and cheerfully engaged to covenant duties. Thus we should commemorate the death of Christ, but remember him as a risen Redeemer. [38]

On the assumption that these accounts of Independent worship are representative of the denomination during this period, there is a clear link between these accounts and those envisaged by the **Directory**; this link is even more clear when some of the unsuccessful demands of the Independents regarding the formation of the **Directory** are taken into account. The practice of two Eucharistic prayers provides a link with the Separatist tradition, and the apparent interest in the fraction and libation provides a link not only with the **Directory**, but with the rite of John à Lasco. It would be correct to say that the late seventeenth and eighteenth century Independent liturgy had its origin in the Puritan and Separatist rites of the sixteenth century. Yet at the same time it was a distinctive rite. It consisted of certain fixed elements which were dictated by the Independent understanding of the Gospel accounts of the Last Supper: the Words of Institution, two Eucharistic Prayers, the fraction and libation, and the delivery. The substance of these prayers--with perhaps the exception of a specific petition for blessing--together with other features such as homilies, exhortations, scripture sentences, psalms and the form of blessing, were all left to the discretion of the minister and his congregation. The Liturgy of the Word was still separate from the Eucharistic liturgy proper.

NOTES

1. R. Tudur Jones, **Congregationalism in England 1662-1962**, 125.

2. "From the Bury Street Records" in CHST 6 (1915), 333-342; at Angel Street, Worcester it was once every two months, William Urwick, **Nonconformity in Worcester**, London 1897, 82-83; at Fetter Lane, London, it was once a month, when a minister could be found. Fetter Lane Independent Church. Church Book. 1782-1820. Ms. 38. 46. Dr. William's Library. Doddridge noted that in the early church it was celebrated "much more frequently among them than with us". **The Works of the Rev. P. Doddridge D.D.**, vol. 5, 338.

3. In the evening by the Baptists at Fenstanton, E. B. Underhill, **Records of the Churches of Christ, gathered at Fenstanton, Warboys and Hexham 1644-1720**, London, 1854, 36, 69; at noon or the afternoon at Bury Street, art. cit.; in the afternoon at Fetter Lane, Ms. cit.; in the morning at Deadmans Place, cited by E. P. Winter, "The Theory and Practice of the Lord's Supper, Among the Early Separatists, Independents and Baptists, 1580-1700", B. Litt. thesis (unpublished) Oxford 1953, 171.

4. **The Works of the Rev. P. Doddridge, D.D.**, vol. 5, 485.

5. Possibly the George Cokayn who was minister during the Commonwealth and Protectorate at St. Pancras, Soper Lane. C. Bernard Cockett, "George Cokayne" in CHST 12 (1933-36), 225-235.

6. Given in Donald Maclean, **London at Worship: 1689-1690**, Manchester 1928.

7. Peter Walkden at Newton and Hesketh Lane, Lancashire records the following items: Prayer, readings from the Psalms, Old Testament and New Testament, prayer, sermon, prayer, psalm and dismissal. K. W. Wadsworth, "An Eighteenth-Century Country Minister" in CHST 18 (1959) 111-124. At Fetter Lane, for the acceptance of the pastorate of Dr. Davies, the order was prayer, discourse, reply, acceptance, sermon, prayer, conclusion, Ms. cit., 9; at a Solemn Humiliation in Suffolk on Thursday September 6th 1744, prayer, psalm, prayer, sermon, psalm, prayer, prayer, singing a hymn composed and read by Mr. Scott, conclusion, in "Copy of the records of the Congregational Church worshipping at the Quay Meeting Woodbridge". Ms. 76.5. Dr. William's Library, p. 37 verso; at Denton on June 16th 1784, "there was a public service in the evening. Mr. Toms began with prayer.

Mr. Harmer preached from Zechariah IV. 7. and Mr. Tozer concluded with prayer". "Copy of the Church Book belonging to the Congregational Church at Denton 1725-89. Ms. 76.17. Dr. William's Library, folio 55.

8. J. Owen, **A Discourse Concerning Liturgies,** Chap. III.

9. **Works,** vol. 5, 294.

10. J. Hay Colligan, **Eighteenth Century Nonconformity,** London 1915, 88.

11. A Guide to Prayer, in **Works,** vol. IV, 125.

12. Ibid., 116.

13. Ibid., 119.

14. **Works,** vol. 5, 469.

15. **Account of the Doctrine and Discipline of Mr. Richard Davis, of Rothwell in the County of Northampton, and those of his Separation,** London 1700, 20. Bury Street Records, art. cit., CHST 6, 334-335.

16. Ed. T. D. Humphreys, **The Correspondence and Diary of Philip Doddridge D.D.,** 5 vols., London 1831, vol. 5.

17. The Diary of Samuel Sewell, 5th Series, **Collections of the Massachusetts Historical Society,** I. 253ff. - Dr. Annesley's celebration at Little St. Helena's London; E. Calamy, **A Letter to a Divine in Germany giving a Brief but true Account of the Protestant Dissenters in England,** 1717, both cited in H. Davies, **The Worship of the English Puritans,** 210, 251-2.

18. Isaac Chauncy, **The Divine Institution of Congregational Churches, Ministry and Ordinances,** London 1697, 96.

19. L. Bouyer, **Eucharistie: Theologie et Spiritualité de la prière eucharistique,** Tournai 1966, comments that the lengthy anaphora of **Apostolic Constitutions** VIII would take no more than a quarter of an hour when uttered by a celebrant in a hurry. ET Notre Dame, Indiana 1968, 250-251.

20. S. Cradock, **Knowledge and Practice, together with the Supplement,** London 1702, 123.

21. Ibid., 123-4.

22. **The Correspondence and Diary,** vol. 5, 326 (6th May 1733).

23. Ibid., 439, (3rd January 1742).

24. One wonders whether "show" deliberately echoes anadeixai found in St. Basil.

25. Thesis cited, 181ff.

26. Chapter XXX paragraph II and VII. Cf. Chauncy op.cit. 95; Cradock, op.cit. 125.

27. Ibid., Chap. XXVIII para. III.

28. R. Davis, **Hymns composed on Several Subjects And on Divers Occasions: In Five Parts with a Table to each Part.** 7th edition corrected by John Gill, 1748. Book III, Hymn X verse 2.

29. Ibid., Hymn XV verse 3.

30. **Works,** vol. IV, 245.

31. Op.cit., 125.

32. **The Correspondence and Diary,** vol. 5, 283. Cf. Matthew Henry (Presbyterian), **The Communicant's Companion,** 1704, 159.

33. Copy of the Records, Ms. 76.5. p. 16.

34. Cf. Chauncy, op.cit., 96-97: "That after Consecration, the Bread broken is to be delivered with the words of Distribution, directed to the whole church at once, and by them divided among themselves, and not carried up and down from party to party, or from seat to seat. After the pouring out the wine and blessing it, it ought to be dispensed with the words of distribution in like manner to the whole church. . . "

35. **The Correspondence and Diary,** vol. 5, 285.

36. Ibid., 309.

37. Ibid., 290 (6th September 1730).

38. Ibid., 297 (November 1730).

Chapter Five

NINETEENTH CENTURY CONGREGATIONALISM: THE CHANGING PATTERN OF "PUBLIC WORSHIP" AND THE EUCHARIST

By 1815 the Congregationalists were a vastly different body from that of 1760. They were far more numerous, far more energetic and far more optimistic.

R. Tudur Jones, **Congregationalism in England 1662-1962**, p. 186.

Whereas the period 1658-1800 represents an era of liturgical obscurity within the Independent or Congregational tradition, the nineteenth century witnessed a Liturgical Movement which in addition to debate on the subject of liturgy and worship, resulted in the production of written liturgical texts. [1]

The main focus of the nineteenth century Congregational Liturgical Movement was "Public Worship", which in fact meant the Morning service. In many Churches and Chapels the service must have remained substantially the same as that described by Isaac Watts. William Hale White, alias Mark Rutherford, who had been a Congregational minister, described the order of service that he remembered from his childhood. Each service consisted of a hymn, a Bible reading, another hymn, a prayer, the sermon, a third hymn, and a short final prayer. [2] "The first, or long prayer as it was called, was a horrible hypocrisy, and it was a sore tax on the preacher to get through it." [3] It commenced with a confession--though not of individual sins--and became a dialogue with God. [4] But changes were taking place. W. H. Willans in 1873 could refer to the "old-fashioned way" of conducting services--hymn, Scripture lesson, Long Prayer, hymn, sermon, hymn and Benediction. [5] In the previous century Job Orton had suggested that the Long Prayer might be divided into two, appropriating the second to intercession. [6] His advice was endorsed by the authors of **A New Directory**, 1812, [7] and according to G. W. Conder, this practice was common by the mid-nineteenth century. [8] Other elements of the service could also be tidied up and improved; the reading of lessons could be performed with care, and the "correct" formula, "Here endeth the lesson" could be used in preference to "Thus endeth the reading of the . . . lesson". [9] Doxologies and the Lord's Prayer could be used, the former to allow the congregation to say "Amen", the latter so that they might join in. [10] G. S. Barrett (1839-1916), minister of Prince Street Chapel, Norwich, advocated the use of intercessory prayer, the Beatitudes and the Creed in public worship. [11]

However, some of the formularies that appeared suggested rather more radical changes in the order of Morning service; they may be considered under two heads: Directories, and the **Book of Common Prayer**.

1. Directories

(a) **A New Directory**, London 1812.

This work, which was by a group of ministers, and included a Preface by the Reverend Samuel Palmer, was addressed to all dissenting members and tutors of Academies. In addition to recommending hints for improving worship, the authors recommended the following outline for Morning worship: [12]

> A Few short passages of Scripture, relating to the Resurrection of Christ, the privileges of Christianity, the institution of the Sabbath, the nature and benefit of divine worship.
>
> A short extemporary prayer, praising God for the Sabbath, creation, the Resurrection, and imploring the divine assistance and blessing in the services of the day, for both minister and people.
>
> A General psalm or hymn of praise.
>
> A lesson. O.T.
>
> The General Prayer, and possibly a psalm as recommended in the **Westminster Directory**.
>
> Second lesson. N.T.
>
> Short extemporary prayer, perhaps grounded on some leading ideas contained in the lesson, and intercession.
>
> Psalm or hymn.
>
> Sermon
>
> Hymn or psalm.

Short extemporary prayer, taking up and applying the leading ideas of the sermon.

(Blessing).

Professor H. Davies has pointed out that the first item of worship is not, as might have been expected, the element of confession. [13] Nevertheless, the order suggested does seem to have been based upon the 1645 **Directory**, the authors having split up the Long Prayer into two, and introduced more singing.

(b) **The Congregational Service Book,** London 1847.

Published in London for the use of Congregationalists, the authorship of this book was not acknowledged. The Preface described the work as supplying a want felt among orthodox dissenters. It explained:

> A creed is not given, because it is now unnecessary; and prayers are omitted because free prayer is undoubtedly the more scriptural and ancient mode of worship.

The only non-scriptural text given was the Te Deum. The recommended service was as follows:

Let us worship God by Singing:
Venite, or Psalm 84, 92, or 122.
Let us Pray.
Short Prayer
Psalm for the Day.
First Lesson.
Te Deum, or Benedictus, or Magnificat, or Nunc dimittis.
Second Lesson (New Testament)
Prayer (Long Prayer). Embracing thanksgiving and intercession for the congregation, the church, and the world, and for the sovereign and the country.
Hymn.
Short Prayer. Sermon.
Benediction.

This service seems to represent a "filling out" of the traditional Congregational service with scriptural elements from the **Book of Common Prayer.** The Long Prayer has been retained before the Sermon.

(c) **Liturgies for Divine Worship,** London 1879.

This liturgy was offered for use for those who wished to use a liturgical service, but who felt those of the Church of England to be too long, though we cannot be certain that it was the work of congregationalists. Five services were offered with the following plan:

A short invocation.
Scriptural statements, with responses, intended to prepare the worshippers for communion with God.
Prayer.
Hymn, chant or anthem.
Praise.

We may presume that these services were to be used in conjunction with readings and a sermon.

(d) **Let us Pray,** London (Second Edition) 1897.

This collection of prayers was prepared by C. S. Horne, minister of Allen Street Chapel, Kensington, and T. H. Darlow of New College Chapel, Hampstead for the use of free churches. Horne and Darlow were both Congregationalists. It consisted of collections of prayers and intercessions grouped under headings such as "Opening Prayers", "Intercessions" and "Collects". It drew freely on the material of the **Book of Common Prayer**. An "Order of Service" and an "Order of Morning Service" were recommended.

Order of Service

Hymn
Prayer - Opening sentences
A Confession
A Collect
The Lord's Prayer
Chant (or Anthem)
I. Lesson
Anthem (or Chant)
Prayer - A Thanksgiving
or An Intercession
or A Short Litany
II. Lesson
Notices (if any)
Hymn (for children)
Prayer - By the Minister
Hymn
Sermon
Offertory (if any)
Hymn
Prayer - Collects
Benediction

Order of Morning Service

Anthem
Prayer - Opening Sentences
A Confession
Hymn
Lesson
Chant
Commandments of Christ with Responses
Prayer - A Collect
The Lord's Prayer
Anthem
Prayer - By the Minister
Children's Hymn
Words to Children
Notices (if any)
Hymn
Sermon
Offertory (if any)
Hymn
Prayer - Collects
Benediction

(e) The "Biblical" Liturgies

In the category of "Directories" may be included the "Biblical Liturgies: **A Biblical Liturgy,** 1855 by David Thomas, Congregational minister of Stockwell, and **A Biblical Service of Prayer for the House of the Lord** which bears no date.

The former consisted of verses of Scripture recited alternately between the minister and the congregation, with psalms and the Lord's Prayer. Each service was centered on a theme such as "The Unity of God". It seems to have been to supplement free prayer rather than to replace it, and the book went through several editions. The later editions included adaptations of services from the **Book of Common Prayer**.

A copy of the second work referred to is to be found in the library of New College, London. It has no date, and no author is given. It is kept with some sermons of John Harris (1802-1850), and it may be presumed to have been Congregationalist. It gives five orders for worship, each with the following outline:

Exhortation to worship.
The Nature of acceptable worship.
A Prayer for Divine assistance in worship.
Portions of Holy Scripture to be read by the minister and people.
A General prayer and thanksgiving.
Lord's Prayer
Benediction.

2. The Book of Common Prayer

Attention has already been drawn to the fact that during the latter years of the eighteenth century the **Book of Common Prayer**, by way of the Countess of Huntingdon's Connexion, came into the Independent tradition on a very small scale. During the nineteenth century its use seems to have become a little more widespread within the denomination, or at least, the use of some of its contents. The influence of the Anglican Morning Prayer upon the Congregational Morning service is already to be seen in **The Congregational Service Book,** 1847. Several liturgies appeared within Congregationalism which were merely adaptations of the Anglican services: **The Book of Common Prayer Adapted for the Use of the Congregational Church, Finchley Common,** 1864; **Free Church Service Book,** 1867; **The Book of Common Prayer and Administration of Baptism and the Lord's Supper, with other Services Prepared for use in the Evangelical Churches by ministers and members of the Established and Nonconformist Churches,** 1867; [14] **A Form of Morning and Evening Service, for the use**

of Free Churches, Manchester 1869; [15] **Forms Submitted for the use of Nonconformist Churches**, 1870; **The Liturgy of the Church of England (Abridged)**, 1874; **Devotional Services for use in Mill Hill School Chapel**, 1895; and **The Free Church Prayer Book**, 1897. The services were merely Anglican Morning and Evening Prayer with variations.

The Morning service thus underwent a change. The "Long Prayer" was being abandoned, and there seems to have been a desire for more participation in the service by the congregation. The old order was filled out with canticles, lessons and shorter prayers. And in some Churches the old style of Morning service, which via the **Directory**, Knox and Calvin, derived ultimately from the Roman Mass and Prone, was given up in favor of a service based upon Morning Prayer of the **Book of Common Prayer**, derived from the choir offices. An interesting feature of some of these liturgies was the use of material in Morning and Evening services which was taken from the Prayer Book communion service. In **A Form of Morning and Evening Service**, in the order of Morning service for the second Sunday, two versions of the Sanctus appear as opening sentences; in **Liturgies for Divine Worship**, the Collect for Purity appears in the first service, and the Sanctus in the second; the Sursam corda and Sanctus, the Prayer for the Whole State of Christ's Church, and part of the Prayer of Oblation, occur in the third, fifth and sixth services of **Devotional Services for use in Mill Hill School Chapel**. There were no inhibitions regarding the traditional use of such material; the prayers could be utilized because they were well-known devotional prayers.

Another interesting feature of some of these works was the recognition of the liturgical calendar. For example, **The Book of Common Prayer adapted for the Use of the Congregational Church, Finchley Common** contained the Prayer Book collects for the temporale. The **Free Church Prayer Book** contained the Prayer Book collects, Epistles and Gospels for the temporale. The twelfth edition of **A Biblical Liturgy** contained the temporale Prayer Book collects, and a special service for Easter Sunday. And **Let us Pray** contained collects for Advent, Christmas, Good Friday, Easter, Ascensiontide, Whitsuntide, All Saints Day, Spring Time, Harvest, New Year's Eve, and In commemoration of the departed. In some Congregational Churches the basic Sunday sequence and festivals of the liturgical calendar were being revived.

In contrast with the Morning service, the Eucharistic liturgy of nineteenth century Congregationalism is made conspicuous by its almost universal omission from the liturgical discussion which occurred within the denomination; very little of the literature on "Public Worship" considered the Eucharist, and only a few of the liturgies which appeared offered an order for the Lord's Supper. This contrast is significant; implicit was a distinction between

"Public Worship" and the Eucharist, suggesting that the Eucharist was not quite so public. The underlying cause of this distinction would appear to have been the prevailing "memorialist" doctrine of the Eucharist within the denomination.

The **Savoy Declaration** of 1658 had restated the firmly Calvinist doctrine of the Eucharist of the **Westminster Confession;** but very different was the weak doctrine expressed in the 1833 **Declaration of the Faith, Church Order, and Discipline of the Congregational, or Independent Dissenters** of the Congregational Union:

> They believe in the perpetual obligation of Baptism, and the Lord's Supper: . . . the latter to be celebrated by Christian churches as a token of faith in the Saviour, and of brotherly love. [**16**]

It was this weak doctrine which R. W. Dale attacked in his essay, "The Doctrine of the Real Presence and of the Lord's Supper". [**17**] The **Savoy Declaration**, so argued Dale, gave

> no sanction to the theory which seems to be generally accepted by modern Independents, and which represents Baptism and the Lord's Supper as having been instituted simply to perpetuate the memory of historical facts, to illustrate spiritual truths, to make an impression on the hearts of those who celebrate the Rites or who witness their celebration, and to afford an authorized symbolic expression of faith in Christ and brotherly love. [**18**]

"There is little doubt", Dale concluded, "that modern Congregationalists, in their extreme dread of high sacramental doctrines, have drifted into pure Zwinglianism; it is possible that some of them have drifted farther still." [**19**]

Dale himself believed that the bread and wine actually convey what they represent. He used the analogy of a besieging army around a city. If a soldier gave the general a key to the city gate, this would merely be a symbolic act of hope; when the governor of the city does the same thing, this is the real transfer of power.

> Christ is present at His table, though not in the Bread and Wine which are placed upon it. He is there--as a Host with his guests. We do not meet to think of an "absent" Lord, or to commemorate a dead Saviour. We receive the Bread from His own hands, and with it all that the Bread symbolizes. We drink the Cup in His presence, and rejoice that we are His friends--that through His Blood we have received "remission of sins", and that

> we "have peace with God" through Him. He is nearer to us now than He was to those who heard from His lips the words of institution. It was "expedient" for us that He should go away; for He has come again, and by the power of His Spirit we abide in Him and He in us. In being made partakers of Christ, we are "made partakers of the Divine nature", and become for ever one with God. [20]

Dale restated the same doctrine in his **Manual of Congregational Principles**, 1884, which was compiled for examination purposes. But as he admitted, his view was a minority view--so much so that the section in the **Manual** on the sacraments had to be withdrawn from the syllabus. Most Congregationalists were of the opinion of J. G. Rogers:

> Our sympathies are distinctly with Zwingle (sic), whom we have always regarded as the most consistent of the Reformers on this point, and strong because of that consistency in following his ideas to their logical issue. [21]

Zwingli's doctrine had been highly praised in an article in The Congregationalist in 1876, [22] and there is little doubt that this was the doctrine of most Congregationalists at this time. Dr. Robert Halley in **The Sacraments** could see no difference between Zwingli and Calvin, believing Zwingli to be the clearer writer, [23] an opinion which J. G. Rogers endorsed. [24] Henry Webb dismissed Calvin's doctrine in favor of a doctrine which was distinctly "Zwinglian". [25] Furthermore, E. Conder explained that such a doctrine was a sign of progress rather than something to lament; Dale's charge of drifting into pure Zwinglianism he wished to describe as being a growth into "Paulinism" or "New-Testamentism". [26]

The typical understanding of the Lord's Supper was given by J. S. Pearsall in his **Public Worship.** It is subjective "memorialism", a mental reflection on the Atonement:

> The Lord's Supper is a commemoration of something that is passed, and therefore the simplest symbol, obeying the law of association, recalls to the mind the name, person, and character, and doings of a friend that has been among us and is gone. The Lord's Supper is not so much to give the idea as to retain it. [27]

For Pearsall, the emphasis was not "Do this in remembrance of me", but "Do this in remembrance of me". [28] The same type of doctrine was expounded by an anonymous writer in the Evangelical Magazine in 1861:

> It is simply a memorial - a memorial of an absent Friend and Lord. [29]

The writer argued that the sacrament enabled us simply and impressively to remind ourselves and the world of Jesus--but only of his death. [30] Though the elements were blessed and administered by the apostles or even by Jesus himself, the soul would be no better by this or any other mere bodily reception; it is God's truth, not bread and wine, which nourishes the soul. [31] A large number of other Congregationalists agreed. [32]

The liturgical corollary of this "memorialist" doctrine was that there was little incentive to question the traditional order of service as inherited from the eighteenth century. The main ingredients for mental reflection were quiet, simplicity, and stillness; [33] if anything, this required a reduction of liturgical forms in the Eucharist rather than any additions. But since the Eucharist was subjective reflection on the Atonement, it did not require the same attention as "Public Worship". Much depended upon the state of mind of the communicant, [34] and not everyone would be in the right state of mind. Again, as a symbol, it was especially fitted and designed to minister to religious emotion; it appealed to the pathetic, imaginative, mystical side of human nature. [35] But depending upon the temperament of the individual, the Lord's presence could equally be realized by a rousing hymn or a sermon. [36] Dr. Pye-Smith of Homerton College had defined the sacraments as "didactic, confirmatory of Divine truths and promises and instructive especially to men of inferior cultivation". [37] The implication of this, as Dale was quick to point out, was that as men became more educated and cultivated, so the need for sacraments would disappear. [38] It might also imply that "respectable" people, persons of "refined taste", were above such sops intended for lesser educated brethren. This would appear to be the underlying reason why, compared with the Morning service, the Eucharistic liturgy in most cases received little attention.

A typical Congregational Eucharist was described by E. G. Herbert in his essay on "The Congregational Character":

> The form is very simple. There is no altar, but the bread and wine are placed on a table covered with a white cloth. A hymn is sung, and then the words of St. Paul describing the Last Supper are read. Sometimes the minister gives a short address, but if he does, his tone is more subdued than at other times. Then, after a short prayer, he repeats the words of the apostle, which tells how our Lord broke the bread, and puts a plate into the hands of each of the deacons, who so carry the broken bread round to the people, as they

> sit in the pews. After a short interval of silence and another prayer, he distributes the cups of wine in like manner, with the words describing how the Lord took the cup. A collection is made for the benefit of the poor members of the church, and, after another hymn, the benediction is pronounced. Thus, not a display of feeling, but a reserve and restraint of all outward expression of emotion, is characteristic of the service. And yet no spectator, observing the pervading stillness which makes audible even the tick of the chapel clock, and the reverent quietness of manner with which the deacons perform their office, and seeing how each communicant after taking the bread and the wine bends the head in silent thought or prayer, could doubt that the occasion was one of the deepest and most solemn feeling. [39]

A very similar order for the Eucharist was recommended by Henry Webb, though in this case he suggested that the bread should be broken before the prayer of thanksgiving. [40] The same order was presupposed by other Congregationalists. [41] The order is still very similar to that of Watts, Davis and Doddridge; the "double consecration" was retained, and the fraction was still symbolic:

> The broken bread shows, how the body of the dear Saviour was broken, when he became a sacrifice for sin. The wine is poured out to intimate, that thus the blessed Redeemer poured out his precious blood on the cross for our salvation. [42]

In some places however, the "double consecration" seems to have been abandoned in preference to one single prayer, a practice for which William Orme could see no scriptural justification. [43] Such a service in an old Independent Chapel at eight o'clock on a summer Sunday evening was described in The Christian World in 1890:

> Silent Prayer
> Hymn. (Come, let us join our cheerful songs).
> Prayer.
>
> "It is the tender pleading of one who feels the goodness of God, the splendid manhood, the saving brotherhood of Christ; that He would come with us and dwell with us, and make us like Himself--loving, gentle, strong to do God's will, and very patient with each other. All the problems of life are brought to the Cross, and grace is asked that in the light which streams therefrom they may be solved in God's time."
>
> 1 Cor. xi Institution.
> Distribution of the Bread, in silence.

"And in like manner he took the cup after supper saying this is the new covenant in My blood. This do as oft as ye drink it in remembrance of Me."
Distribution of wine, in silence.
Collection
Doxology sung.
Benediction. [**44**]

However, just as the Morning service had been affected by the Anglican **Book of Common Prayer,** in some instances the Eucharist was influenced by the same source. This may be seen with reference to four liturgies compiled by Congregationalists which included an order for the communion.

1. The Book of Common Prayer Adapted for the Use of the Congregational Church, Finchley Common, 1864.

A copy of this liturgy is to be found in the Congregational Library, Memorial Hall, London. It has no introduction or Preface, and is anonymous. It gives orders of Morning and Evening Prayers, and the Holy Communion.

The Order of the Administration of the Lord's Supper, or, Holy Communion.

Anthem. Rev. 1:5, 6. or the Easter Anthems, 1 Cor. 5:7; Rom. 6:9; 1 Cor. 15:20; Rev. 5:13.
Lord's Prayer.
Collect for Purity.
Commandments.
Collect for the Day.
Epistle.
Gospel.
Anthem. from Rev. 5.
Creed.
Prayer for the Church Militant.
Collects (Post-Offertory Collects).
The Grace.
Sermon.
Invitation, "Ye that do truly".
Confession.
Collective Absolution.
Comfortable Words.
Sursum corda.
Easter Preface.
Sanctus.
Humble Access.
Prayer of Consecration.
Words of Administration.

Prayer of Oblation.
Gloria in excelsis.
Hymn.
Collection for the poor.
Blessing.

The order followed that of the **Book of Common Prayer,** the only significant textual variations being in the Prayer for the Church Militant, where "Bishops and Curates" was replaced by "all the Ministers of thy Church", a collective absolution, "have mercy upon us", and the words of administration where thee/thou was replaced by you/your.

2. **Free Church Service Book,** 1867.

The **Free Church Service Book** with a Preface by Christopher Newman Hall was used in Surrey Chapel where Newman Hall was minister. In a previous chapter we have already noted Newman Hall's own attachment to the **Book of Common Prayer,** and the Anglican liturgy is the sole source of the **Free Church Service Book.** Surrey Chapel had had a liturgical tradition before Newman Hall's pastorate. The Chapel had been built in the previous century for Rowland Hill who at one time was in close association with the Countess of Huntingdon's preachers. [45] Although ordained deacon in the Church of England, on account of his itinerant preaching, Hill was unable to obtain Priest's Orders. Later he fell out of favor with the Countess of Huntingdon, and seceded from the Church of England. Surrey Chapel was built for his use, and there he used the **Book of Common Prayer** with a few verbal alterations. [46] In this respect, Newman Hall's liturgy was a continuation of the liturgical tradition of the Chapel, being the **Book of Common Prayer** services with minor verbal alterations.

The book contained five services, four for ordinary Morning or Evening worship, and the fifth for the Communion. The fourth service was the Ante-communion of the **Book of Common Prayer,** and was recommended to be used when the Communion was to follow.

For the Lord's Supper, or Holy Communion.

Sentences of Scripture, or Exhortation "Ye that do truly".
General Confession, "Almighty God, Father of our Lord Jesus Christ".
Absolution, "Almighty God . . . have mercy upon <u>us</u>".
Comfortable words.
Sursum corda, Easter preface and sanctus.
Prayer of Humble Access.
Prayer and Thanksgiving (Prayer of Consecration).

Words of Delivery.
Prayer of Oblation.
Gloria in excelsis.
Hymn and Free Prayer.
Blessing.

This order was a slavish copy of the Anglican order, omitting most of the rubrics, and with minor verbal alterations: the absolution was collective, avoiding a priestly conception of absolution; the wording of the "Comfortable Words" was slightly altered; and only the Easter preface was used. The Words of Delivery were also slightly altered:

> The Body of our Lord Jesus Christ, which was given for us, preserve our bodies and souls unto everlasting life. Let us take and eat this in remembrance that Christ died for us, and feed on him in our hearts by faith and thanksgiving.
>
> The Blood of our Lord Jesus Christ, which was shed for us, preserve our bodies and souls unto everlasting life. Let us drink this in remembrance that Christ's blood was shed for us, and be thankful.

There is little significance in the changes here, other than perhaps to indicate that the presiding minister is also a guest at the Supper. Newman Hall's views on the eucharist are not at all clear. He was able to affirm a "real presence":

> We, too, believe in the real presence of Christ. The bread and wine are emblems of it. His actual body is in heaven; it is not in the Sacrament. The bread is not flesh. He will come hereafter, but He is not yet corporeally present. "As often as ye eat this bread, ye do show the Lord's death till He come". But, by His appointment, the bread and wine represent His body and blood; and we, by receiving them, represent and, as a means of grace, spiritually aid, our very union with Him. [**47**]

This qualification of "real presence", when taken with a further statement that

> We may be real partakers of the body and blood of Christ, though we may never have received the bread and wine; [**48**]

would seem to suggest a "Zwinglian" position, and would place Newman Hall in the main stream of nineteenth century Congregational thought on the Eucharist. It is interesting that Newman Hall seems to have regarded the Prayer Book liturgy as an adequate expression of his beliefs.

3. **Let us Pray**, 1897.

Although for the Morning service Horne and Darlow offered only an outline for worship together with collections of prayers for the minister to construct his own service, a full order for the Communion was provided.

(Address).
Sentences.
Hymn.
Brief exhortations from Scripture for a right attitude for communion.
Prayer (Collect for Purity).
Lesson. 1 Cor. 11:22-26.
Comfortable Words (2 from BCP; 4 additional).
Exhortation to confession (Ye that do truly).
Prayer (Prayer of Humble Access).
Lord's Prayer
Distribution: The bread which we break, is it not the communion of the body of Christ?

or The Lord said: This is My body which is given for you: this do in remembrance of Me.

The cup which we bless, is it not the communion of the blood of Christ?

or The Lord said: This is My blood of the new testament, which is shed for many for the remission of sins. This do ye, as oft as ye drink it, in remembrance of Me.

Adding, As often as we eat this bread and drink this cup, we do show the Lord's death, till He come.

(or words of administration from the BCP).

Silent Prayer, or A Prayer by the Minister, or
Post Communion Litany (Scripture sentences).
Closing Hymn, with offertory.
Benediction.

This order exhibits some most interesting features. The provision of an address suggests that as in all other cases, the Communion was not regarded as part of the Liturgy of the Word, though of course it may have followed it. The order is a combination of traditional Independent and **Book of Common Prayer** material. The Independent features are the first exhortation to a right attitude, 1 Cor. 11:22-26 as a warrant, the first set of words of administration, the silent prayer of Scripture sentences after communion, and the position of the offertory. The Anglican material which was freely utilized is the Collect for Purity, the "Comfortable Words" (adapted), the exhortation to confession, and the Prayer of Humble Access, as also the alternative words of administration. The opening sentences may have been suggested by the Anglican Morning Prayer, or possibly by John Hunter's **Devotional Services.** [49]

A fascinating question is raised by the apparent absence of the Prayers of Thanksgiving and Blessing. The traditional double consecration was neither provided for, nor hinted at; nor at first sight does it appear to have been replaced by a single prayer, suggesting perhaps a pronounced "memorialist" doctrine. However, providing that our judgment is not colored by an Anglican liturgical fundamentalism, another explanation is possible, namely, that a single prayer of consecration has been provided by the "Prayer of Humble Access".

This prayer has its origin as a pre-communion devotional prayer, being included in the 1548 **The Order of the Communion** where it came after the Latin Canon of the Mass, and then in the 1549 **Book of Common Prayer** where it followed the new English Canon. In the 1552 **Book of Common Prayer** it was used in a new position, after the Sursum corda and Sanctus and before the prayer which in the 1662 Prayer Book was entitled "The Prayer of Consecration". Although the rubrics of the 1662 Prayer Book imply that the Prayer of Humble Access was regarded as a pre-communion devotional prayer prior to the consecration, it could in the 1552 book have been intended as part of the Canon. Only a knowledge of its original use in 1548 and a knowledge of the shape of the anaphora in the Classical rites could give rise to the opinion that it must only ever be a pre-communion devotional prayer. Horne and Darlow seem to have had no inhibitions in this respect; they have simply entitled it "Prayer", but it seems to have been intended as a prayer of blessing:

> Grant us therefore, gracious Lord, so to eat the flesh
> of Thy dear Son Jesus Christ, and to drink his blood . . .

If this interpretation of Horne and Darlow is correct, then it provides an interesting new use for Cranmer's prayer.

4. **The Free Church Prayer Book**, London 1897.

This liturgy was compiled by the Reverend J. Mountain, minister of St. John's Road Free Church, Tunbridge Wells, one of the Churches of the Countess of Huntingdon's Connexion. However, it properly belongs to the Congregational Church. By this date most of the Countess' Churches were indistinguishable from Congregationalism, [50] and Mountain was a Congregational minister, having been trained at the Nottingham Congregational Institute and Cheshunt College. [51] He was assisted in the compilation of the liturgy by the Librarian of the Congregational Union, T. G. Crippen. [52]

As a minister of one of the Countess of Huntingdon's churches, Mountain would have inherited the use of the **Book of Common Prayer**. However, he explained in his Preface that he felt that certain parts of it needed revising, and in his liturgy--which is merely an adaptation of the Anglican liturgy--he made use of the proposals for revision of 1689 **(The Liturgy of Comprehension)**, the revision of John Wesley, **(A Biblical Liturgy** by David Thomas, Newman Hall's **Free Church Service Book**, which perhaps suggested the title for Mountain's compilation, and **The Protestant Prayer Book**, 1894 by Charles Stirling.

The order for the Communion follows that of the **Book of Common Prayer**, but contains some significant variations:

Lord's Prayer, with doxology.
Collect for Purity
Ten Commandments, or Ten Beatitudes
Collect
Epistle
Gospel: Glory be to Thee, O Lord.
Thanks be to Thee, O Lord,
for this Thy Holy Gospel.
Nicene Creed.
Prayer for the Whole Estate of Christ's Church.
A General Thanksgiving (BCP).
The Grace.
Hymn or Anthem.
Sermon.
(Hymn and Dismissal).
Offertory Sentences.
(Hymn and Dismissal).
An Address (exhortation).
Invitation, "Ye that do truly".
Confession of Sins, or Absolution.
An Exhortation.
A General Thanksgiving.
Comfortable Words.
Sursum corda, Easter Preface and Sanctus.
Prayer of Humble Access.
Prayer of Institution.
Fraction.
Delivery.
Lord's Prayer.
Prayer of Oblation.
Gloria in excelsis.
Blessing.

A Biblical Liturgy can have been of little help with the Communion service, but the four other acknowledged sources have all been drawn upon, in particular **The Protestant Prayer Book** of Charles Stirling.

(a) **Liturgy of Comprehension**, 1689.

This liturgy suggested the Ten Beatitudes which Mountain provided as an alternative to the Ten Commandments. The 1689 liturgy gave eight Beatitudes, Jeremy Taylor's Communion Office 1658 appearing to have been the ultimate source. Mountain used the 1689 proposals, including the responses, but added two further Beatitudes to balance with the Commandments:

> Blessed are those servants, whom the Lord,
> when He cometh, shall find watching.
> Blessed are they that hear the Word of God,
> and keep it.

(b) **Wesley's Sunday Service**, 1784.

Mountain, like Wesley, was writing for a non-episcopal Church; in the Prayer for the Whole Estate of Christ's Church, Wesley had changed the petition "Give grace, O heavenly Father, to all Bishops, and Curates" to "all Ministers of thy Gospel". Both Newman Hall in his fourth service, and Charles Stirling, were faced with the same problem. Mountain changed the wording to "all Christian Ministers, Missionaries, and Teachers".

Again, following Wesley, as had Newman Hall and Stirling, the absolution was made collective, "have mercy upon us".

(c) **Free Church Service Book**, 1867.

Mountain followed Newman Hall in providing only the Easter preface after the Sursum corda.

(d) **The Protestant Prayer Book**, 1894.

By far the most important source of Mountain's Communion service was that of **The Protestant Prayer Book**, the product of Evangelicals of the Church of England who had become exasperated by the failure of the bishops and ecclesiastical courts to eradicate Anglo-Catholic doctrine and ritualism. Stirling together with a number of clergy seceded from the Church of England, and carried out a revision of the **Book of Common Prayer** in such a manner as to exclude a catholic interpretation of cermonial or doctrine. Concerning the Eucharistic liturgy, Stirling had explained in the Preface:

> The Communion Service has been purged of every doubtful phrase, and not a syllable has been retained that can possibly be quoted as suggestive, or permissive, of any "real" or "essential", or "corporal" Presence in, or with, the elements of bread and wine. [53]

The influence of Stirling's liturgy is to be seen in the following features:

1. The responses before and after the Gospel.
2. The text of the invitation to confession.
3. An Exhortation with A General Thanksgiving.
4. Additional Comfortable Words: John 14:27; 1 John 1:7, 8.
5. The altered text of the Prayer of Humble Access.
6. The alteration in the Prayer of Consecration:

   "and grant that we, receiving these thy creatures of bread and wine, according to thy Son our Saviour Jesus Christ's holy institution, in remembrance of his death and passion, may realise, by faith, our oneness with Him".

Mountain also made alterations in the offertory sentences, the words of administration, the Prayer of Oblation and the text of the Gloria in excelsis. The words of administration were as follows:

> Our Lord Jesus Christ, whose Body was given for you, preserve your body and soul unto everlasting life. Take and eat this in remembrance that Christ died for you, and feed on Him in your heart, by faith, with thanksgiving.
>
> Our Lord Jesus Christ, whose Blood was shed for you, preserve your body and soul unto everlasting life. Drink this in remembrance that Christ's Blood was shed for you, and be thankful.

These words which exclude any notion of Christ's presence in the elements are in keeping with the changes made by Stirling, but are not from his liturgy, nor do they occur in 1689, Wesley or Newman Hall. The words do, however, occur in **The Book of Common Prayer . . . for use in The Evangelical Churches**, 1867, with the exception that the latter has thee/thou instead of you/your. This may have been an unacknowledged source here.

In summary we may say that from the writings on the subject of worship, and from the printed liturgies themselves, the Morning service in nineteenth century Congregationalism underwent a change in its structure and content. Sometimes this change was limited to the division of the Long Prayer into two; in some

Churches it involved more congregational participation, including versicles and responses; in a few Churches the older pattern of service was abandoned for one based upon Anglican Morning Prayer. The Eucharist appears to have been regarded as a separate service, and was less "public" than Morning worship. The prevailing memorialist view of the sacrament was an important factor in Eucharistic liturgy, remaining substantially the same as that in the previous century. However, some ministers do appear to have abandoned the older pattern for a printed liturgy using material from the communion service of the **Book of Common Prayer.** It is strange that they seem to have looked no further than the Anglican liturgy for their material, their results being a slavish reproduction of the Anglican formularies, or appearing to be amateur scissors and paste work. Nevertheless, in a denomination which had had no written liturgy since 1645, these orders represent a remarkable liturgical revolution.

NOTES

1. Supra, Chapter 1.

2. W. Hale White, **The Autobiography of Mark Rutherford,** London 1881, 6.

3. Ibid.

4. Ibid.

5. W. H. Willans, "Attendance at Public Worship", 59.

6. J. Orton, **Letters to Dissenting Ministers,** ed. S. Palmer, London 1806, 2 vols., vol. 2. 60.

7. **A New Directory,** 53.

8. G. W. Conder, **Intelligent and True Worship,** 5.

9. J. S. Pearsall, **Public Worship,** 105.

10. Ibid., 134-5.

11. G. S. Barrett, "Congregational Worship", in CYB 1897, 87-8.

12. **A New Directory,** 82-87.

13. H. Davies, **Worship and Theology in England 1850-1900**, 78.

14. Strictly speaking this appears to have been prepared for all nonconformists rather than purely Congregationalists. The British Quarterly Review states: "Nothing can be more admirable than the emendations of this Prayer Book; nothing more Christian and amiable than the Spirit of the Introduction"; but the reviewer thought that it would be of little avail. "The Book of Common Prayer" in BQR 47 (1868) 69-128, 126.

15. The services in this volume were praised in the British Quarterly Review for being "simple and beautiful". BQR 50 (1869), 591-592, 591.

16. Declaration of Faith, article XVIII, in W. Walker, **Creeds and Platforms of Congregationalism**, 1893, (reprint Boston 1960), 550-551.

17. In ed. H. R. Reynolds, **Ecclesia**, London 1870, 315-390.

18. Ibid., 368.

19. Ibid., 371.

20. Ibid., 390.

21. J. G. Rogers, "Sacramentalism" in The Congregationalist 13 (1884) 980-989, 981.

22. T. H. Gill, "Ulrich Zwingli" in The Congregationalist 5 (1876) 321-336.

23. R. Halley, **The Sacraments**, (2nd edition) 2 vols., London 1844 and 1851, vol. 2, 227ff.

24. J. G. Rogers, "Sacramentalism", 989.

25. H. Webb, **The Ordinances of Christian Worship**, London 1873, 184ff.

26. E. R. Conder, "The Lord's Supper" in The Congregationalist 14 (1885), 169-179, 175-6.

27. J. S. Pearsall, **Public Worship**, 89-90.

28. Ibid., 91.

29. Anon., "An Invitation to Communion" in Evangelical Magazine, N.S. 39 (1861) 862-867, 862.

30. Ibid.

31. Ibid.

32. See also J. Pye-Smith, **First Lines of Christian Theology**, 2nd edition,

London 1861; J. Angell James, "The Sacraments" in Evangelical Magazine N.S. 20 (1842), 215-221; E. G. Herbert, "The Congregational Character" in Religious Republics, London 1867, 108-109.

33. J. S. Pearsall, op.cit., 94; E. G. Herbert, op.cit., 109; H. B. S. K. "A Quiet Communion Service" in The Christian World, 25th September, 1890, 763: "How still everything is! Not a whisper disturbs the solemn quiet".

34. J. Angell James, op.cit., 218.

35. E. Conder, "More thoughts concerning the Lord's Supper" in The Congregationalist 15 (1886), 128-135, 135, 133.

36. Ibid.

37. J. Pye-Smith, **First Lines of Christian Theology**, 666-667.

38. R. W. Dale, "The Doctrine of the Real Presence and of the Lord's Supper" in op.cit., 369-370.

39. E. G. Herbert, op.cit., 109-110.

40. H. Webb, op.cit., 38.

41. R. Halley, **The Sacraments**, vol. 2, 338; William Orme, **The Ordinance of the Lord's Supper Illustrated**, London 1826, 38-39.

42. B. H. Draper, **Solemn Recollections, Before, At, and After, the celebration of the Lord's Supper**, Southampton 1825, 11.

43. William Orme, op.cit., 39.

44. H. B. S. K., "A Quiet Communion Service", The Christian World, September 25th, 1890, 763-764.

45. **The Life and Times of Selina, Countess of Huntingdon**, vol. 2, 317.

46. **Newman Hall. An Autobiography**, London 1898, 120.

47. Newman Hall, Address in CYB, 1867, 88.

48. Ibid.

49. For the liturgical work of John Hunter, see the following chapter.

50. John W. Grant, **Free Churchmanship in England 1870-1940**, nd., 97.

51. See the list of Free Church ministers in **The Christian World Year Book**, 1883. In CYB 1898 it was reported that he had become a Baptist.

52. **The Free Church Prayer Book,** Preface vi.

53. **The Protestant Prayer Book,** 1894, Preface xii.

Chapter Six

THE COMMUNION ORDER IN DR. JOHN HUNTER'S "DEVOTIONAL SERVICES FOR PUBLIC WORSHIP" 1886-1901

It is now used freely in many Congregational churches up and down England.

Dr. P. T. Forsyth's Tribute in The Christian World, September 20th, 1917, p. 4.

By far the most outstanding and influential liturgical compilation of nineteenth century Congregationalism was the **Devotional Service** of Dr. John Hunter, which, according to one Congregational writer, may be regarded as the first Congregational liturgy worthy of the name. [1] It was certainly the first viable alternative to the **Book of Common Prayer**, and its wide influence, which lasted well into the twentieth century, separates it from all other nineteenth century Congregational liturgies.

Dr. John Hunter (1849-1917) was very much an "independent" figure. Although he ministered at York (1871-1882), Hull (1882-1886), and at the King's Weigh House, London (1901-1904), most of his pastorate was spent across the border at Trinity Church, Glasgow. [2] During his pastorate in England, Hunter often found himself at odds with the Congregational Union, believing that modern "Congregationalism" had little to do with Independency. Yet in spite of his Scottish domicile and his individualism, his **Devotional Services** were extremely popular in England. Originating in 1880 as a few pages of intercessions, confessions and thanksgivings, together with responses for the use of the congregation at York, the work was gradually enlarged to reach its final form of 327 pages in the seventh edition of 1901. After this date it went through many impressions, and at the time of Hunter's death in 1917, it was claimed that the collection was in use "in many parts of the world, and in almost every denomination. Hundreds of ministers who have not introduced it either to pulpit or pew carry it with them to funerals, marriages, or baptisms". [3] The reason for its success, so it has been argued, was its unusual combination of the traditional with the modern; stylistically it is traditional, but equally it is the expression of nineteenth century theology, of Divine immanentism and emphasis on the historic Jesus as mankind's greatest exemplar, and upon the Social Gospel. [4] But its success must also lie in its originality; most of the prayers were Hunter's own composition, [5] and the result provided nonconformists with a rich and dignified alternative to the Anglican liturgy.

Hunter was born in Aberdeen, his father being a member of the Church of Scotland and his mother an Episcopalian, and he was well acquainted with the worship of both these Churches. Although at first attracted to the Church of Scotland, Hunter became more and more involved in the Congregational Church, and eventually trained for its ministry at the Nottingham Congregational Institute (1866-68) and Spring Hill College, Birmingham (1868-71). It was at Birmingham that he was first introduced to the writings of F. D. Maurice, which, together with a fondness for Carlyle, Ruskin and Kingsley, accounted for his immanentism and Christian Socialism. The influence of immanentism on his liturgical work was recognized by a reviewer of the fourth edition of **Devotional Services**, 1890, in The Christian World, who, referring to the Communion Order, suggested that even R. W. Emerson might have been saved to the Christian Church by such a service as this. [6] The influence of Christian Socialism is to be seen in the social concern of his intercessions, and his conception of the Eucharist as first and foremost a fellowship meal.

Another influence was that of Unitarianism. According to a college friend, Hunter took great pains to acquaint himself with the forms of worship of that body, and was greatly impressed by a little book of prayers by John Page Hopps. [7] This influence is most marked by Hunter's use in his **Devotional Services** of James Martineau's **Common Prayer for Christian Worship**, 1861, and by the fact that all Hunter's prayers were addressed to the Father.

Another stimulus seems to have been the Church Service Society. This society was founded in 1865 by a number of ministers of the Church of Scotland to promote liturgical study and to produce forms of worship for the use of ministers in public services. In 1867 it published the **Euchologion**, a collection of services. This was mainly the work of G. W. Sprott, S. Story and J. Tulloch. Principal Tulloch became a personal friend of Hunter. Furthermore, in 1893, at the instance of some fellow-ministers, Hunter promoted a Congregational Church Service Society, of which the objects were to be "to promote the regular and systematic culture of the devout life, the revival of worship and reverent observance of Christian ordinances in families and congregations of Christ's Church", and for many years he acted as its secretary. [8]

Believing that the worship of the Free Churches suffered by a lack of congregational participation, Hunter strove to strike a better balance between free and liturgical prayer. Although he was widely travelled and had attended services in Roman Catholic, Coptic, Armenian, Greek and Russian Churches, this experience seems to have had no obvious textual influence on his liturgical work. There is no indication of an interest in liturgical history or ancient texts. Rather,--and here in part lies the success of the **Devotional Services**--he was content to draw upon the traditional Congregational pattern of worship, clothing the framework with his own prayers.

In the earlier editions of the **Devotional Services,** Hunter had given collections of various types of prayers which could be put together by the minister to form a service, though he did recommend an outline for worship which varied from edition to edition. In the fourth edition, 1890, he suggested:

> Voluntary
> The reading of introductory sentences inviting to worship.
> Collect. (To which may be added a general confession and thanksgiving).
> Hymn.
> Scripture reading.
> Psalm or Canticle chanted (closed by organ chord).
> Silent meditation.
> Prayer (extempore).
> Anthem.
> Scripture reading.
> Responsive prayer, from Book of Services.
> Hymn.
> Lord's Prayer.
> Sermon.
> Offertory.
> Hymn.
> Benediction.
> (Amen sung at the end of the hymns and prayers, and at the close of the benediction by choir and congregation.)

By the seventh edition Hunter had rearranged the material to form thirteen separate services.

Not until the third edition of the **Devotional Services,** 1886, did Hunter include a Eucharistic liturgy, suggesting the familiar nineteenth century Congregationalist division between "Public Worship" and the Eucharist. The order continued to be developed, reaching its final form in the seventh edition, 1901.

Like many nineteenth century Congregationalists, Hunter's

Eucharistic doctrine seems to have been a subjective "memorialism". In **A Plea for a Worshipful Church,** 1903, he defined the Supper as a poetic symbol; [9] in **The Coming Church**, 1905, he insisted that in its original form the Eucharist was no ecclesiastical or mystical rite, but a social meal, and he pleaded for a sympathetic understanding toward those who had no use for sacraments. [10] The language of his Eucharistic liturgy was therefore of commemoration and fellowship, symbol rather than sacrament, though in later life mysticism played around the symbol. [11] Something of this latter combination is expressed in a passage in **A Plea for a Worshipful Church;** the Supper is

> the Holy Commemoration, a quickening and inspiring remembrance of the Saviour's Holy Living and Dying; the Holy Eucharist, a service of thanksgiving for all the blessings which have come to us and our race through Jesus Christ our Lord; the Holy Communion, the sign of our communion with God our Father and Jesus Christ His Son, and a help of its realisation--the sign of our communion with all disciples of Christ, with the Church of all ages and lands, and with the Church triumphant, especially with our own dear and holy dead, in a Love from which neither life nor death, things present nor things to come, can separate us. [12]

Nevertheless, in his Eucharistic liturgy the dominant idea was that of symbol.

The Order of Communion Service, third edition, 1886. The structure of the service was as follows:

Sentences.
Collect (three provided).
Hymn. "Bread of the World".
Readings. Psalm 103:1, 2, 4, 5, 8, 10-12;
Psalm 116:12-14, 17; Matt. 26:26-28.
Responses: verses of Scripture concerned with the two great commandments, faith, love, peace and joy, with responses.
Pause for silent meditation.
Prayer: The victory of the Cross, confession of sin, Thanksgiving, commemoration of the dead and living.
Institution: 1 Cor. 11:23-25.
Words of administration.
Offertory. "Let us do this in remembrance of Christ, for inasmuch as we do good to one of the least of His brethren we do it unto Him".
Hymn.
Lord's Prayer.
Benediction (Grace).

The Communion service was quite separate from the Morning services, and although **Devotional Services** provided collects for the festivals of the Christian year, there was no provision for their inclusion in the Communion. The only borrowing from the **Book of Common Prayer** was the Collect for Purity, which was one of the three collects provided. Nothing appears to have been borrowed from the **Euchologion** of the Church Service Society, the most recent edition for Hunter being that of 1884. However, several features were suggested by, or borrowed from, Martineau's **Common Prayer for Christian Worship:**

(a) The opening rubric and sentences.

> Martineau: The Minister, standing by the Lord's Table, shall say one or more of the following sentences:
>
> Hunter: The Minister, standing by the Table, shall say one or more of the following sentences:-

The first sentence, Matt. 5:6, was the same in both, and Hunter used three other sentences which Martineau had used--Matt. 11:28; Rev. 3:20; Rev. 22:17.

(b) The second collect, "O God our Heavenly Father", adapted from the "Prayer of the Veil" which occurs in the Syriac liturgy of St. James, may have been suggeted by its use in Martineau's Eighth Service.

(c) The Commemoration of the Dead and Living.

> Martineau: We remember the fathers from the beginning of the world; the patriarchs, prophets, apostles, martyrs, and all who have wrought righteousness . . . We remember the whole family of man;
>
> Hunter: We remember all who from the beginning of the world have wrought righteousness and walked with Thee. We remember prophets, apostles, and martyrs . . . We remember in this sacred hour of communion the whole family of man; . . .

(d) The words of administration were the first set provided by Martineau:

> Take and eat this in remembrance of Christ.
> Drink this in remembrance of Christ.

Only a single Eucharistic Prayer (of consecration) was provided, which was by no means unknown in Congregationalism, [13] though this may represent the more general influence of Scottish Presbyterianism. Although there seems to have been no conscious attempt at imitating the classical Eucharistic Prayers, many of the themes found in the latter are found in Hunter's comprehensive prayer before the Institution Narrative. The themes of the commemoration of the Dead and Living, suggested by Martineau's service, were developed into a rich commemoration of the communion of saints, a concept which was especially dear to Hunter. [14]

The Prayer provides some interesting insights into Hunter's understanding of the Person of Christ and of the Eucharist. Phrases such as "the gracious beauty of His life", "the charity of His Cross", "our knowledge of Thy Fatherhood, our human brotherhood", recall the ethos of Ernest Renan's **La Vie de Jesus.** Many of the nineteenth century "Lives", in attempting to strip away the myth from the man and questioning the pre-existence of Christ, came very close to the Unitarian position with which Hunter had much sympathy. Many of the "Lives" presented the atonement as merely a display of love and an example to be followed, and questioned the reality of the resurrection. Inevitably, they tended to reinforce a "memorialist" concept of the Eucharist. It is tempting to conclude that in Hunter's Prayer, the "Quest of the Historical Jesus" finds its liturgical expression. [15] The Prayer itself, together with the Unitarian words of administration amply illustrate Hunter's memorialism:

> Help us to yield ourselves to the influence of this hour of holy memories and immortal hopes . . . We would remember Christ--the gracious beauty of his life, His obedience unto death, the charity of His Cross, and His victory over the world's sin and sorrow. We would remember all that we owe to Him . . . Impress and quicken our hearts with the memory of our Master and Saviour . . .

This is contrasted with

> We confess with shame that we often forget our Lord. We forget Him in our fear and anxiety . . . We forget Him in our indolence and weariness in Thy service . . . Forgive, O God, our forgetfulness. Help us so to enter into the spirit of this service, that we may go out into the world better prepared to remember Christ amid the care and strife and sorrow of our common days.

And Hunter prayed:

> Help us to think as He thought, to believe as He believed, and to trust as He trusted . . . we pray for grace to learn the lessons of His Cross . . .

And at the administration of the bread and wine,

> Take and eat this in remembrance of Christ.
> Drink this in remembrance of Christ.

Unlike the Last Supper, the elements in Hunter's communion had nothing to do with the Lord's body and blood.

No rubrics for the fraction were given. Possibly it was intended to be made during the recital of the institution. But its omission may have been deliberate; immanental theology tended to regard the atonement only in terms of a moral example of self-sacrifice and love, and the language of Hunter's Prayer suggests that this was the focus of his memorialism. To remember the life and example of Jesus and the brotherhood of mankind was the object of this liturgy; it was a symbol of commemoration and of moral fellowship.

Hunter continued to develop this liturgy, the definitive text being that of the seventh edition, 1901.

Fourth Edition, 1890.

Only minor changes were made in this edition.

(a) A new Scripture sentence was added, John 15:15.

(b) A fourth collect was added.

(c) The sequence of order after the administration was rearranged:

> The Lord's Prayer
> Hymn
> Offertory

(d) The Grace was replaced with the Blessing from the communion service of the **Book of Common Prayer**.

Fifth Edition, 1892.

Rather more changes were made in this edition.

(a) Three new Scripture sentence were added, John

15:12 with Matt. 5:23-24; part of 1 Cor. 12:13 and 10:17; 1 Cor 5:7-8.

(b) A completely new item was introduced after the sentences, entitled "Address". It was a short devotional invitation to communion of three paragraphs. The first paragraph was based on the Invitation of the **Book of Common Prayer**, "Ye that do truly and earnestly repent", though with a suitable anti-sacramental alteration: "draw near with reverence, faith, and thanksgiving, and take the Supper of the Lord to your comfort". This was followed by two paragraphs which would seem to have come from Hunter's pen: his monumental invitation, "Come to this sacred Table, not because you must, but because you may", which was later utilized in the official compilations of the denomination, and a paragraph which recalls the paraphrase of the Sursum corda of Farel and Calvin: [**16**]

> And now that the Supper of the Lord is spread before you, lift up your minds and hearts above all selfish fears and cares; let this bread and this wine be to you the witnesses and signs of the grace of our Lord Jesus Christ, the love of God, and the communion of the Holy Spirit.

(c) The collects were increased to six, the fifth being the Prayer of Humble Access suitably altered: "Grant therefore, gracious Lord, that, in hunger and thirst after righteousness, we may be filled with Jesus Christ, and ever more dwell in Him, and He in us. Amen".

(d) The hymn "A holy air is breathing round" as an alternative to "Bread of the world".

(e) The Eucharistic Prayer (of consecration), which reached its final form in this edition, was slightly altered in the second paragraph and enlarged by the addition of four paragraphs:

> Holy Father, we pray that we may have communion . . .
> Father of our spirits, God of love . . .
> O God, who art love . . .
> Almighty God, who hast called and redeemed . . .

(f) Martineau's words of administration were replaced by new words, though ones which were hardly less "memorialistic":

> Let us eat of this bread in remembrance of Christ;
> and may the life which was in Him be in us also.
> Let us drink of this cup in remembrance of Christ;
> and may the spirit in which he died be our spirit.

The words underline the immanentist idea that the spirit of Jesus--his outlook and example rather than the Holy Spirit--is also potentially present in everyone, the sacrament serving as a picturesque reminder of the supreme example of Christ and an encouragement to his followers. [17] There is no Divine presence here; Jesus is spoken of in the past tense.

(g) A slight change in the sequence after the administration:

Lord's Prayer
Offertory
Prayer
Hymn, "Beneath the shadow of the Cross"
Benediction

Two post-communion prayers were provided, the first being a précis of the Prayer Book "Prayer for the whole state of Christ's Church". An alternative Benediction was given.

Sixth Edition, 1895.

A crucial stage of development was reached in the sixth edition. The Communion Order of 1892 was given with only minor changes: the hymns were omitted; the collects were reduced to four; a rubric for silent meditation was removed; and a doxology was added to one of the post-communion prayers. However, in this edition Hunter introduced a second Eucharistic liturgy, based upon that of the Scottish Episcopal Church. [18]

Second Order

Sentences (1 Cor. 5:7b-8; Rev. 3:20)
Collect for Purity
The Two Commandment with response
Collect for Grace and strength to keep the commandments
Epistle
Gospel with response "Glory be to Thee, O God"
Offertory. Sentences and ascription of glory.
Prayer for the Whole Estate of Christ's Church (including reference to the saints and departed)
1 Cor. 11:23-25
Invitation
Confession
Absolution (collective)
Comfortable Words. Matt. 11:28-30; John 14:27; John 10:11, 16.
Sursum corda, Preface and Sanctus

Prayer of Humble Access: "so to partake of this holy communion of the Saviour's body and blood, that we may be filled with Jesus Christ, and evermore dwell in Him and He in us. Amen".
Prayer (of consecration)
Hymn
Words of administration
Lord's Prayer
Thanksgiving
Abbreviated Gloria in excelsis
Hymn
Benediction

Hunter made small changes to the text, for example in the "Prayer for the whole estate of Christ's Church" where "Bishops and curates" was replaced by "all ministers of Jesus Christ". Hunter also abbreviated the post communion thanksgiving and the Gloria in excelsis.

Hunter's main innovation in this order was the rearrangement of the "Prayer of Consecration". In the Scottish liturgy the Words of Institution in this prayer were preceded by a petition for consecration in imitation of the epiklesis in the classical anaphora. This petition in the Scottish rite can be traced back via the Non-juring divines to the 1637 liturgy for Scotland, and beyond that to the Prayer Book of 1549. After the institution narrative, the prayer continued with the 'Prayer of Oblation" in imitation of the anamnesis of the classical prayer; again this was ultimately derived from the book of 1549. The use of the Institution Narrative as part of the Eucharistic Prayer was not usual Independent practice, and thus Hunter subtracted it from the Scottish prayer, and inserted 1 Cor. 11:23-25 before the invitation to communion as a warrant for the whole rite. Even so, compared with the position of the narrative in his first order, this was a new position; in the first order the institution followed the Eucharistic Prayer.

Hunter retained the remainder of the Scottish prayer without much further modification, including the petition for consecration, and an anamnesis. This had the textual result of providing a liturgy with a much "higher" eucharistic doctrine than that expressed in his first order.

Seventh Edition, 1901.

The final form of Hunter's Eucharistic liturgy was that of 1901. A considerable amount of rearranging took place, the two orders of the sixth edition being merged to form a single order. In this new order the material from the Scottish Episcopal liturgy was used only sparingly to supplement Hunter's own order. It is of some significance that none of those elements of the

Scottish rite which represented a high sacramentalism were retained; the petition for consecration and the anamnesis which had meant so much to the Non-jurors and the Scottish Episcopalians were apparently of little importance to Hunter.

(a) The opening sentences were greatly reduced in number, only one of which had been retained from the original communion order of 1886.

(b) The Address was now followed by the confession from the **Book of Common Prayer** (used in the second order of the sixth edition), "Almighty God, Father of our Lord Jesus Christ".

(c) The collects were increased to five.

(d) After the collects, Hunter inserted the Comfortable Words, using here some of the redundant opening sentences from the earlier communion orders.

(e) After the Comfortable Words, Hunter included the Sursum corda, Prefacé and Sanctus.

(f) The "Reading" was now said antiphonally, the verses referring to the Institution being removed.

(g) After the Responses, now entitled "Commandments", Hunter placed the Institution Narrative as a warrant, followed by an introduction to prayer, "In Communion with Jesus Christ and with all His disciples and friends, let us offer our prayers together to the God of our salvation".

(h) Only parts of the Eucharistic Prayer need be said, or an extempore prayer may take its place.

(i) The Offering was expanded.

(j) A new thanksgiving was provided.

(k) Only the **Book of Common Prayer** communion blessing was provided.

The second order of the sixth edition had provided the Confession, the Comfortable Words, Sursum corda, Preface, and Sanctus.

Although in the **Devotional Services** Hunter provided for some observance of the liturgical calendar (e.g. the fourth edition provided collects for Advent, Christmas, The Close of the Year, The New Year, Lent, Palm Sunday, Good Friday, Easter, Whitsunday, Trinity Sunday, All Saints, The Spring and the Harvest), there were no provisions for its observance in the Eucharistic liturgy. In tracing the growth of Hunter's Eucharistic liturgy through the various editions, it will be seen that in his first order of 1886 he had simply clothed the outline of the usual Congregational type of service. In the succeeding revision this order was expanded, in particular by adding material from the **Book of Common Prayer.** This tendency which was most noticeable in the definitive text of 1901, was rather unfortunate, for what had started as an Independent liturgy came to look like yet another adaptation--albeit a drastic one--of the Anglican liturgy. The liturgy which preceded the Eucharistic Prayer became rather too long with the unnecessary addition of the Comfortable Words, Sursum corda, Preface and Sanctus. Yet for those who were satisfied with a memorialistic concept of the eucharist, it provided a dignified order of service. According to P. T. Forsyth, through the **Devotional Services** Hunter "helped to wear down the Nonconformist tradition against liturgical forms, and even where he did not wholly succeed in that crusade he certainly promoted a higher standard of worshipfulness in public services". [**19**]

NOTES

1. H. Davies, "Liturgical Reform in Nineteenth Century English Congregationalism" in CHST 17 (1954), 73-82, 76.

2. For biographical details, L. S. Hunter, **John Hunter, D.D. A Life,** London 1921.

3. Tribute from Scotland in The Christian World, 20th September 1917, 7. After 1901 **Devotional Services** was published by J. M. Dent, London. The following information supplied by the publisher gives some indication of its popularity and influence: It was published in 1904 at 3s. 6d. and simultaneously an abridged edition at 1s. 6d. References in the publisher's catalogue do not distinguish between these two editions which were in fact only impressions. In 1920, 1,000 copies were printed; 1924, 1400; 1930, 1,025; 1935, 1,025; and in 1943, 1,500. The book went out of print towards the end of 1949. The writer, in his duties as Registrar of Marriages, found the 1903 edition in use at Stambourne Congregational Church, Essex, in August 1975. The influence upon the denomination is seen in successive orders which drew upon the **Devotional Services.**

4. H. Davies, **Worship and Theology in England 1850-1900,** Princeton 1962, 231.

5. "Most of the prayers, I believe, are my own". Preface, **Devotional Services** Fifth edition 1892, vii.

6. The Christian World, 18th September 1890, 734. R. W. Emerson (1803-1882), Essayist, Poet and Philosopher, and former American Unitarian minister, was a leading exponent of the idea of spirit immanent in nature.

7. A. J. Griffith, "A Reminiscence", in L. S. Hunter, **A Life,** 27. The book by Hopps was probably **Prayers for Private Meditation and the Home,** 1866.

8. Ibid., 92.

9. J. Hunter, **A Plea for a Worshipful Church,** London 1903, 59.

10. J. Hunter, **The Coming Church,** London 1905, 15, 57-58.

11. L. S. Hunter, **A Life,** 208.

12. Op.cit., 59.

13. Supra, chapter 11.

14. L. S. Hunter, **A Life,** 201-3; 285.

15. Cf. E. Renan, **The Life of Jesus,** ET 1864, 83, 85, 127, 175, 215ff; D. Strauss, **The Life of Jesus,** 2 vols., ET 1879, vol. 1, 282-3, 388ff; J. Seeley, **Ecce Homo,** 1866, 130ff, 173ff. It is not being suggested that Hunter was a disciple of these writers, but his prayer represents the wide diffusion of many of their basic themes. No doubt many of the "Lives" were to be found in Hunter's large library. See "Ministerial Libraries. Dr. John Hunter's Library at the King's Weigh House", in The British Monthly, June 1904, 303-306.

16. See Bard Thompson, **Liturgies of the Western Church.**

17. Cf. R. J. Campbell, **The New Theology,** London 1907, 174: "Until His spirit becomes our spirit His Atonement has done nothing for us, and, when it does, we, like Him, become saviours of the race".

18. Text in W. Jardine Grisbrooke, **Anglican Liturgies of the Seventeenth and Eighteenth Centuries.**

Chapter Seven

DR. WILLIAM EDWIN ORCHARD'S "DIVINE SERVICE", 1919 AND 1926

> They believe that the New Testament authorizes every Christian Church to elect its own officers, to manage all its own affairs, and to stand independent of and irresponsible to, all authority, saving that only of the supreme and divine Head of the Church, the Lord Jesus Christ.
>
> Principles of Church Order and Discipline, **Declaration of Faith,** 1833.

As a Congregationalist, Dr. W. E. Orchard (1877-1955) remains something of an enigma. Ordained an evangelical Presbyterian and first minister of St. Paul's Church Enfield, he drifted into Liberalism and the "New Theology", thence to the Free Catholic Movement, and finally into Roman Catholicism. From 1914 - 1932 his spiritual journey took him to the King's Weigh House, and, nominally, Congregationalism. It was whilst as a Congregationalist that his liturgical work flowered--liturgical work which was marked by its radical departure from the ethos of Congregationalism.

During his short ministry at the Weigh House, Dr. John Hunter had introduced his **Devotional Services,** and these services were still in use when Orchard accepted the pastorate in 1914. But as he himself recalled:

> I declared from the outset that while I was willing to use Dr. Hunter's liturgy for the ordinary services, I could never take his Communion Service; for in this he had not only broken away from all historic forms, but he had prefaced it by a series of affirmations as to what it did not mean, which I could never take on my lips. [1]

At first therefore, Orchard continued with the Morning and Evening services of Hunter's **Devotional Services;** at a later date these were replaced with ten different orders of Orchard's own composition, which like those of the **Devotional Services,** were variations on the pattern of Morning and Evening Prayer of the **Book of Common Prayer.** [2] On the other hand, Hunter's communion order was immediately discontinued.

When at Enfield, Orchard had already compiled a liturgical service for the communion service, [3] but his last years there had been marked by a growing love of catholic forms of worship. This was to be demonstrated by the special "Reformed Eucharist" he drew up for his first service at the Weigh House on the 4th October 1914, reported fully in The Christian World. [4] It had an Introit, Prayer of Invocation, Confession, Kyrie eleison, Absolution, Lord's Prayer, Epistle, the Gradual (Goss's "O taste and see), the Gospel, and the Te Deum sung as a Creed. After the notices had been read, two deacons brought in the communion bread and wine, which the minister covered and placed on the communion table at which he stood later to receive "the offerings and oblations". After a prayer for the whole state of Christ's Church and the sermon, the communion service continued with the Sursum corda, Sanctus, the Prayer of Humble Access, the Benedictus qui venit, Eucharistic Prayer, Silent Adoration, the Agnus Dei, the commemoration of the Living and the Dead, closing with the Nunc dimittis, and the benediction "Now unto Him that is able to keep you from falling" (Jude 1:24-25). "The Service was remarkable" said The Christian World, "-a complete departure, in fact, from the ordinary usage of Free Churches". [5] On the "Order of Service" sheet for the week commencing 4th October, 1914, Orchard explained:

> It will be noticed that a special Order of Service has been compiled for the celebration of the Communion. This is entirely tentative and experimental, but it is hoped that we shall be able to adopt something along these lines for the purpose of a devout and worthy observance of the Lord's Supper. [6]

The adoption was swift; by December copies of the new communion service were available priced threepence, and it was celebrated on the first Sunday of each month. [7]

Whereas Hunter's communion service had stood between a Congregational pattern and the **Book of Common Prayer,** Orchard's rite lay between the **Book of Common Prayer** and the Roman Catholic Mass. [8]

In the years that followed, Orchard gravitated nearer Roman Catholicism, and his spiritual pilgrimage was reflected in the ceremonial of the services. In 1914 for the Eucharist, he had worn a surplice and white stole. Later he adopted the traditional Western eucharistic vestments, incense was used, and later still, the service of Benediction or Exposition of the Sacrament was introduced into the Weigh House. All this could be justified by the independent nature of Congregational church polity; each congregation was free to determine its own rites and ceremonies.

By 1917 Orchard was working on an entirely new service book, and in September of that year the Weight House Publication Committee was considering the question of its publication; [9] in February 1918 it was announced that the Oxford University Press had agreed to publish it. [10] **The Order of Divine Service** finally appeared in 1919; an abridged edition was issued in 1921, [11] and a revised edition in 1926. An American edition was also published.

In the **Divine Service** Orchard provided two Eucharistic liturgies. The first was entitled "A Simple Observance of the Lord's Supper", and the second, "The Order for the Celebration of the Eucharist or Sacrament of Holy Communion". With the advent of the new book the services for Sunday were changed. In a leaflet circulated to the congregation, Orchard suggested the following:

(1) There should be no "general" communicating at the monthly 11 a.m. Festal Eucharist.

(2) There should be a 10 a.m. celebration every Sunday.

(3) The "Simple" service to be celebrated once a month after Morning or Evening Service. [12]

This plan was adopted in March 1919, with the "Simple" service being celebrated on the first Sunday in the month, and the Festal celebration on the third Sunday. [13] In July it was decided to use the "Simple" service on the fifth Sunday evening also. [14]

The "Simple" service had been designed so that the individual communion cups and other customs of the Free Churches should be preserved, but in which there should be no attempt to consecrate the elements, they being regarded purely as symbols, each recipient acting as his own priest and the service being simply a memorial. [15] It took the form of Scripture interspersed with rubrics. The "President" commenced by reading the Institution, Matt. 26:20, 21-23, 26-27, supplemented by phrases from 1 Cor. 11:24-26. The rubrics suggested self-examination, confession, silent invocation of the Holy Spirit, the fraction, adoration and thanksgiving. The bread and wine were administered separately.

After the communion, prayer was suggested, pleading the sacrifice of Christ and making self-oblation, followed by the offering for the poor (in its traditional Congregational position), 2 Cor. 8:9, and "The High Priestly Prayer" - John 17:1, 9-10, 20-21 - with rubrics suggesting a remembrance of the saints and departed, the living, and the unity of the Church. Matt. 26:30a introduced a hymn, with John 14:27 as the benediction.

As far as Orchard was concerned, the "Simple" service was a concession to Free Church tradition; the main Eucharistic liturgy was the second order. It provided for

1. A Low Celebration, without music.
2. A Festal Celebration, with Choral Setting; omitting the Kyrie Eleison, but including the Gloria in Excelsis.
3. A Solemn Celebration for Penitential Seasons or Requiems; omitting the Gloria in Excelsis but including the Kyrie Eleison.

Writing in 1933, Orchard claimed that this liturgy had been "carefully compiled from the most ancient sources, and taking advantage of recent research and discussion". [16] It is difficult to determine exactly what Orchard understood by "most ancient sources" and "recent research and discussion". By 1917 when he was preparing the work, some important liturgical material had been made available, notably the **Euchologion of Serapion**, and the **Apostolic Tradition** attributed to Hippolytus. [17] At a more popular level, W. H. Frere's **Some Principles of Liturgical Reform** (1911) was available. But there is nothing in the Eucharistic liturgy of the **Divine Service** to suggest that Orchard had taken these into consideration. In the **Divine Service** he conveniently gave the sources of many of his prayers, and the majority of these were taken from collections by other compilers, for example, Dr. Bright's **Ancient Collects** and Dr. Selina Fox's **A Chain of Prayer Across the Ages**. It would seem that Orchard was more accurate in a statement he made earlier when still at the Weigh House, that it consists "almost entirely of a compilation from other sources". [18] As the following table illustrates, most of the material was taken from the **Book of Common Prayer** and the Roman Catholic Mass.

	Source - probable or acknowledged
Introit or Hymn	
In the Name of the Father, and of the Son, and of the Holy Ghost. Amen	Roman

	Source - probable or acknowledged
V. I will go unto the altar of God	Roman
R. Unto God, my exceeding joy	
Psalm 43. Judge me O God	Roman
V. Our help is in the Name of the Lord	Roman
R. Who made heaven and earth	
Confession	Syriac James (text from Neale Littledale)
Kyrie Eleison	Roman
Absolution, or	BCP
Gloria in Excelsis	Roman; BCP
Prayer of the Veil	Syriac James (Priest's Book of Private Devotion)
Epistle	
Gradual	(Roman)
Gospel	
Nicene Creed or	BCP
Te Deum	BCP Morning Prayer
Notices	
Invitation to communion	
Hymn	
The Bidding Prayer	
The Address	
The Offertory:	
Collects	
At the Offering of the Bread	
At the Mixing of the Chalice	
At the Offering of the Chalice	
Versicles and Responses	Probably suggested by the Roman Oblation of the Faithful, the Offertory Incensation, and the Lavabo.
The Offertory Prayer	BCP; Didache
Communion Hymn	
Collect for the Day	
Collect for Purity	BCP
Sursum corda, Proper Preface	BCP
Sanctus	BCP

	Source (cont)
Orate Fratres	Roman
Suscipiat Dominus	Roman
Benedictus qui venit	Roman
The Eucharistic Prayer	St. John's Gospel and "Ancient Liturgies"
Silent Adoration	
The Prayer of Oblation	BCP; Roman *Canon missae*, *Unde et memores* and *Supplices*
The Lord's Prayer	
Agnus Dei	Roman
The Communion:	
(1) Distribution	(Free Church Practice)
Humble Access	BCP
Words of Administration:	
The Communion of the Body/Blood of Christ	
(2) Communicants come to the Table	(Roman and Anglican practice)
Lord, I am not worthy . . .	Roman
The Body of our Lord Jesus Christ preserve my soul unto everlasting life	(Roman)
What shall I render . . . ?	Roman
The Blood of our Lord Jesus Christ preserve my soul unto everlasting life	Roman.
Invitation, "Ye that do truly"	BCP
or. "Come ye people; the holy and immortal and undefiled mystery is celebrated; approach with faith and fear; with hands cleansed by penitence partake of the gift; for the Lamb of God is set forth as a sacrifice for us.	

	Source (cont)
or, "Holy Things for the holy"	
Words of Administration:	
The Communion of the Body/Blood of Christ	
or. The Body/Blood of our Lord Jesus Christ preserve thy soul unto everlasting life	Roman/BCP
The Commemoration of the Living, the Saints and the Departed	
The Post Communion Prayer	(Various collects)
Nunc dimittis	BCP Evening Prayer Luke 2:29-32
Benediction	BCP, or Jude 1:24-25
It is finished: depart in peace	Roman

The Introit, Gradual, Epistle and Gospel were left to the celebrant's choice, and the Commemoration of the Living, the Saints and the Departed was left for extemporary prayer. The Eucharistic Prayer, "in accordance with early usage", could also be extemporary, "care however being taken to invoke the Holy Spirit, and to use the Words of Institution recorded in the Gospels, or in Saint Paul's First Epistle to the Corinthians".

Despite the heavy dependence upon the **Book of Common Prayer** and the Roman Mass, Orchard's rite was no mere catholic counterpart to the liturgy of J. Mountain considered earlier; [**19**] this liturgy was not simply a scissors and paste job. This is most clearly to be seen in the Eucharistic Prayer and the Prayer of Oblation.

Orchard very skilfully used St. John's Gospel to provide a Christological thanksgiving, emphasizing the continuity between the Word of God in the Old Testament with the Word made flesh. The Eucharistic Prayer opened with the word "Holy", a feature of the Post-sanctus of the West Syrian Anaphora, though since Orchard had broken connection with the Sanctus by the Orate fratres, this may be purely coincidence. The Epiklesis appears in the Egyptian position, before the Words of Institution, the terminology being of the West Syrian type, but with distinct echoes of the Scottish Communion Office and the American **Book of**

Common Prayer; the petition "that they may become unto us the most blessed Body and Blood" still allowed a Reformed interpretation of the Spirit working in the communicant rather than on the elements. The "Prayer of Oblation" was a careful blending of the **Book of Common Prayer** "Prayer of Oblation" with the Unde et memores and Supplices of the Roman **Canon missae.** Orchard here presented a rite in which the Liturgy of the Word and Sacrament were restored in unity, in which the Eucharist was linked to the liturgical calendar, and in which a rich variety of classical Western forms, with some Eastern elements, were reintroduced into the Congregational liturgical tradition.

Orchard's interest was not, however, solely liturgical. The prayers he used and those he composed from sources, betray his doctrinal interest, namely the doctrines of sacrifice and presence in the Eucharist. The sacrificial aspect was emphasized by the use of the Roman Offertory prayers, the versicles and responses which stressed sacrifice and the altar, the Orate fratres and Suscipiat Dominus, and the "Prayer of Oblation" in which "the Bread of eternal life, and the Cup of everlasting salvation" were offered to the Father. The Eucharistic presence was stressed particularly by the Epiklesis and Words of Institution where the words "This is My Body which is broken for you", "This is My Blood of the New Covenant which is shed for many unto remission of sins", were printed in large Gothic script. Orchard's gravitation towards Rome meant that these two doctrines became more and more pronounced in his thought.

In his **Foundations of Faith,** Orchard explained the Eucharistic sacrifice as follows:

> The Sacrifice of the Mass is explicitly declared to be neither an addition to, nor a repetition of, Calvary, but the very same offering as that made on Calvary. Since Christ offered Himself by an eternal spirit, this can be continually represented in time as it was on Calvary; save that in the Mass it is now an unbloody sacrifice that is offered, for it is one with the eternal offering which Christ is now making for us in heaven; wherefore it is not so much that Christ comes down to us upon the Altar, but through the Sacrifice of the Altar we are brought into touch with the offering which Christ ever lives to make for us in the heavenly realm, and at the Mass we are actually partaking in the worship of the Lamb once slain and now standing upon the throne. [20]

Elsewhere he maintained that the word "remembrance" (Do this in remembrance of me) meant an objective offering of the sacrifice of Christ's Body and Blood; our offering is one with

Christ's eternal offering in heaven, illustrated first in the elevation of the "Sacred Species", and then in the Prayer of Oblation. [21] On the subject of the Eucharistic presence he wrote:

> All that we do in the Mass is to repeat Christ's words, "This is my Body"; "This is my Blood", praying that this may be fulfilled to us, and then treating the elements as if our prayer had been answered. [22]

In **Foundations of Faith** Orchard defended the doctrine of Transubstantiation.

It is not surprising, therefore, that in the revised edition of **Divine Service**, 1926, in addition to minor rearrangements in the second Eucharistic liturgy, various changes and additions were made in order to heighten the Catholic conceptions of sacrifice and presence.

The minor alterations were mainly in the rubrics, but included the placing of the collects for the day and for Purity in the more traditional position before the Epistle, and the Orate fratres and Suscipiat Dominus were placed before the Offertory Prayer, so removing any interruptions from Sursum corda to the conclusion of the Prayer of Oblation. The latter prayer now made mention of "his coming again in glory", and included a petition for the Holy Spirit to come down upon the communicants.

The Offertory of the Bread and Wine was stressed by the addition of the Prayer of the Veil, and two further Roman Offertory collects, In Spiritu humilitatis and Veni Sanctificator, increasing the three collects of 1919 to a total of six. The concepts of sacrifice and presence were given further emphasis in the new Eucharistic Prayer. In the second edition Orchard explained the new Prayer thus:

> In particular the Eucharistic Prayer has been entirely re-shaped in accordance with the most recent liturgiological research, making use of the earliest available material, so that it now represents a conflation of the Greek, the Egyptian, and the Roman Rites.

But the sacrificial aspect was now emphasized by the optional inclusion of a conflation of the Roman Te igitur, Memento Domine, Communicantes, Hanc igitur and Quam oblationem: "accept and bless this offering", "for all whom, and for all concerning them, we offer up to thee this sacrifice of praise" and "which oblation . . . make . . . blessed, approved, ratified reasonable, and acceptable".

The Eucharistic presence was likewise accentuated. There

was a subtle change in the Epiklesis: "that they may become for us" would appear to refer to the elements as in the Quam oblationem, "ut nobis . . . fiat", replacing the more subjective words "unto us" of the 1919 text. Furthermore, the optional use of the Roman Quī pridis and Simili modo would seem to suggest not so much an ecumenical approach to liturgy as an indication that like-words mean like-doctrine.

Orchard explained a change in the Prayer of Oblation as follows:

> The insertion of a second petition for the Holy Spirit in the Prayer of Oblation, put here for the preparation of the communicants, as seems to have been the original purpose of an Epiclesis at this point, rather than for the sanctification of the elements, which should come beforehand, may perhaps serve to indicate how the ideas underlying the Greek and Roman liturgies may be reconciled by including both.

Orchard's Eucharistic liturgy was a complete return to the classical rite, though with a decidedly Western bias, and including many late features such as the Roman Offertory collects. It was a rich liturgy, and in particular, the Eucharistic Prayer of 1919 illustrated how a very Scriptural prayer could be composed without departing from the classical shape of the anaphora. Had its author been concerned primarily with the restoration of the traditional pre-Reformation shape of the Eucharistic liturgy within Congregationalism, and shown a little more diplomacy, it might have been of some influence within the denomination. But the liturgy could not be separated from Orchard's own advance towards Roman Catholicism. The ultimate reason for the lack of influence of the **Divine Service** was not so much its liturgical forms as the ceremonial and doctrines with which it became inextricably bound. When its author was wearing traditionally catholic vestments and using incense, and was expounding and defending the Sacrifice of the Mass and Transubstantiation, it was hardly likely that many Congregationalists would look with sympathy at this liturgy. In fact, as Orchard himself admitted, some of the Weigh House congregation were offended by the advances, and dropped away. [**23**] Various Congregational liturgical books borrowed individual prayers from **Divine Service**, but its Eucharistic liturgy was tacitly ignored. Writing in 1927 Orchard admitted of the **Divine Service**

> We have actual knowledge of only one or two Churches here or in America who have adopted it. This would seem to indicate that our preference is merely a peculiarity. [**24**]

In 1933 Orchard became a Roman Catholic. The **Divine Service** remained in use at the Weigh House, though the ceremonial fell into disuse. Later parts of the liturgy were also abandoned. In 1965 the Weigh House congregation amalgamated with the Whitefield Memorial Church, Tottenham Court Road. [25] The surviving copies of **Divine Service** from the Weigh House remained on the hymnbook shelves of the Whitefield Memorial Church--unused. Yet in spite of its lack of influence, it remains a quite remarkable rite belonging to the Congregational tradition.

NOTES

1. W. E. Orchard, **From Faith to Faith,** London 1933, 118; "affirmations" may refer to Hunter's Invitation.

2. An extremely beautiful illuminated manuscript book of Orchard's Ten Orders is now in the custody of Dr. Williams' Library, London.

3. See B. D. Spinks, "A Precursor to Dr. W. E. Orchard's Divine Service", Journal of URC History Society, 2:3 (1979), 73-75.

4. "At the Weigh House. Dr. Orchard's New Ministry. The Communion with a Liturgy", in The Christian World, October 8th, 1914, p. 9.

5. Ibid.

6. For this Service sheet, see **Scrap Book, 1905-1917**, Dr. Williams' Library, Ms. 209.

7. Order of Service sheet, week commencing December 6th, 1914, in **Scrap Book, 1905-1917.** I have been unable to locate a copy of this order.

8. In **From Faith to Faith,** 119, Orchard stated that in this service he had followed largely the order, though not always the words, of the Anglican liturgy. In "The Priestly Sacrifice", **The New Catholicism and Other Sermons,** London 1917, 9, he made the strange claim that it was "either scriptural or moulded on Eastern forms". A comparison of the summary from The Christian World, with the BCP and the Roman Mass will show our estimation to be correct.

9. Church Committee Meetings Minutes, 1915-1925, September 3rd, 1917, Dr.Williams' Library Ms. 209.

10. Ibid., February 11th, 1918.

11. Ibid., May 11th, 1921. It was reported that a number of churches would have preferred **Divine Service** to the **Book of Congregational Worship,** 1920, had the former been procurable at a lower price.

12. "The Distribution of the Sacrament". Copy in Church Minutes, 1916-1926, March 26th, 1919. Dr. Williams' Library, Ms. 209.

13. Ibid.

14. Ibid., July 2nd, 1919.

15. W. E. Orchard, **From Faith to Faith,** 134-135.

16. Ibid., 134.

17. F. E. Brightman, "The Sacramentary of Serapion of Thmuis" in JTS 1 (1899-1900), 88-113, 247-277; R. H. Connolly, **The so-called Egyptian Church Order**, Cambridge 1916.

18. W. E. Orchard, "Our Liturgy" in The King's Weigh House Monthly, February 1927.

19. See Chap. 5, 101ff.

20. W. E. Orchard, **Foundations of Faith,** 4 vols., London 1924-27, vol. 3, Ecclesiological, 126.

21. W. E. Orchard, "Our Offering of Christ's Sacrifice", in The King's Weigh House Monthly, December 1928.

22. W. E. Orchard, "The Meaning of the Mass", in The King's Weigh House Monthly, August 1928; cf. "The Real Presence" in ibid., August 1931.

23. W. E. Orchard, **From Faith to Faith,** 135-136.

24. W. E. Orchard, "Our Liturgy", in op.cit. But he himself regarded it as a contribution to the quest for a perfect liturgy. Ibid.

25. For details see Elaine Kaye, **The History of the King's Weigh House,** London 1968.

Chapter Eight

WHAT MEAN YE BY THIS SERVICE?
THE CONGREGATIONAL UNION LITURGIES, 1920 and 1936

> If we only see in Christ a supreme case of human religion, or if we see in the Cross but a manifestation of love and not its grand crucial action of judgment and grace, we cannot see in the Supper the meaning the Church has found in it . . .
>
> P. T. Forsyth, **The Church and the Sacraments** 1917, p. 248.

Nearly fifty years were to pass before the Congregational Union, on behalf of the whole denomination, felt able to take up the suggestion made in 1873 by W. H. Willans, that the Union should itself prepare an order for worship. [1] Liturgical services were becoming more common amongst Congregationalists, and in 1916 a liturgical service was used at a meeting of the Union. [2] The **Congregational Year Book** of 1919 reported that a committee had been appointed to compile a book of liturgical services for use at option. [3] One of the members of the Committee, Sir John McClure, LL.D., D.Mus., was elected Chairman of the Union in 1919, and in his Spring Address took the opportunity of speaking about public worship. According to McClure, there was a steadily growing conviction among Congregationalists that the advantages of a liturgy greatly outweigh its defects. [4] However, any compilation that the denomination produced should not be a mere pasticcio:

> Any liturgy prepared for the use of Congregationalists becomes in some measure their contribution to the worship of the Church Universal, and must bear on it the impress of their spiritual experience and religious conceptions. . . our liturgy if it is to be sincere, cannot be a mere copying or even adaptation of others, but a real expression of the best thoughts and highest aspirations to which our faith and order have enabled us to attain. [5]

In 1920 the slender volume appeared, entitled **Book of Congregational Worship.** Its scope was limited, and the Literature Committee of the Union had to supplement it with special orders for laying foundation stones and the dedication of a Church. [6] In 1936 it was replaced by a new compilation, **A Manual for Ministers.** Both books contained Eucharistic liturgies.

To compile orders of Morning worship for optional use by Congregationalists was in itself not a particularly difficult task. But the compilation of a Eucharistic liturgy for the whole denomination was an entirely different matter. When Hunter and Orchard compiled their Eucharistic liturgies, they were able to use what material they wished and to express what doctrine(s) they wished. If other Congregationalists, or even other Churches, liked the services and doctrines expressed, they were free to use them. However, the liturgies of Hunter and Orchard did not pretend to represent anyone's views other than those of the author. While it was true that no one would be forced to use the compilations of the Congregational Union, nevertheless they appeared as the official liturgical forms of the denomination, and as such were bound to reflect and influence the mind of the denomination. Here was the great difficulty; what was the mind of the denomination on Eucharistic liturgy and doctrine?

In 1936 a commission on the sacraments of Baptism and the Lord's Supper reported that a very wide variety of views were to be found within the denomination, ranging from a "high" view to those whose attitude approximated to that of the Quakers. Some Churches seemed to have had no considered doctrine of the sacraments at all. [7] The situation had in fact changed very little from that described by R. W. Dale some fifty years before.

In theory the Roman Catholic views of W. E. Orchard had a legitimate place in the denomination, simply because Congregational church polity allowed such; on the whole, however, Orchard was alone in his views. A "high" view of the sacraments was taught by Dr. P. T. Forsyth (1848-1921). Forsyth had studied in Germany under Ritschl, and in his early years had been a noted liberal; gradually he moved toward orthodoxy, and in 1901 he became Principal of Hackney Theological College. An extremely rich doctrine of the Eucharist was put forward in **The Church and the Sacraments,** 1917. Forsyth rejected a mere memorialistic conception of the Eucharist; how can we have a mere memorial of one who is still alive, still our life, still present with us and acting in us? [8] Mere memorialism was, so Forsyth argued, a more fatal error than the Mass, and a far less lovely one. [9] Symbol was a better word than memorial, but even this was not adequate; sacrament, insisted Forsyth, meant that something is done; it is an act of Christ really present by his Holy Spirit in the Church. [10] A sacrament is an <u>opus operatum</u>. [11]

> . . . it is an act of the Church more than of the individual. Further still, it is an act created by the eternal Act of Christ which made and makes the Church. At the last it is the act of Christ present in the Church, which does not so much live as Christ lives in it. It is Christ's act offering Himself to men rather than the act of the Church offering Christ to God. [12]

According to Forsyth, the important part of the Eucharist was the action which was symbolized, the breaking rather than the bread, the outpouring rather than the wine. [13] Thus the fraction was important, and the signs really convey what they signify.

Another "high" view was implied by C. H. Dodd in an article on Eucharistic symbolism in St. John's Gospel, where Dodd argued that the discourse on the Bread of Life in chapter six is an exposition of Christ's words "This is my Body", teaching a mystical doctrine of salvation, "not so much because Christ does something for us, as because He gives Himself to us". [14]

However, Forsyth and Dodd were not typical of the denomination. Most Congregationalists were "Zwinglian" in belief, often asserting a "real presence", but with so many qualifications and negations that, to use Orchard's words, "the meaning becomes almost 'this is not my Body; this is not my Blood' ". [15]

Principal A. E. Garvie of New College, in an article in The Christian World affirmed a "real presence" in the Eucharist, but rejected the Roman Catholic, Lutheran, Calvinist and Zwinglian conceptions of the sacrament, preferring "personal presence" to a metaphysical or spiritual explanation. [16] In **The Holy Catholic Church from the Congregational Point of View**, he maintained:

> He is really present at the Lord's Supper without any such limitation to the elements unless we are prepared to maintain that the material is more real than the spiritual. It is the whole Christ who presents Himself to faith, so that the believer has communion with Him. [17]

But the "whole Christ" was certainly not the humanity of Christ which had been laid in the grave and was no more. [18] Garvie accepted the authenticity of the command to repeat the rite, but he was far less certain that Jesus had meant any more than that he should be remembered at every common meal.

> He never meant the ordinance, so significant in its simplicity, to be transformed into a sacred mystery, set apart from the daily life of believers. At every meal believers can and ought to remember and commune with Christ. [19]

The presence of Christ at the Supper was such as could be enjoyed at any meal; thus the elements of bread and wine were not essential to the rite.

A very similar train of thought was to be found in the communion addresses of J. G. Greenhough in **Eden and Gethsemane.** Greenhough affirmed a "real presence", but denied that it had anything to do with the bread and wine:

> The bread was blessed and the cup was blessed, not in the sense that their nature was changed, but as He blessed almost every common thing He touched, making them sacred in their suggestiveness, investing them with the power of lifting human thought up to the heavenly level. [20]

The analogy with "almost every common thing He touched" led Greenhough to state:

> The Communion Supper only brings into prominence that which is always going on, without which we should lose all power to love and serve; [21]

Presumably other things could also bring this into prominence; there could be unlimited sacraments, because it was the thoughts, feelings, and spirit in which we do something, which make a sacrament. [22]

> Wherever bread is eaten, and wherever men take some simple drink to allay their thirst, and that is much the same as to say, wherever human beings live, there the materials for this highest religious service are found, and there the memory is helped to recall and realise once more the Divine sufferings which were endured for human sin, and the pitiful dying love which brought the world salvation. [23]

The bread and wine were a help to the memory; no doubt other things would do just as well. According to B. J. Snell, the bread and wine are symbols which are not essential either to commemoration or to communion, but merely helps to both. [24] The logical conclusion to this type of thought was in fact suggested by Bertram Smith of the famous Wrigley and Smith partnership at Salem Chapel, Leeds. In an interview with The Christian World Smith suggested that sometimes it would be good to change the symbols at the monthly communion service:

> I should like to have them sit and look at a picture sometimes. [25]

Here was the realization of Dale's fear of a drift beyond "Zwinglian-ism".

By the early decades of the twentieth century, "memorial-ism" had found a new powerful ally in New Testament Higher Criticism. It exerted influence in three particular ways.

1. In more general terms the Liberal Theology which resulted from Higher Criticism weakened the Eucharist by attacking the traditional doctrines of the Atonement and the Resurrection.

Liberalism came to the fore in Congregationalism with the "New Theology" which appeared in 1907, and again in the early 1930's with the Blackheath Group; both movements attempted to express the Christian faith in contemporary language and ideas.

The New Theology was associated with R. J. Campbell, T. Rhondda Williams, J. Warschauer and K. C. Anderson, and made its debut in a series of books in 1907. [26] Its main theme was that God is immanent in all things, and that an incarnation was therefore unnecessary. Christ was a man in whom God appeals to us as never before; he is the unique standard of human excellence, a standard which men must attempt in order to fulfill their destiny. Jesus is "Friend", "Guide" and "Brother". The Atonement cannot be understood in terms of a ransom or a sacrifice, for these terms were no longer meaningful. The Cross was merely an example of self-sacrifice; it is not something that Christ has done for us, but something which, if we are willing, He may do in us. [27] Wherever love is ministering to human necessity, and the very same spirit which was in Jesus is seen--the spirit which heals and saves--there is the Atonement. [28] For Atonement to be effective, it has to be repeated on the altar of human hearts. [29]

The Resurrection was also interpreted in subjective terms, either as a vision, or, according to T. Rhondda Williams:

> The first disciples could, I believe, come upon their faith through the tremendous influence which Jesus had had upon them. We do not easily surrender to death those we love--we tend naturally to believe in their survival; this is still more especially the case with the great souls; it would be very specially the case with some personality that entirely dominated our lives; it must have been inevitable in the case of Jesus. [30]

There was no divine presence at the Eucharist, or at least, no more than in any other part of God's creation; certainly Jesus could not be present. The Eucharist was a memory of Jesus and an expression of brotherhood; the fraction was only a symbol of the example of love. The New Theology reinforced the argument of J. Morgan Gibbon (1855-1932), minister of Stamford Hill Church, London, that the great significance of the Supper was as a means of pledging each other in Jesus Christ, solely on the grounds of faith and service. [31]

The same themes of the New Theology were updated and repeated by the Blackheath Group. This was a group of liberal Congregationalists formed in 1933 and concerned to re-state Church thought to take into account the changes demanded by the modern age. [32] God may be apprehended by all the common and normal endowments of our nature as human beings, and the same divine power which was available for Jesus is available for all men. [33] In Frank Lenwood's **Jesus--Lord or Leader?**, the Atonement and Resurrection were given a subjective interpretation similar to that of the New Theology. For Lenwood, the Communion service was "the most perplexing of our ritual". [34] As well as being a memorial of the death of the Master, it was also a sacrament of the "divine hospitality" which carries with it the brotherhood of those who receive it. [35] His obvious embarrassment with the Eucharist led Lenwood to point out that the Quakers had maintained the spiritual life without any sacraments. [36]

If these two movements had any influence on Eucharistic thought in the denomination, it was to reinforce a "memorialist" concept.

2. The nature of the Eucharist was called in question by the Religio-historical school of thought. German scholars such as Otto Pfleiderer, Albert Eichhorn and Wilhelm Heitmuller had suggested that the Pauline view of the sacraments, and those which subsequently developed in the early Church, were the result of Hellenization, in particular, the direct influence of the mystery cults. Since this approach tended to throw suspicion on the Catholic understanding of the Eucharist, it appealed to some Congregationalists. A leading article in The Christian World explained the Christian sacraments as having their origin in the Eleusinian Mysteries from the East, and the Persian cult of Mithras. [37] The sacrament became a mystery because the peoples to whom Christianity was preached had already a religion of such mysteries, had minds already filled with prepossessions concerning them, mental moulds which were bound to shape the doctrine this way. [38] The article pointed out that the mental conditions which shaped the doctrine had no claim to control the views of Christians now; scholars of the first rank agreed with the Quakers that Jesus had no thought of the perpetuation of the Eucharist. The writer added that the Quakers appeared not to have done badly in adhering to that view.

The mystery cult argument was used--though with more

caution--by J. V. Bartlet, Professor of Church History at Mansfield College, Oxford, and by E. J. Price, Professor and Principal at Yorkshire United Independent College, Bradford. [**39**] It was also used by Harry Bulcock who was associated with the Blackheath Group and was chairman of the Union of Modern Free Churchmen. In **A Re-stated Faith: Positive Values,** Bulcock was cautious: the influence of the mystery cults was an open question. The meal of the early Christian community was in the nature of a Church social gathering, but with his doctrine of the revelation of an Inward Christ, Paul stated in 1 Cor. 11 what he believed Christ intended the meal to be, namely, a solemn religious communion. [**40**] But in **A Modern Churchman's Manual** Bulcock was more definite. The actual forms of the sacrament could be traced to a circle of animistic and magical ideas. The Last Supper does not seem to have been intended by Jesus to have become a recurring rite, or to have had a "communion" significance. There are grounds for believing that the development of meaning was due to Paul who combined the Agape meal with the sacramental doctrines of the Mystery cult communion meals. [**41**]

For those who accepted the implications of this school of thought, the Supper should probably have never been repeated, and at best was an ecclesiastical custom expressing fellowship.

3. Although as late as 1941 Harry Bulcock was still propounding the mystery cult theory, most scholars recognized that it was a theory which went beyond the available evidence. But Higher Criticism still questioned the authenticity of the command of Jesus for the rite to be repeated. Several Congregational scholars had doubts regarding its authenticity. C. J. Cadoux, Vice-Principal of Mansfield College and a New Testament theologian explained:

> In regard to the question whether Jesus gave instructions for the rite to be repeated, the difficulty lies in the fact that, while such instructions are reported by Paul (1 Cor. xi. 24 fin., 25 fin.) and in the ungenuine text of Lk. xxii. 19 fin., they are omitted in Mk. and (most strangely) in Mt. It is almost equally hard to believe that (i) the Disciples would have practised the rite constantly and Paul have twice written, "Do this in remembrance of me", if Jesus had not given any such injunction, and (ii) that Mk. and Mt. would have omitted this injunction if he had. We must, for the reasons given, leave the question undiscussed and undecided here, observing only that the act of Jesus in distributing the bread and wine was emphatically a communal act, and that, if he was known among his Disciples and friends by his special manner of breaking bread and sharing wine when at table with them (Lk. xxiv. 30f., 35L; 1 Cor. xi. 24f. ["This

> do", not "This eat", "This drink"]), the solemn circumstances of the Last Supper might suggest to the Disciples the repetition of the act in his memory, even if Jesus himself had not explicitly enjoined such repetition in actual words. [42]

The same agnosticism was expressed by Dr. R. Mackintosh, Edward Grubb and A. D. Martin. [43] The implications were put quite bluntly by Dr. Albert Peel, the editor of The Congregational Quarterly, historian and a minister:

> No one today would claim categorically that the two sacraments were instituted by Christ and that He ordered them to be perpetually observed. No one could claim that the sacraments were indispensable, in so far as the like grace can be otherwise mediated. No one could deny that Christians have lived faithful and devout lives without the use of sacraments. The repetition of the words of blessing (Institution) savours of magic and is something entirely aloof from the spirit, the simplicity, of Jesus Christ. The experience of the Society of Friends and others has shown that symbols are not necessary. [44]

The overall impact of Higher Criticism may be summarized as follows:

(a) If Jesus instituted the Eucharist, it was merely as a social meal expressing solidarity and fellowship.

(b) It was doubtful whether Jesus did in fact institute the rite. It may have been perpetuated by the early Church, as a reminder of Jesus and as a fellowship meal. It could be justified on psychological grounds, for many found it a helpful symbol. [45] But it was not necessary, and for some it was a tiresome custom.

(c) Ideas of Divine Presence of mystical communion with God were derived from Paul or the mystery cults (or both), and were a departure from the Gospel meaning of the Supper.

It is impossible to estimate how widespread these views were in the denomination, but clearly they served to reinforce the already dominant subjective memorialist conception of the Eucharist. Nor did they stimulate study of the early liturgy by members of the denomination. When Congregationalists did turn a scholarly eye to liturgy, the Jewish table prayers and the **Didache** were interesting in providing a background to the rite, but later liturgies could not be taken seriously. [46]

The shape of the Congregationalist Eucharistic liturgy was also being affected, from an entirely different and unexpected quarter. In the nineteenth century the movement for total abstinence grew very quickly within the denomination, [47] and it demanded that at the Communion service unfermented grape juice should be used rather than alcoholic wine. But the adoption of grape juice raised the question of hygiene, for it did not possess the sterilizing properties of alcohol which gave some protection in the use of common cups. In answer to the problem, trays of individual Communion cups came into vogue at the turn of the century. "Hygienic Communion Services" were advertised in the **Congregational Year Book** 1905 by Geo. Bambridge of Sunderland, and in an advertisement in 1912, Townshends Limited of Birmingham claimed that five hundred Congregational Churches used their trays of cups. "Why use the insanitary common cup at the Lord's Table which courtesy would forbid at your own?" asked the advertisers. The advantages were listed as purity, safety from infection, unhindered devotion, and permanently increased attendance at the communion. Trays were also provided for individual portions of bread. Since the trays had to be prepared beforehand, it meant that where they were adopted, the fraction and libation were lost; from P. T. Forsyth's point of view, the heart of the Eucharistic action was torn out of the rite.

It was the culminative effect of these various factors which led A. D. Martin (1869-1940) to suggest a new order for the Lord's Supper. [48] Martin was extremely critical of the individualism of the new communion trays which he described as "suggestive of the laboratory of a chemistry class", [49] and he recalled with nostalgia the celebrations at Lewisham High Road Church which he had attended as a youth. But such nostalgia certainly did not suggest to Martin a return to Calvinistic orthodoxy; Martin was uncertain that Christ had in fact instituted the Eucharist, and therefore the Church was not bound by the very form of the original supper in the Upper Room:

> In the first place, the Church is at liberty, if a spiritual convenience require it, to re-shape the Communion service according to modern experience. In the second place, in such re-shaping we should preserve the largest possible measure of continuity with the past, and of community with contemporary believers. [50]

There could be no return to the common cup; in order to recapture the communal aspect of the Supper, Martin was prepared to surrender the Reformation protest against the Roman Catholic practice of communion in one kind, and to advocate communion in bread only. The order of service which he proposed was as follows: [51]

> Introductory sentences, or, occasionally, the recital of what has been called John's "alternative sacrament", the story of the washing of the disciples' feet.

Hymn
Various prayers, including always a prayer for the blessing of all the departed.
Mark's Narrative of the Supper
Salvator Mundi and Gloria in excelsis
Jesus said: John 6:27-29, 33, 35, 37, 48, 51, 63
Bread distributed
Private prayer
Triumphant hymn and offertory

It is unfortunate that Martin did not reveal "the past" with which this liturgy was supposed to be continuous.

In a situation of such diverse views a suitable solution would have been for the Congregational Union to have provided a selection of Eucharistic liturgies which would cater for the whole denomination: perhaps a rite based upon the classical liturgies, such as Orchard had compiled, that of John Hunter which was obviously popular within the denomination; an outline of an order for those who stood firm on free prayer; and possibly an order of an experimental nature for those liberals who felt unable to use more traditional rites. But this comprehensive course was not followed by the Union; the **Book of Congregational Worship,** 1920, contained a single order for the Communion; **A Manual for Ministers** contained two orders of a similar nature. In both instances the Congregational Union presented a particular type of Eucharistic liturgy as a norm for the denomination.

Book of Congregational Worship, 1920

Under the chairmanship of the Rev. B. J. Snell, M.A., B.Sc., the committee responsible for the compilation of this book comprised the following persons: Sir John D. McClure, LL.D., D.Mus.; A. D. Snow, J.P.; the Revs. T. H. Darlow, M.A., E. M. Drew, B.D.; P. T. Forsyth, M.A., D.D.; C. Bentley Jutson; T. H. Martin, M.A., W. Charter Piggott; Arthur Pringle; Richard J. Wells, and Thomas Yates. Darlow had to retire because of ill-health.

Some of the members of the committee had previously produced liturgical compilations: Sir John D. McClure, Headmaster of Mill Hill School, may have been responsible for **Devotional Services for use in Mill Hill Chapel,** 1895, [52] and compiled **Devotional Services for use in the Tiger Kloof Native Institution,** Vryburg 1912; [53] T. H. Darlow, with C. S. Horne, had compiled **Let us Pray** - (second edition 1897); P. T. Forsyth, **Intercessory Services for aid in Public Worship,** Manchester 1896, and Arthur Pringle had produced some litanies for his church at Purley. [54] Only **Let us Pray** had contained a Eucharistic liturgy.

The 1920 book contained ten orders of worship, which were of a similar type to those of Hunter and Orchard, being based loosely upon Morning and Evening Prayer of the **Book of Common Prayer**, with canticles, collects, versicles and responses.

The Eucharist, entitled "Holy Communion", came immediately after the tenth order of worship, but was a quite separate service, having no obvious link with the "Liturgy of the Word".

Hymn
Scripture sentences: John 3:16; Romans 8:32; 1 Tim. 1:15; Matt. 11:28; John 6:35b; John 6:37b; Matt. 5:6; Rev. 3:20
Invitation, "Ye that do truly and earnestly"
Confession: Psalm 51:1-3, 10-12
Sursum corda, Preface and Sanctus
Institution: 1 Cor. 11:23-26
Prayer of Commemoration and Thanksgiving
Silent Prayer
Distribution: This is My body which is broken for you.
This cup is the New Testament in My blood.
Lord's Prayer
Collect, "O God of unchageable power and eternal light" or, Didache 9, prayer over the bread
Collect for the departed
Hymn of praise and thanksgiving, or Gloria in excelsis
John 13. Selected verses, The Washing of the disciples' feet, or other suitable passages. The Offertory
Blessing. Hebrews 13:20-21

Of the eight scripture sentences provided, three were suggested by the "Comfortable Words" of the **Book of Common Prayer**, and two by Hunter's order in the seventh edition of **Devotional Services.** The **Book of Common Prayer** had supplied the Invitation, the Sursum corda, preface and sanctus, most of the substance of the Prayer of Commemoration and Thanksgiving, the collect for the departed (part of the final collect in the burial service and part of the 'Prayer for the Church Militant") and the Gloria in excelsis. A Gelasian collect, part of **Didache** 9 and Scripture completed the rite.

The Prayer of Commemoration and Thanksgiving commemorated both the Supper and the sacrifice of the Cross, made oblation of the sacrifice of praise and thanksgiving, and of ourselves, and had a petition for a fruitful communion. The material was mostly from the Prayer Book,--the prayers of Consecration, Oblation and Humble Access. The Commemoration of the sacrifice and the petition for a fruitful communion including the indwelling of Christ, together with the words of administration which stressed "broken for you", and "The cup of the New Testament in My blood" perhaps reflect the influence of P. T. Forsyth, for there was rather more in these words than a bare memorial. Nevertheless, in liturgical terms the rite was very timid and unimaginative. Apart from the instance of the use of the **Didache** which was then in vogue, and a Gelasian collect which Orchard had included in the **Divine Service**, the committee does not seem to have been able to look beyond the **Book of Common Prayer**. The order lacked the originality of Hunter and the wide catholic sources of Orchard. There was no link with the liturgical calendar, nor were there any lections in the rite. If this book was a landmark in the history of the Congregational Union, it was hardly likely to be regarded as a landmark in christendom's liturgical literature; with regard to the Eucharist, McClure's words had falled on deaf ears. [**55**]

A Manual for Ministers, 1936

The precise origin of **A Manual for Ministers** is not clear. In the **Congregational Year Book** 1932, the Literature Committee reported that it was having to supplement the 1920 book with special services for occasions such as the dedication of a Church. [**56**] In the **Year Book** of 1935 it was again the Literature Committee which reported that the 1920 book was being expanded into the form of a manual or a directory, and that the first draft was then under consideration. [**57**] It was a completely metamorphosed book which appeared in 1936, with a foreward by the Secretary of the Congregational Union, S. M. Berry. No actual committee was named as being responsible for the work, but Berry referred to a "group of men", and singled out for special mention Mr. H. W. Lyde, and the Reverends H. Bulcock, Maldwyn Johnes, W. J. McAdam, John Phillips, W. Charter Piggott and Malcolm Spencer. Of these, John Phillips, the chairman, had studied under A. E. Garvie at London, and described himself as a liberal evangelical; [**58**] Charter Piggott had served on the committee responsible for the 1920 book; H. Bulcock, whose liberal views have already been noted, had compiled **Orders of Service for Free Church Use** for Prenton Church; [**59**] and Malcolm Spencer was Secretary of the Social Service Committee. [**60**]

The minutes of this "group of men" were taken down by Maldwyn Johnes, but no longer survive. However, according to the Rev. John Phillips, the Chairman, the Literature Committee had wanted a different kind of book from that of 1920. [**61**] It was not a question of expert liturgiologists compiling a liturgy based upon any traditional order; it was deliberate policy to break with the more traditional liturgies. The Committee simply accepted what it thought would form reasonable guidelines for the use of ministers. Current Anglican thinking on liturgy--in particular the 1928 proposed Prayer Book--had no influence on the compilers.

The **Manual** drew on many sources, and made special acknowledgement of Hunter's **Devotional Services,** Orchard's **Divine Service** and his book of private prayers, **The Temple,** and A. S. T. Fisher's **An Anthology of Prayers.**

Part 1 of this work provided material for Morning and Evening worship; as in **Let us Pray** and the earlier editions of **Devotional Services,** the material was arranged in groups with headings from which a service could be compiled: Service with the Choir and Additional Prayers; Introductory Sentences and Prayers; Additional Introductory Sentences; Additional Prayers suitable for Morning or Evening; Additional Morning Prayers; Additional Evening Prayers; Offertory Sentences; Offertory Prayers; Prayers before the Sermon; Closing Prayers; Benedictions and Ascriptions.

The two services of Holy Communion were placed in Part II, Ordinances and Offices of the Church. The first order was basically that of 1920 with some additions and omissions, and was mainly the work of Charter Piggott. [**62**] The changes were quite significant, for they suggested a move toward a more liberal evangelical interpretation of the Eucharist.

<u>First Order</u>

Hymn
Sentences (1920 and additions. John 3:16, 1 John 4:10, 1 Tim. 1:15, Matt. 11:28, John 6:35b, Matt. 5:6. For an evening communion, Luke 24:13-16, 28-31)
Invitation (Hunter)
Confession: Psalm 51, selected verses. (1920)
Petition for Pardon (BCP collect for 21st Sunday after Trinity)
Institution 1 Cor. 11:23-26
Prayer by the minister (no text provided)
Prayer of Humble Access (BCP altered)
Words of Administration: The Lord Jesus said,
This is My body which is broken for you.
This do in remembrance of me.
The Lord Jesus said, This cup is the new testament in My blood; this do ye as oft as ye drink it in remembrance of Me
Silent prayer
Prayers (3 from 1920, 2 new prayers)
John 13, selected verses or other suitable passage. Offertory (1920)
Blessing (1920)

The traditional Eucharistic elements, the <u>Sursum corda</u>, Preface and <u>Sanctus</u> were dropped, and the Invitation from the

Book of Common Prayer was replaced by Hunter's longer Invitation. Although this indicates the popularity of **Devotional Services,** it also strengthened a "memorialist" concept of the Supper--"Come not to testify that you are righteous, but that you sincerely love our Lord Jesus Christ, and desire to be His true disciples". Certainly the Invitation added "come not to express an opinion, but to seek a Presence and pray for a Spirit", but what presence and which Spirit?

The 1920 Prayer of Commemoration and Thanksgiving, with oblation and petition for a fruitful communion, was removed and replaced by free prayer by the minister. It seems strange that at this point no guidance whatsoever was offered as to what the prayer should contain. One is tempted to wonder if the 1920 prayer was too "high" for the 1936 revisers. A sample of what the prayer (and service) might not include was given by B. L. Manning:

> Have you ever been at a Communion service where the bread and wine, handed to us from the Upper Room itself, were treated as tiresome, rather unspiritual and adjuncts to a service, impedimenta to be disposed of as rapidly and inconspicuously as possible lest they should hinder us (God forgive us) from spiritual flights on our own account? . . . The bread and the wine are sometimes huddled round to us before the service proper begins, or perhaps under cover of some hymn. The bread is not broken. The wine is not poured out. Prayer, thanksgiving, and the invocation of the Holy Ghost do not precede the distribution of the Elements . . . Let me not be thought to exaggerate. I bring no general charge against our churches, but I say that in some places and at some times these things are done; and everyone knows that that is true. [**63**]

The provision for free prayer was immediately followed by the Prayer of Humble Access (optional), but with significant emendations:

> Grant therefore, gracious Lord, that we may come with confidence to the throne of grace, that we may be strengthened with power through Thy Spirit in the inward man: that Christ may dwell in our hearts through faith: to the end that we, being rooted and grounded in love, may be strong to apprehend with all saints what is the breadth and length and height and depth, and to know the love of Christ which passeth knowledge, that we may be filled with all the fullness of God.

The Prayer Book reference to feeding on Christ's flesh

and blood was removed. Now the emphasis is on the communicant, on the "inward man" in whom Christ dwells "through faith", that "being rooted and grounded in love" the communicant "may be filled with the fullness of God". The words are no doubt capable of several interpretations, but the same words were used in the service of the formation of a Church; the presence here was no different and no more special than that at any gathering of Christians. The authors of the New Theology could not have faulted it.

In view of the doubt of some Congregationalists on the authenticity of the command to repeat the rite--including at least one of the "group of men", Bulcock--it is strange that the 1920 words were replaced by the Pauline words. It is possible that the 1920 words were regarded as too "high", for they might infer that the Lord's presence was connected with the elements. In the new words, "The Lord Jesus said" was prefixed, and the command to repeat the rite stressed "in remembrance". There was no fraction mentioned, and no hymn after communion. Various collects could be used, and the 1920 narrative of the washing of the disciples' feet was retained, stressing the social gospel.

Second Order

Exhortation
Sentences: Matt. 11:28, John 6:37b, Matt. 5:6, Rev. 3:20
Collect for Purity
Lord's Prayer
Hymn
Short exhortation: Brethren, in remembrance of our Lord we take our common meal of fellowship, and know that where two or three are gathered in His Name, there is He in the midst.
Short silence
Prayer by the minister
Prayer of Humble Access as in first order, if desired.
1 Cor. 11:23-24
Words of delivery (Hunter's fifth edition)
1 Cor. 11:25-26
Words of delivery (Hunter's fifth edition)
Short silence
Prayers (Seven provided)
John 13--selected verses, or another suitable passage
Hymn
Benediction, Aaronic, or as in first order

The second order was, according to the chairman of the committee, purely the work of Harry Bulcock, put in at his request--and pressure--to represent the group of Modern Churchmen in Congregationalism. [64] Liberal memorialism was blatantly set forth in the opening exhortation:

> We are gathered together to observe the Sacrament of the Lord's Supper, and we call to remembrance that this holy custom of the Church has been a source of strength, comfort, and inspiration to the people of Christ in all generations, and a means of realizing the presence and power of our Lord in the fellowship of His Church.
>
> Therefore we would reverently repeat the solemn acts and words which keep fresh in our hearts the memory of our Lord's sacrifice, His redeeming love, His faith and hope in the triumph of His Gospel over evil and death.
>
> We would renew our pledge of affection and service for the Church, for which He gave Himself in love that it might be a holy Church without blemish.
>
> And in repentance and faith we would open our hearts to our Lord that He may enter and dwell therein; and in such communion with Him we would deepen our sense of fellowship not only with one another here present, but with all the saints of God on earth and with all the company of heaven.

The Supper, according to Bulcock's thinking, was a "holy custom" rather than a Divine Institution, "a source of strength, comfort and inspiration" rather than an encounter with the Living God, and a useful opportunity of renewing our pledge of affection to the Church. Whereas the exhortations of the liturgies of the Reformation emphasized what God in Christ had done for mankind, this exhortation seems to be obsessed with what man can do for God at the Supper. Later, almost in parody of the Catholic Orate fratres used by Orchard, we find:

> Brethren, in remembrance of our Lord we take our common meal of fellowship, and know that where two or three are gathered in His Name, there is He in the midst.

The Supper is a fellowship meal, at which God is present as at any gathering of Christians; the bread and wine are incidental to the rite. The words of delivery were Hunter's immanentist words:

> Let us eat this bread in remembrance of Christ, and may the life which was in Him be in us also.
>
> Let us drink of this cup in remembrance of Christ; and may the spirit in which He died be our spirit.

There is no presence here, only a memorial.

Finally, two of the collects provided, reinforced a liberal view of the sacraments: that we may "realize" the holy mystery of communion; and that our breaking of bread in common may be with gladness and singleness of heart; that we may have grace of fellowship and concord; that our hearts may be filled with kindliness, goodwill and the spirit of service, and that God would manifest to all men the "gracious spirit" of the Master.

The same symptoms of Liberal theology were to be found in the service of Infant Baptism, where the central fact was not that Christ was doing something for the child, but that the child was being dedicated by men to God; and in the "Order of Service for the Opening of a Bazaar or Sale of Work" (!), where the occasion was depicted as a conscious effort by men to establish the Kingdom of God. The Hymn provided treated the items as sacramental.

In these two communion rites, the compilers had not wandered far from their own tradition, but had simply rewritten material to express what they believed to be a modern understanding of the Supper. There was no liturgical scholarship, but rather the New Testament and dogmatic theology of a minority expressed in prayer. Memorialism, either in evangelical or modernist terms was set forth as the norm for the denomination. The compilers were, no doubt, satisfied with their work, and since by 1937 two thousand copies of **A Manual for Ministers** had been sold, it may be assumed that many Congregational ministers were equally satisfied. [65] The Christian World expressed surprise that in neither order had a prayer of consecration been provided, but on the whole regarded it as "a rich collection of devotional material". [66] According to the Literature Committee Report, someone had described it as "the finest book of its kind ever produced for Free Church ministers". [67] But others, recognizing the blatant liberal tendencies, were not impressed. In the Church Quarterly Review it was contrasted with a collection of essays from Mansfield College, published the same year, entitled **Christian Worship.**

> We feel sure that the Mansfield fathers would have compiled an Order for Holy Communion far more consonant with biblical and catholic tradition than either of the two given in this Manual. They are surprisingly meagre and far removed from the noble traditions of some of the ancient Evangelical churches on the Continent. The notes of intercession and thanksgiving can scarcely be heard, the main stress being laid upon the benefits to man conferred in the sacrament. The element of Offertory is entirely absent. . . . Surely there never was a more unscriptural book than this. [68]

This last statement, which has considerable justification, is ironical when it is remembered that the Independent tradition had stood for complete obedience to "God's Word written".

NOTES

1. "Attendance at Public Worship", CYB 1874, 59.

2. CYB 1917, 44.

3. CYB 1919, 20.

4. "The Public Worship of God" in CYB 1920, 56.

5. Ibid.

6. Report of the Literature Committee, CYB 1932, 164.

7. The Report of the Commission on the Sacraments of Baptism and the Lord's Supper, 1936 in CYB 1937, 94-119. For a detailed study see J. K. Gregory, "The Understanding of the Lord's Supper among English Congregationalists 1850-1950", D.Phil. Thesis, Oxford University, 1956 (unpublished).

8. P. T. Forsyth, **The Church and the Sacraments**, London 1917, 228-229.

9. Ibid., xvi.

10. Ibid., 177.

11. Ibid., 229.

12. Ibid.

13. Ibid., 240.

14. C. H. Dodd, "Eucharistic Symbolism in the Fourth Gospel" in The Expositor, 1911, 530-546, 546.

15. W. E. Orchard, **Foundations of Faith**, vol. III, Ecclesiological, 115.

16. A. E. Garvie, "The Valid Sacraments" in The Christian World, February 13th, 1936, 8; Ibid., **Studies in the Inner Life of Jesus**, London 1907, 367-368.

17. A. E. Garvie, **The Holy Catholic Church from the Congregational Point of View,** London 1920, 114.

18. Ibid.

19. Ibid., 103; **Studies in the Inner Life of Jesus,** 367.

20. J. G. Greenhough, "The Meaning of the Feast" in **Eden and Gethsemane. Addresses for Communion Services,** Manchester, 1903, 60.

21. Ibid., 64.

22. J. G. Greenhough, "The Sacramental Aspect of Common Things", **Eden and Gethsemane,** 117.

23. Ibid., 116.

24. B. J. Snell, "The Lord's Supper", in **Eden and Gethsemane,** 128, 131.

25. Rev. B. Smith of Salem Chapel Leeds, in The Christian World, September 24th, 1925, 12.

26. R. J. Campbell, **The New Theology,** London 1907; T. Rhondda Williams, **The New Theology,** Bradford 1907; J. Warschauer, **The New Evangel,** London 1907; K. C. Anderson, **The New Theology,** London 1907.

27. J. Warschauer, **The New Evangel,** 158.

28. R. J. Campbell, **The New Theology,** 168.

29. Ibid., 166.

30. T. Rhondda Williams, **The New Theology,** 120.

31. J. Morgan Gibbon, "The Social Value of the Lord's Supper", in **Eden and Gethsemane,** 203.

32. See the letter to the editor, The Christian World, February 9th, 1933, 7. J. W. Grant, **Free Churchmanship in England 1870-1940,** 303-304.

33. See the Group's Statement in The Christian World, February 9th, 1933, 7.

34. F. Lenwood, **Jesus--Lord or Leader?,** London 1930, 301.

35. Ibid., 302.

36. Ibid.

37. Anon., "Sacraments" in The Christian World, February 13th, 1908, 11.

38. Ibid., 10.

39. J. V. Bartlet, "The Eucharist in the Early Church", in **Mansfield College Essays,** London 1909; E. J. Price, "The Eucharist in History and Experience" in The Congregational Quarterly, 5 (1927), 135-148.

40. H. Bulcock, **A Re-stated Faith: Positive Values,** London 1934, 58-60.

41. H. Bulcock, **A Modern Churchman's Manual,** London 1941, 30-31.

42. C. J. Cadoux, **The Historic Mission of Jesus,** London 1941, 311; Cf. ibid., **Catholicism and Christianity,** London 1928, 397.

43. R. Mackintosh, **Proceedings of the Fifth International Congregational Council,** ed. A. Peel, London 1930, 139-140; Edward Grubb, "The Last Supper" in The Congregational Quarterly, 8 (1930), 57-63, 60-61; A. D. Martin, "The Administration of the Communion Service" in The Congregational Quarterly, 10 (1932), 73-81, 76.

44. A. Peel, **Christian Freedom,** London 1938, 67-84.

45. For this justification see "Sacraments" in The Christian World, February 13th, 1908, and H. Bulcock, **A Modern Churchman's Manual.**

46. J. V. Bartlet, "The Eucharist in the Early Church"; E. J. Price, "The Eucharist in History and Experience".

47. A. Peel, **These Hundred Years,** London 1931, 280-283.

48. A. D. Martin, "The Administration of the Communion Service".

49. Ibid., 75.

50. Ibid., 77.

51. Ibid., 79.

52. McClure became Headmaster in 1891, and was responsible for the new chapel. See K. M. J. Ousey, **McClure and Mill Hill,** London 1927.

53. A Copy is to be found in the British Museum.

54. A. E. Peaston, **The Prayer Book Tradition in the Free Churches,** 188.

55. See supra.

56. CYB 1932, 164.

57. CYB 1935, 202.

58. Letter to the writer, 27th August, 1975.

59. Copy in the Congregational Memorial Library, London. Bulcock later compiled **The Modern Churchman at Prayer. Some Orders of Worship,** London 1943.

60. Spencer's **The Social Function of the Church,** London 1921, presented the liberal idea that men could build the Kingdom of God.

61. The information in this paragraph is from a taped interview with the Rev. J. Phillips, in his ninetieth year, in 1976.

62. Letter cited.

63. B. L. Manning, **Essays in Orthodox Dissent,** London 1939, 61ff.

64. John Phillips has emphasized this point both in conversation and in correspondence.

65. CYB 1938, 213.

66. The Christian World, June 25th, 1936, 6.

67. CYB 1937, 257.

68. Church Quarterly Review, 123 (1936-37), 386.

Chapter Nine

MORE INDEPENDENT EUCHARISTIC LITURGIES 1909-1930

> Although we, as Nonconformists, claim freedom from stereotyped ceremonies in our worship, yet there are times when fixed forms are helpful to the minister and beneficial to the people.
>
> C. H. Davis, **Orders of Service**
> Newport, Isle of Wight, 1909, Preface 3

Although lacking the success of Hunter's **Devotional Services,** the novelty and sensationalism of Orchard's **Divine Service,** and being less prestigious than the publications of the Congregational Union, other Congregationalists, perpetuating the right to independency in matters of worship and liturgical forms, continued to compile their own liturgies. Some of these contained Eucharistic rites, and here we consider five such rites: C. H. Davis, **Orders of Service**, Newport, Isle of Wight, 1909; E. D. Cecil, **Prayer and Praise**, Penge, 1914; G. H. Russell, **Intercession Services** 1923; **A Service Book for Use in Bishop's Stortford College**, 1925; and C. E. Watson, **The Rodborough Bede Book,** Woodchester, 1930. These formularies all shared the same theological milieu as those of the Congregational Union of 1920 and 1936.

1. **Orders of Service for the Solemnization of Matrimony, The Baptism of Infants, The Burial of the Dead and the Ordinance of the Lord's Supper**, 1909.

This short volume was compiled by the Rev. C. H. Davis, B.A., (1864-1940) when minister at Newport, Isle of Wight. Davis had trained for the ministry at Paton College, Nottingham under Dr. J. Paton, and at New College, London.

In the Preface Davis explained that the **Orders of Service** were issued with the view to supplying a want among ministers and lay preachers in the denomination, for there were certain times when fixed forms were helpful to the minister and beneficial to the people. Although Davis provided full services for Marriage, Baptism and Burial, only a brief outline for the communion was given, together with a selection of suitable scripture passages from the Revised Version.

> An Order of Service for the Ordinance of the Lord's Supper. To be modified according to the desire or circumstance.
>
> Hymn
> Address
> Portions of Scripture relating to the Bread
> Prayer
> Bread passed around to communicants
> Portion of Scripture relating to the Wine
> Wine passed around to communicants
> Hymn
> Offertory on behalf of the Poor Fund
> (Here reference may be made to any cases of affliction or need)
> Prayer and Benediction

The passages of scripture provided were 1 Cor. 5:7-8; Matt. 26:20-30; Mark 14:17-26; Luke 22:14-20; 1 Cor. 11:23-28; 1 Cor. 10:16-17.

In this recommended outline Davis preserved what was probably the type of service found in many Congregational churches at the time. It is remarkably similar to that described by M. L. Harper at Grange Park Congregational Church, Leyton: [1]

> Hymn
> Passages of scripture, and the Institution, 1 Cor. 11:23-26
> Minister gives thanks
> Administration of bread
> 1 Cor. 11:25
> Administration of cups
> The glasses of wine are retained until all are served. When the deacons have reseated themselves, the minister, reciting a few appropriate words, invites the members to drink "in remembrance of Him". The members all drink at the same time, and then, as after receiving the bread, they offer silent prayer
> Hymn
> Benediction
> Collection for the poor

Orchard's "Simple Observance of the Lord's Supper" could easily have been arranged in a similar way.

2. **Prayer and Praise**, 1914.

Compiled by E. D. Cecil, this liturgy was for use at Penge Congregational Church. In the Preface the compiler stated the view that for decency and order, some form or method in public worship was necessary. There was a "gradually increasing desire for "common prayer", to accompany and supplement the common praise of hymn and chant". It was hoped that its usefulness might extend to other Churches in the same and similar denominations. Full advantage had been taken of the "beautiful prayers and collects of the Anglican Prayer Book". Acknowledgments were given to P. T. Forsyth, W. E. Orchard (of St. Paul's Presbyterian Church, Enfield--presumably **Service Book** [2]) and B. J. Snell of Brixton Independent Church.

The Communion Service or The Ordinance of the Lord's Supper

Hymn
Scripture Sentences
Reception of new members, and a prayer
1 Cor. 11:23-26
The minister's prayer for a right and worthy participation in the Lord's Supper
Distribution of the bread.
Short term of silent prayer
Distribution of the wine
Short term of silent prayer
Minister's prayer of thanksgiving
Lord's Prayer
Scripture sentences and offertory
Hymn
Blessing

As with the order of C. H. Davis, this rite provided only an outline for the structure of the service, with rubrics and scripture sentences. The first set of sentences--Matt. 11:28-30, Lk. 15:10, Matt. 5:6, Rev. 3:20, Matt. 7:7, Lk. 11:13, John 10:14a, 15b, 16a, c,--are exactly the same sentences and in the same order, including the selection from John 10:14-16, as were to be found in Hunter's seventh edition for the first part of the "comfortable words". A coincidence seeming unlikely, it appears that Hunter was the source. The offertory sentences--Gal. 6:10, Matt. 6:19-20, Matt. 7:12, 2 Cor. 9:6-7, 1 John 3:17, Heb. 13:16--are all found among the offertory sentences in the **Book of Common Prayer**. The text of 1 Cor. 11:23-26 was provided, but no prayers were given. As with the order of Davis, this rite provided just a framework for extemporary prayer; it gave the form of the service, but not the substance.

3. Intercession Services for Congregational Use in Public Worship, 1923.

This liturgy was the work of G. H. Russell (?-1932?) while minister at Matlock Congregational Church. Russell had trained at Hackney College under P. T. Forsyth and A. E. Garvie, and with C. Bentley Jutson he contributed an article on worship in the Congregational Quarterly. [3]

Containing a Foreword by Dr. J. H. Jowett, this book presented services on particular themes of Intercession, such as "The Coming of God's Kingdom", "The Revival of the Church" and "The Missionary Work of the Church". These consisted of scripture sentences, a congregational prayer, provision for silent prayer and short litany with responses and the Lord's Prayer, and were designed to supplement free prayer. However, the book also contained an order for the Eucharist, prefaced by an invitation to "all who love our Lord Jesus Christ", and thoughts for meditation.

The Holy Communion

Scripture sentences. Matt. 11:28, John 6:35, John 14:18, Matt. 28:20, Luke 24:30-31

That the experience of the Real Presence of Christ may be ours here and now, let us spend a few moments in silent prayer

Silent Prayer (Short collect for the presence of Christ)

Communion Hymn

Sentences. John 3:16, Rom. 8:32, 1 Tim. 1:15, 1 John 1:5-7, Matt. 5:6, Matt. 7:11, Rev. 3:20, John 6:37

Invitation (Either first two or last paragraph of Hunter's)

Prayer of Confession. Psalm 51:1-3, 10-12

Lord's Prayer

A silent prayer (for a quiet mind, reverent and devout heart, and assurance of the Divine mercy)

Prayer. O God, our Heavenly Father, draw near to us now as we remember the passion and death of Thy Son, our Saviour Jesus Christ; and as we receive this bread and this wine, the symbols of His broken body and shed blood, may we be quickened and nourished in that life which is divine, and made of one spirit with Him who was obedient unto death. Amen

or,

We do not presume (Hunter's text)

Institution 1 Cor. 11:23-26.

Distribution of the bread: This is My Body which is broken for you.

or,

The body of our Lord Jesus Christ, which was broken for thee, preserve thy soul unto everlasting life. Take and eat this in remembrance that Christ died for thee, and feed on Him in thy heart by faith with thanksgiving.

Silent communion

Distribution of the wine: This is My Blood of the New Covenant which is shed for many unto the remission of sins.

or,

The Blood of our Lord Jesus Christ, which was shed for thee, preserve thy soul unto everlasting life. Drink this in remembrance that Christ laid down His life for thee, and be thankful.

Silent communion

Thoughts for meditation

General Thanksgiving

Prayer of self-oblation, or free prayer

Offertory for the poor

Special requests for intercession

Prayer of intercession for the world, the Church, the sick and the departed

or,

Prayer for fellowship

Luke 2:29-30

Blessing. Hebrews 12:20-21.

Much of this Eucharistic rite was a synthesis of material from Hunter's **Devotional Services,** the **Book of Congregational Worship,** 1921, and the **Book of Common Prayer.** Hunter had supplied the invitation and the version of the "Prayer of Humble Access"; all eight Scripture sentences of the 1920 communion order were used, together with the confession from Psalm 51. The Anglican liturgy provided the basis of the second set of words of administration, the General Thanksgiving, and some of the substance of the Prayer of intercession.

The rite was a strange composition, there being no lections, and no specific thanksgiving until after the communion, though there were several petitions for the presence of Christ and for a true communion. The use of silent prayer and meditation gave to this liturgy a mood of contemplation and quiet.

4. **A Service Book for Use in Bishop's Stortford College,** 1925.

This compilation was the work of Mr. F. S. Young, M.A.,

the Headmaster of this Congregational school. In the Preface, Young explained that for many years he had made use of Hunter's **Devotional Services**, and later had used his own manuscript copies of forms of service based upon those of Hunter and Orchard, and using Bright's **Ancient Collects.** As these manuscripts were inconvenient, he had produced the service book. The book was compiled on the principle that for schools a liturgical form of service was the most suitable, and Young acknowledged a great debt to the **Book of Common Prayer**, "without which no Service Book for a British Congregation could be compiled". The book provided thirteen orders for Sunday Morning worship. For the communion service, Young had looked no further than the Anglican liturgy.

The Communion

The collect (for purity)
Collect of the day, if not previously used
Epistle) Optional
Gospel)
Exhortation: Ye that do truly
Confession: Almighty God, Father of our Lord Jesus Christ
Prayer for Pardon
Comfortable words
Sursum corda, Preface and Sanctus
Prayer of Humble Access
Prayer of Consecration
Words of administration
Prayer (of oblation)
Gloria in excelsis
Benediction

Apart from minor alterations such as a collective absolution and words of administration (Let us take and eat), the order was that of the **Book of Common Prayer**, and perpetuated the slavish copying of the previous century as found in the **Book of Common Prayer for use of the Congregational Church at Finchley Common,** and the **Free Church Service Book** of Newman Hall.

5. **The Rodborough Bede Book**, 1930.

C. E. Watson (1869-1942) [4] was minister of the Rodborough Tabernacle, Gloucestershire, from 1909 until his death in 1942, the church itself having originated with the preaching of George Whitefield. Watson had been brought up as an Evangelical Anglican in Lincolnshire, and his parish church had been involved in the Ritual charges which were brought against the Bishop, Edward King. This incident led Watson to consider the subject of ministry in the New Testament, and he became convinced of

Congregationalism. He trained at Lancashire Independent College under Dr. Caleb Scott and A. S. Peake.

Watson was extremely interested in tradition and customs, and this interest was reflected in the **Bede Book** in which, as the title suggested, Anglo-Saxon words were used in preference to those of Latin derivation, and in which he presented to his church the devotional and liturgical heritage of past ages. The book was a collection of collects, prayers and litanies grouped together for the opening, middle and end of services--Fore Bedes, Mid-Bedes and End Bedes. The book also contained a section on the sacraments, with five orders for "Eucharist". The orders presupposed that the minister would provide a suitable hymn and free prayer at appropriate places in the service as required.

The orders for the Eucharist were short, and varied in the exact sequence of items. They contained common features, namely versicles and responses said by minister and people, short collects and ascriptions of praise, the use of silence, and separate communion of the bread and wine. The elements were distributed beforehand, and so the fraction was eliminated. Orders I, II and IV were composed of material from St. John's Gospel, the Four Gospels and the Pauline writings respectively. In Orders III and V Watson made ingenious use of more traditional liturgical material. Order III was based on the anaphora of St. James, with an expanded Sursum corda, a Preface with thanksgiving for creation, "the sun, the moon, the stars; the earth and the sea also; the first-born whose names are enrolled in heaven", and the Sanctus. This was followed by a short post-sanctus and Words of Institution, and a prayer modeled on part of the Acts of Thomas calling upon the name of Christ and the petition "Come Thou and communicate with us in this eucharist, which we celebrate in Thy name, and the love-feast wherein we are gathered together at Thy behest", which may in fact preserve a primitive form of the classical Epiklesis. [5] After the communion there was a version of the traditional West Syrian anamnesis acclamation, "Thy death, O Lord, we will proclaim", and an offering of "this our oblation and service".

In Order V the prayers from **Didache** 9 and 10 were used to provide a Eucharist. **Didache** 10:6 was used as the opening dialogue, followed by 10:3-5. After extemporary prayer, and a prayer with an Institution narrative came the communion of the bread, then **Didache** 9:3-4, the communion of the wine and **Didache** 9:2 and 10:2.

In these orders Watson combined scriptural material with more traditional liturgical material, and the latter without the doctrinal and ceremonial offence found in Orchard's **Divine Service.** Had the orders been available separately without the pedantic "Bedes", they would have provided the denomination with short but worthy liturgical forms for the Eucharist.

From the survey of these five liturgies, it is apparent that for liturgical material, most compilers would not look beyond the **Book of Common Prayer**, Hunter's **Devotional Services** and the 1920 book; there was no sign of serious liturgical scholarship, either with regard to classical rites or those of the Reformed tradition. The only exception appears to have been C. E. Watson, though his motives seem to have been antiquarian rather than liturgical. The double administration, (rather than consecration) persisted, and there was no obvious connection with the Morning service with lections and a sermon. The mood of the Eucharist was quiet and meditative, and the service simple.

NOTES

1. M. L. Harper, **The Communion Service**, London 1926, 10-12.

2. See Chapter 7, note 3.

3. G. H. Russell and C. Benley Jutson, "Public Worship" in CQ 3 (1925), 456-467.

4. For biographical details, A. T. S. James, **A Cotswold Minister**, London 1944.

5. See S. P. Brock, "The Epiclesis in the Antiochene Baptismal Ordines", in **Orientalia Christiana Analecta** 1974 ("Symposium Syriacum 1972") 183-218. Bryan D. Spinks, "The Consecratory Epiklesis in the Anaphora of St. James", in SL 11 (1976), 19-38.

Chapter Ten

THE NEO-ORTHODOX, OR "GENEVAN" LITURGIES 1948-1969

> We cannot without peril break our continuity with God's work in history, with God's Church in history. We cannot just clear two thousand years by a huge somersault and land with a splash in the New Testament, with its polity, practice, or habit of mind. That jars everything. It grieves the Spirit. It denies historic providence. It repudiates the Kingdom of God in history. It robs us of most of the sainthood, sacrifice, and devotion of the whole Church, and often leaves our public prayers to be but pious journalese.
>
> P. T. Forsyth, **Congregationalism and Reunion,** London 1919, p. 55.

In 1948 from the Oxford University Press there appeared a new liturgical compilation for the use of Congregationalists, **A Book of Public Worship,** by W. J. F. Huxtable, J. Marsh, E. R. Micklem and J. M. Todd. This work represented an important landmark in the history of Congregational liturgy, and its underlying principles and ethos were perpetuated in J. M. Todd's **Prayers and Services for Christian Festivals,** 1951, and the Congregational Union's **A Book of Services and Prayers,** 1959 and 1969.

These works, which we may conveniently, and justifiably, term Neo-Orthodox, or "Genevan", liturgies, must be seen as the culmination of two distinct movements.

A Manual for Ministers of 1936 had represented a liturgical triumph for Liberal Modernism; but not all Congregationalists were so enthusiastic about the advances of this theological movement. The check on Liberal theology is generally associated with the name of Karl Barth, the Swiss theologian, whose work represented a return to the orthodoxy of the Bible, the Catholic Creeds, and the Reformation Fathers. The Word of God, Barthianism asserted, was not simply the written words of the Bible upon which a theological faculty could perform critical analysis; the Word of God was nothing less than the proclamation of the Living God to his Church, in which God becomes present with his people. Barth emphasized the transcendence of God and the Divine action in history. His call to the Reformed Churches that they should return to the orthodoxy of the Reformation Fathers did not go unheeded in English Congregationalism. It produced a group of "Genevan" men who wished to recall Congregationalism to the inheritance of the Reformation and the early Catholic Church. They traced their churchmanship through John Owen to Calvin and Geneva, and they emphasized the value of order in Church life. [1]

The Liberalism of the Blackheath Group of churchmen in the 1930's called forth a protest from these "Genevan" men. At the Autumnal Assembly of the Congregational Union in 1931 an unfriendly critic "discovered a 'sharp turn to the right' in Congregational Theology, and snapshotted Dr. J. D. Jones, Dr. N. Micklem, and Professor J. S. Whale all stepping to the right together". [2] Nathaniel Micklem, Principal of Mansfield College, Oxford, challenged the orthodoxy of the Blackheath Statement of 1933, and in **What is the Faith?** 1936, he attacked those who consciously or unconsciously abandoned the Word of God contained in Scripture as the standard and rule of faith, and who had substituted for it human reason or "the modern mind". [3] Redemption, Micklem stressed, was not by a man, not even by a perfect man, but by the "mighty act" of God. [4] He emphasized the objectivity of the Atonement and the Resurrection.

The same concern with the integrity of Scripture was to be found in C. H. Dodd's **The Apostolic Preaching**, 1936. [5] Dodd showed that the preaching of the early church was kerygma, not didache; it was concerned with the mighty acts of God--the life, death, resurrection and exaltation of Jesus Christ. He maintained that the preaching which is the Word given to the Church to proclaim, stubbornly refuses to be moulded in conformity with the Zeitgeist. It cannot therefore be expressed in sermons designed to fit modern tastes, or in scientific "restatements". Furthermore, Dodd and W. D. Davies [6] failed to find the great chasm that the Liberals claimed existed between the Gospels and the teaching of St. Paul. Professor J. S. Whale and A. G. Matthews recalled Congregationalists to their Reformed traditions and to Calvin, and orthodoxy was further defended by B. L. Manning and Daniel Jenkins. [7] These "Genevan" men used The Presbyter as their regular journal, and formed the Church Order Group for mutual consultation. [8] **A Book of Public Worship** was the work of four members of the Church Order Group.

The insights of this "Genevan" school of thought led to a revaluation of the Eucharist:

(a) The relationship between Word and Sacrament.

The "Genevan" school reiterated the Reformation principle that the Word of God is alone the vehicle of grace. The Sacraments convey grace because they are modes of the Word, the verba visibilia of Augustine. [9] The sacraments complete and fulfill the preaching of the Word. [10] They do not add anything to the Word, any more than in marriage the kiss and the ring add anything to the plighted troth; but they do movingly reiterate it and give effect to it. [11] They are sacred pledges and seals of the promises of God. [12] According to Nathaniel Micklem, they are acts of God in his Church, whereby that opus operatum of Christ, never to be repeated, is, as it were, extended and brought home to believers. [13] They set forth in action what the preacher sets forth in words. Professor Whale drew the conclusion:

> Thus, in the full diet of public worship in every Church throughout Christendom, two permanent elements together constitute "the means of grace"; first, the preaching and hearing of the Word; second, the Sacrament of the Eucharist, where the highest is not spoken but acted; where the promises of the Gospel are visibly sealed by the Yea and Amen of a ritual act. [14]

This had two particular implications. The Congregational practice of separating the Morning worship from the Eucharist was theologically defective. Furthermore, the Eucharist was not an optional extra; the Quaker neglect of the sacraments was judged to be defective. [15]

(b) The integrity of the Institution of the Eucharist.

Whereas the Liberal school gave the impression of being concerned mainly with what could not be believed about the Eucharist, the "Genevan" school took a more positive approach.

C. H. Dodd thought it unlikely that Jesus gave instructions at the Last Supper that the sacrament should be repeated in remembrance of him, primarily because Christ did not think beyond the Resurrection. [16] However, there was no reason to conclude that it was the invention of St. Paul; Jesus often had meals with the disciples, and he used the Jewish symbol of the Kingdom of God as a great feast. The Kingdom of God was present with Jesus; at the Last Supper he proclaimed that the bread of the coming Kingdom was present in him, "This is my Body".

> His act, like the symbolic acts of the prophets, not

> merely declares, but helps to bring about that which God has willed. It is a signum efficax. [17]

The remembrance of the Passion was easily associated with the meal, and it expressed the Church's expectation of the Lord's Advent. The sacrament provided an anchorage for the historical element in the Christian faith, along with the more mystical sense of the Lord's abiding presence and with the hope of glory. [18]

In **Paul and Rabbinic Judaism**, W. D. Davies took seriously the Jewish background of St. Paul. Davies accepted the priority of the Marcan account of the Institution; Paul's account in 1 Cor. 11 was a refinement of the tradition, bearing "the mark of the Rabbi who has moulded what he has found in the tradition into a form palatable to his own delicate sensibilities". [19] In particular Davies drew attention to Paul's introductory words, "For I have received of the Lord that which I also delivered unto you": the Greek words paralambanein and paradidonai correspond to two technical terms used in Rabbinic literature for the two activities mentioned, namely qibbēl and māsar. [20] The delivery of tradition included the interpretation and explanation of what was implicit. [21] Paul moulded what he had received in such a way as to reveal its inner meaning. [22] He altered the saying over the cup, and added the command to repeat the rite. However, Davies accepted the argument of Vincent Taylor that the command to repeat the rite was not innovating, but that Paul was true to the mind of the Master in making explicit what was quiescent before. [23] Eis anamnesin, so Davies claimed, represented l^{e} zēker or zēker of the Passover Haggadah, except that "Christ" was substituted for "the day thou camest forth out of Egypt". [24]

Another Congregationalist scholar, A. J. B. Higgins, also vindicated the command to repeat the rite. [25] Following the work of the Lutheran scholar, Joachim Jeremias, Higgins accepted that the Last Supper was a Passover meal, and that Mark preserves the best account. Higgins also accepted Davies' assessment of the Pauline account, that the command to repeat the rite was implicit in the Passover context of the Supper. He was prepared to accept that the first command to repeat the rite was in the tradition received by Paul, the apostle himself adding only the second command after the cup.

Once again, the implication here was that the Gospels and St. Paul were not at variance with each other, and even if Jesus had not himself given the command to repeat the Eucharist, the Church had rightly interpreted her Master in continuing to celebrate it. The Eucharist was not an optional extra.

(c) The Meaning of the Eucharist.

If it was admitted that the command to repeat the rite was a correct inference from the nature of the Last Supper, then what did it mean to "do this in remembrance"?

The subjective "memorialist" concept had been challenged by the Lutheran scholar, Joachim Jeremias. He had argued that the word anamnesis meant remembrance by God; to celebrate the Eucharist was to bring the Messiah's life and death before God: "Do this that God may remember me". When God remembers, he acts. [26]

Another interpretation was put forward by the Anglican liturgical scholar, Gregory Dix. Dix suggested that anamnesis meant "re-present", a re-calling of the past, implying a dramatic re-enactment and a presence. [27] Both these views repudiated the idea that the remembrance involved was subjective, and both views emphasized that the Eucharist was an action--a view which was in complete harmony with the "Genevan" view of sacraments.

Professor J. S. Whale reflected Dix's assessment of anamnesis in **Victor and Victim**; the Eucharist was a "paschal drama", meaning "ye do re-enact the drama of him who was Victor because he was Victim". [28] The bread and wine are not bare signs or mere illustrations; they convey what they signify, namely the grace of Christ's finished work.

> The redeeming death with which the Lord here identified his followers was the death of a sacrificial victim. In the ritual action of the Supper he declares that he is about to die that death, making the broken bread and outpoured blood of the grape the acted parable and efficacious sign of the breaking of his body and the shedding of his blood. From the mysterious words den bisri (This my body) and den idhumi (This my blood) the command "Do this" is plainly indissociable. [29]

Dix's views also received endorsement from R. S. Paul, at one time minister of Leatherhead, Surrey, in **The Atonement and the Sacraments:**

> . . . it is calling an event back to life, the action of bringing an event out of the past into the present. This is not "mere memorialism" in the weakened sense we have come to know it. If this is the meaning of the remembrance of our word in the Eucharist, it has less to do with pious memories than with the "Real Presence", for if in this sense we do this in remembrance of him, we bring the event which we remember out

> of the past and make it effective--re-present it--in the present by dramatic action. [30]

C. H. Dodd described the Eucharist as a Signum efficax; [31] it may be regarded as a dramatization of the advent of the Lord, which is at once His remembered coming in humiliation and His desired coming in glory, both realized in His true presence in the Sacrament. [32] At each Eucharist we are there--we are in the night in which He was betrayed, at Golgotha, before the empty tomb on Easter day, and in the upper room where He appeared; and we are at the moment of His coming, with angels and archangels and all the company of heaven, in the twinkling of an eye, at the Last trump. [33] Nathaniel Micklem asserted that in the Supper the sacrifice on calvary is as it were extended into time and applied to the heart of each believer; it is the seal and ratification of the Gospel. It is God who recalls and regenerates, and who comes and gives Himself to us. [34] The action of the Supper was stressed, and in particular the fraction; it was the bread broken which was important. [35]

One Congregationalist who dissented from the emphasis on the fraction was A. J. B. Higgins. Following Jeremias' assessment that the Supper was a Passover meal, Higgins observed that the first words of Institution were said not at the breaking of the bread but at its distribution. [36] In any case, it was customary in Palestine to break the bread at any meal. The wine was poured from the mixing bowl into the cup before it was offered by Jesus to the disciples. The fraction and libation were therefore of no significance. [37]

> What is to be emphasized is not the eucharistic elements themselves but the sacrificial act they call to mind. Christ's death is preached, not his dying re-enacted. [38]

Nevertheless, Higgins emphasized the Divine presence; the Church's Eucharist is at one and the same time a remembrance of the death of Christ, and the expectation of perfect joy with him in the Kingdom, which is already in a measure anticipated at each celebration by the experience of his risen living presence. [39]

Calvin had written:

> In His sacred Supper He bids men take, eat and drink His body and blood under the symbols of bread and wine. I have no doubt that He will truly give and I receive. [40]

The "Genevan" school endorsed this view. A Eucharistic liturgy worthy of the name would express more than pious meditations on the death of Christ.

The second movement from which the Neo-orthodox liturgies derived was the Liturgical Movement. [41] In an article in 1933, B. M. Peake drew the attention of Congregationalists to the Continental Liturgical Movement. [42] However, the compilers of **A Manual for Ministers** had paid no attention to the insights of the movement, and had ignored liturgical scholarship. The Neo-orthodox liturgies made up for this deficiency, and a renewed interest in liturgical history and its principles among Congregationalists is represented by the collection of essays edited by Nathaniel Micklem, **Christian Worship**, 1936; Horton Davies's **The Worship of the English Puritans**, 1948; and Raymond Abba's **Principles of Christian Worship**, 1957.

Particularly influential among Congregationalists was the work of the Scottish Presbyterian liturgiologist, W. D. Maxwell. [43] In 1931 Maxwell produced an annotated edition of John Knox's **Genevan Service Book**, tracing the liturgy from the Mass through Bucer and Calvin to the **Book of Common Order** 1562 of the Church of Scotland. Later, in 1936, in **An Outline of Christian Worship**, Maxwell presented a brief consideration of the historic Eucharistic liturgies of the main Churches of Christendom. In these works Maxwell stressed three points:

(a) Historically the Calvinist liturgical tradition is derived from the Roman Mass. The main service was a Eucharistic liturgy; when communion was not celebrated the service was in fact the synaxis or ante-communion. The practice of some Reformed Churches of basing the morning worship on the choir office of Anglican Matins was a mistake and a departure from the true pattern of Reformed worship. [44]

(b) Historically, the Eucharistic liturgy consisted of two parts, the Liturgy of the Word and the Liturgy of the Upper Room. This was the basis of Calvin's liturgy, and it was his intention to keep them together. He was prevented from having a weekly Eucharist by the Genevan Magistrates, but he himself regarded this as defective. True Calvinist worship consists of Word and Sacrament united as one service. [45]

(c) The Eucharistic Prayer in the classical Eucharistic rites has a particular structure: an opening dialogue, a thanksgiving for creation and redemption, the words of Institution, an anamnesis and epiklesis, self-oblation and intercessions. Maxwell had a prejudice in favor of the Eastern rites, particularly the West Syrian, and he regarded the Roman **Canon Missae** as a dislocation and fragmentary, of inferior composition and style. [46]

The first two of these points harmonized with the theological stance of the 'Genevan' group that Word and Sacrament belonged together, both being a proclamation of the mighty acts of God.

The influence of Maxwell was to be seen in J. S. Whale's essay on Calvin in **Christian Worship.** [47] Whale asserted that the separation of Word and Sacrament was a vicious practice, and that Calvin's liturgy was a Reformed Mass, not a choir office. [48] Other Congregationalists have reiterated Maxwell's points. [49]

A second important influence was the collection of Mansfield College essays, **Christian Worship**, edited by Dr. Nathaniel Micklem, being both an expression of and a contribution to the Liturgical Movement. The Foreword claimed that the collection was "A systematic study of Public Worship" and expressed the hope that the historical studies would be accepted as a serious contribution to the subject, and that the later chapters would serve as an interpretation and a vindication of the common traditions of their Reformed Churches. The essays included Biblical, historical, and contemporary studies.

Professor Horton Davies has said of this work:

> It was the first time that as notable a group of Free Church Scholars (Congregationalists, Presbyterians, and a Baptist) had surveyed the history of the great Christian tradition of worship and indicated its primary importance for their Communions, which hitherto had been thought by others (and perhaps even by neglect among themselves) to emphasize preaching to the derogation of prayers and sacraments. Apart from its intrinsic importance, the volume was a portent. [50]

Another influence upon Congregational thinking was **The Book of Common Order**, 1940, of the Church of Scotland. Since the formation of the Church Service Society in 1865, there had been a movement to restore to Scottish worship the pattern of the classical and Reformed rites. In the **Book of Common Order** 1940 a Eucharistic liturgy was given having a Eucharistic Prayer based upon the West Syrian anaphoras. The book was influential in that it represented an English liturgical compilation other than the **Book of Common Prayer**, and it was the product of a Reformed Church.

A further stimulus to the Neo-orthodox liturgies was Gregory Dix's **The Shape of the Liturgy**, 1945. In this detailed discussion of the history and development of the Eucharistic liturgy, the Anglican scholar argued that the Last Supper had consisted of a seven action shape which every historical liturgical rite (the **Didache** being discounted) had reduced to a four action shape, viz. He took (offertory of bread and wine), He gave thanks (Eucharistic Prayer), He broke (fraction), and He gave (communion). Though this has not passed without criticism, [51] it was extremely influential. The emphasis on the Eucharist as a series of actions appealed to those Congregationalists who argued that the sacrament was essentially action. [52]

A Book of Public Worship 1948.

In his book **Congregationalism To-day**, Dr. Nathaniel Micklem attacked the Liberalism which at that time seemed to dominate Congregationalism. At one point he turned to consider **A Manual for Ministers.** He noted its lack of orthodoxy: on Easter day it celebrated not the triumph of the Lord, but the immortality of the human soul. He also commented upon the two Eucharistic orders:

> In this book we are offered two alternative orders of communion. The Great Thanksgiving is omitted from them both! It is small satisfaction to the denomination to discover that it has produced two communion services without parallel in Christendom. [53]

The 1948 **A Book of Public Worship** was designed to oust **A Manual for Ministers;** it would be orthodox, and have parallels in Christendom.

The compilers of the 1948 book, E. R. Micklem, J. W. Todd, John Marsh and W. J. F. Huxtable, were all "Genevan" men. E. R. Micklem was the younger brother of Dr. Nathaniel Micklem, and had been chaplain and tutor at Mansfield College, 1922-38; Marsh and Huxtable had been trained at Mansfield, and Marsh succeeded E. R. Micklem at the college in 1938; James Todd had trained at Cheshunt College, Cambridge under J. S. Whale, the latter being Professor of Ecclesiastical History at Mansfield 1929-1933 before becoming President of Cheshunt College.

In the Introduction to **A Book of Public Worship,** written by John Marsh, the liturgical principles of the compilers were clearly set out. The early Congregationalists, so Marsh claimed, had pleaded for liberty, but their worship had been orderly. They were concerned not that they might do as they pleased, but that they might worship as they ought. Standards of worship could not be fixed by the State; they had been determined by the Gospel. [54]

Christian worship derives from two sources, the Jewish Synagogue and the Upper Room. The readings and sermon, derived from the Synagogue, and the Supper are together a dramatic representation of the great themes of the Christian story. The sermon seeks to do what the simple rite of the Lord's Table does in action--take us back to that place where we learn anew what God has done to redeem us from sin and death, but so to take us back as to make us know that the same God is still active in the same way in the same world to save the sinful race of men. [55]

Marsh explained that Word and Sacrament belong together. Calvin's aim had been to keep these two together: "For him the full order, Word and Sacrament, was normal; anything less was an unfortuate if unavoidable deprivation". [56] Since Congregationalism derives from Calvinism, their worship is to be understood in terms of Holy Communion, not of Matins and Evensong. [57] Maxwell's influence is easily discernible.

The compilers also felt it important to draw upon their own Puritan liturgical heritage:

> We have not ceased to draw freely from all manner of sources for our material, but we have tried to include some from such works as the Middleburg Prayer Book and Baxter's Reformed Liturgy. [58]

The main principles of the compilers were to return to the classical and Calvinist tradition of Word and Sacrament, and to draw upon all sources including their own Reformed liturgical tradition.

The fact that the Congregationalist custom was monthly communion [59] meant that the services of Word and Sacrament were still set out as distinct services. Nevertheless, the intention of the compilers was that Word and Sacrament should be understood as a unity. The book provided five orders of worship, four orders for communion, and a short order for communion. The Introduction stated:

> We believe, as the recent statement of the Life and Work Committee suggests (Some Considerations on Worship, presented to the Council, 24th March 1941), that not until Congregationalists come to envisage Sermon and Supper, Word and Sacrament, as belonging together, will they experience that revival of public worship that all desire and need. We have therefore adopted for the setting out of the orders of service on Sundays a device which will make plain and constantly remind us of this fundamental unity of Christian worship. We print five orders of worship, which can be used on any Sunday, whether the service is to include the Lord's Supper or not. When the service includes Communion the appropriate ending of the "ministry of the Word" should be used, after which the minister may continue with any one of the four orders provided for that part of the service coming from the Upper Room. [60]

Each of the five orders of worship contained the following rubrics:

> When the foregoing Ministry of the Word is followed by Holy Communion the service then proceeds according to one of the Orders for the administration of the Sacrament of the Lord's Supper.
>
> When the Service is not completed with Holy Communion a Prayer, appropriate to the special message of the Sermon, may be offered; or the following Prayer may be used. **[61]**

Each order of Communion began with the rubric:

> The Service proceeds after the usual Order of Worship to the point indicated by rubric in the foregoing Services.

The five orders for worship were thus to be considered as the Ante-communion, or synaxis. Since each order of worship could be linked with any of the four orders of communion, the book provided a combination of twenty services of Word and Sacrament, as well as the single short order.

The orders for worship represented a break with the tendency found in some previous books of imitating Anglican Matins and Evensong. Following Maxwell's strictures, these orders were a return to the structure of Reformed Worship. The precise sequence varied, but in overall structure they consisted of a call to worship with scripture sentences, adoration, confession and absolution (from the old confiteor and Introit), the lections, and the great prayer with thanksgiving, supplication, intercession, and the Lord's Prayer (from the old intercessions) which was essentially the same as the order found in Calvin's rites. The only deference to Anglican tradition was that in the first three orders, the sermon came after the intercessions at the end of the service. However, in the last two orders the old Reformed tradition was followed, the sermon being placed after the lections.

For the lections three lessons were suggested, an Old Testament reading and two from the New Testament, one of which should be from the Gospels. A lectionary was provided which followed the liturgical calendar. The use of the lectionary would ensure that the preacher would not air his own prejudices, but through the year would proclaim the mighty acts of God. The liturgical calendar served the same purpose; Daniel Jenkins pointed out:

> the commemoration of the significant "moments" of our redemption in the Christian Year, while not itself one of the "Gospel Ordinances", is obviously solidly based on the apostolic testimony . . . **[62]**

The traditional Temporale was provided for, together with special observances such as All Saints and Harvest Festival.

In the compilation of the orders for the communion, the authors paid careful attention to three things:

(a) Their own Reformed tradition, Calvin and the Puritan liturgies.

(b) Other Reformed churches, particularly the Church of Scotland's **The Book of Common Order**, 1940.

(c) The classical Eucharistic rites.

Dix's thesis of a four-fold action was not entirely accepted; the offertory of bread and wine was omitted, the preparation taking place before the service. A rubric advised:

> The Minister and Deacons take their places at the Lord's Table; and the bread and wine, which have previously been prepared on the Table, are uncovered.

The offertory of money, which in the Anglican tradition was associated with the preparation of the bread and wine, was placed in the traditional Congregational position after the communion. Since the preparation of the bread and wine was not emphasized as part of the Eucharistic action, the compilers, consciously or unconsciously, followed Baxter's three-fold action of thanksgiving, fraction and communion.

First Order

After a communion hymn, the order began with the reading of the Words of Institution as a warrant, 1 Cor. 11:23-26, introduced by words from the Scottish **The Book of Common Order**, only the punctuation being different. Then came Scripture sentences of assurance, again based upon the Scottish order. In the latter, however, the words of assurance precede the presentation of the bread and wine, and the Words of Institution. Of the four sentences, Matt. 11:28, Matt. 5:6 and John 6:35, 37b are in the Scottish book; the fourth, Rev. 3:20 is found in Hunter and in the second order of **A Manual for Ministers.** At this point came the Eucharistic Prayer molded upon those found in the classical rites with the Sursum corda, Preface, Sanctus, thanksgiving, epiklesis and oblation. Much of the phraseology has parallels with that of the main order of the Scottish book (118-120). The Scottish Eucharistic Prayer was based loosely upon the West Syrian anaphora of St. James, together with several phrases from the "Prayer of Consecration" of the Anglican rite. [**63**] Some phraseology was also taken from the second order in the Scottish book (127).

The Sursum corda, Preface and Sanctus have been taken from the **Book of Common Prayer**, and the Scottish prayer had been followed in the Post-sanctus. This latter use resulted in the thanksgiving for creation, which in the Scottish prayer came in the Preface, being placed in the Post-sanctus, a feature which W. D. Maxwell criticized in his review of **A Book of Public Worship.** [64]

As in Calvin, the **Directory** and **The Book of Common Order** 1940, the Words of Institution were not part of the Eucharistic prayer, but were read as a warrant; consecration was by Word and prayer. The Epiklesis in this prayer, taken from the Scottish book, is to be seen in this context. The petition did not ask for a change in the elements, but requests their sanctification, and for the communicants' sanctification, "that we, receiving them, may by faith be made partakers"; this adequately expresses Calvin's doctrine of communion by faith and the working of the Holy Spirit. The Congregational version had also made a slight addition, "that the bread which we break may be to us"; this addition, in the light of Cranmer's explanation of "unto us" in the 1549 Canon, could be regarded as a more subjective understanding of the Epiklesis than in the Scottish prayer.

After the Eucharistic Prayer, again following the Scottish order, the Lord's Prayer was recited by Minister and people. Continuing the parallel with the Scottish rite (and their common ancestor, the Westminster **Directory**), came the fraction.

The "Genevan" school emphasized the fraction, and attacked the widespread practice of individual cups. [**65**] Where individual cups were used, the chalice also should be placed upon the table, and the bread should not be so cut up before the service that there is none for the Minister to break. [**66**] "It is his duty to take bread and break it in the sight of the assembled communicants, and likewise to take the cup and present it as he speaks the words concerning it". [**67**]

Since the "Genevans" insisted that the essential fact in the Eucharist is not man's remembrance and commemoration of Christ's death, but that Christ gives himself to man, [**68**] the words of administration reflected the Calvinist belief that what Christ promises, this he gives in the communion of the bread broken and the wine poured out:

> Take ye, eat ye: this is the body of Christ which is broken for you; do this in remembrance of him.

> This cup is the new covenant in the blood of Christ, which is shed for the remission of sins; drink ye of it.

Once again, the wording was almost the same as that given in **The Book of Common Order**; the Post-communion prayer was also from the same source with a minor alteration to the final sentence. After the offering for the poor and a hymn, the first order concluded with the Grace.

Second Order

In this order the compilers borrowed material from the **Book of Common Order**, 1932, of the United Church of Canada. This Church had been formed in 1925 by a union of Canadian Congregationalists, Methodists and Presbyterians; the communion rite of the united church reflected Anglican and Scottish liturgical usage.

After the communion hymn, the minister said the "Prayer of the Veil" which was in the Canadian rite and had been used in earlier Scottish rites. The Eucharistic Prayer which followed was that of the Canadian rite, but without any Proper prefaces. The Canadian prayer [**69**] was based on the Canon of the 1549 **Book of Common Prayer**, having Sursum corda, preface, Sanctus, thanksgiving, Institution Narrative, anamnesis, epiklesis, oblation of worship and self, and doxology.

Of particular interest here was the form of the anamnesis:

> Wherefore, having in remembrance his precious death and passion, his glorious resurrection and ascension, and pleading his eternal sacrifice, we thy servants do set forth this memorial which he hath willed us to make, giving thee thanks that thou hast counted us worthy to stand before thee.

This extends into the epiklesis: "so sanctify with thy Word and Spirit these thine own gifts of bread and wine which we set before thee". This same anamnesis is also to be found in the Scottish **Book of Common Order**, 1940.

In the classical anaphoras, the anamnesis often interprets "Do this in remembrance" as "Offer this in remembrance", and includes a specific offering of the bread and cup. Thus in **Apostolic Constitutions** Book VIII:

> Therefore, having in remembrance his passion and death, and resurrection, and his return into heaven, and his future second advent, . . . we offer unto thee, our

> King and our God, according to his appointment, this bread and this cup, giving thanks unto thee through him that thou hast counted us worthy to stand before thee and to sacrifice unto thee.

And in the Roman **Canon missae:**

> Mindful, therefore, O Lord, not only of the blessed passion of the same Christ, Thy Son, our Lord, but also of His resurrection from the dead, and finally His glorious ascension into heaven, we, Thy ministers, as also Thy holy people, offer unto thy supreme majesty of thine own gifts, a pure sacrifice, a spotless sacrifice, the holy bread of eternal life and the cup of everlasting salvation.

One of the foremost targets of the Reformers' attacks was the medieval doctrine of the sacrifice of the mass, which the Roman anamnesis was thought to countenance. The Reformers held that the only sacrifices that Christians could offer were praise and thanksgiving, alms and themselves. The Eucharistic elements were not an offering to God, but a gift to men which could only be received. [**70**] Since most Reformation liturgies replaced the entire **Canon missae**, the anamnesis disappeared. [**71**]

In the **Book of Common Prayer**, 1549, Cranmer carefully redrafted the Roman anamnesis:

> Wherefore, O Lord and heavenly Father, according to the instruction of thy dearly beloved son, our Saviour Jesu Christ, we thy humble servants do celebrate, and make here before thy Divine Majesty, with these thy holy gifts, the memorial which thy son hath willed us to make, having in remembrance his blessed passion, mighty resurrection, and glorious ascension . . .

All reference to the bread and wine being offered was omitted. In 1552 the 1549 Canon was rewritten, and "anamnesis" appears to have been interpreted as the actual act of communion which followed immediately after the Words of Institution. After the communion, the minister asked God to accept the sacrifice of praise and thanksgiving, and continued with an oblation of "ourselves, our souls and bodies" - though this prayer was one of two alternatives. Later Anglican divines, comparing the Prayer Book communion with the earlier liturgies such as **Apostolic Constitutions**, interpreted the sacrifice of praise and thanksgiving as including the Eucharistic elements. According to John Cosin, Bishop Overall (d. 1619) used to transfer the "prayer of oblation" so that it followed the Institution Narrative and came before the administration; Cosin himself even suggested that the printers may have placed it in the wrong place. [**72**] The Non-jurors and the Scottish Episcopalians restored the 1549 sequence of prayers in their liturgies (i.e. as with Overall, the "prayer of oblation" followed on immediately after the Institution Narrative), and inserted an oblation of the elements in imitation of the classical rites. On the whole, however, churches in the protestant tradition have avoided any reference to Eucharistic Sacrifice in their liturgies.

In the present century there has been a growing consensus among Roman Catholic and Reformed scholars on the question of Eucharistic sacrifice in sacramental terms. The Faith and Order Report 1951, **Ways of Worship**, stated:

> It is well known that both Luther and Calvin rejected this conception on the ground that the sacrifice of Calvary had been offered once for all and was not to be repeated. But recent studies of both the New Testament and the patristic evidence have led to a re-opening of the question, and it is asked whether sacrificial language does not appear in a new light when the idea of re-presentation replaces that of repetition, and when communion and offering are seen as two sides of the same thing. . .
>
> . . . Doubt is cast upon the interpretation of the Epistle to the Hebrews traditional in Calvinist Churches, according to which the sacrifice at the heavenly altar is held to imply the abolition of sacrificial practice on earth. The Epistle is interpreted as justifying the idea, traditional in Orthodox liturgical worship, that in the Eucharist the crucified, risen and ascended Lord unites His worshippers with Himself in His eternal self-offering to the Father. [73]

This latter idea of entering into the eternal sacrifice of Christ has been accepted by a number of continental Reformed scholars. [74] It has also been accepted by some Scottish Presbyterian scholars, [75] and it underlies the thought of the anamnesis in question. W. D. Maxwell commented upon the identical Scottish form:

> The determinative words are "pleading His eternal sacrifice, we thy servants do set forth this memorial". The Scottish rite lays emphasis not upon "the oblation once offered", though this of course, is there in recollection and theology, but specifically upon the eternal quality of our Lord's sacrifice: it happened once for all time, but it belongs to eternity where He continually presents Himself before the Father. Similarly, the Eucharist is of eternity, and when we plead "His eternal sacrifice", we desire Him to unite our offering and prayers with His, which is eternal, and "this memorial" in time and

> space is a part of that eternal memorial. His sacrifice is not repeatable, but it is continually renewed; the "remembering" is not mere recollection in the psychological sense (which, in fact, is never the biblical sense), but a real uniting, possible by grace and through faith, faith which is not mere intellectual assent, but a committal of the whole person to Him. It is, thus, as Calvin declares, a vera communicatio with Him. [**76**]

Although not identical, a similar idea of Eucharistic sacrifice was expounded by C. H. Dodd. He argued that the words of the Last Supper indicate a self-offering. Whatever relation the sacramental breaking of the bread at the Last Supper had to his sacrifice, with his death in prospect, that relation the breaking of bread in the Sacrament has to his sacrifice, with his death in retrospect; the sacrament unites us with Christ in his sacrifice, and by virtue of that union we dedicate ourselves to God. [**77**] J. S. Whale has also stressed that in the Eucharist we have sacramental identification with the Redeemer's perfect sacrifice. [**78**]

In adopting the wording of the Canadian anamnesis, the "Genevan" compilers accepted that "remembrance" was not merely subjective, but rather the memorial included the pleading of the eternal sacrifice of Christ before God. This includes setting before him the bread and the wine.

The Institution Narrative was contained within the prayer, and the epiklesis, similar to that in the first order, petitioned for sanctification by the Word and Spirit.

After the Eucharistic Prayer came the Lord's Prayer, the fraction, administration, Post-communion prayer (based on that in the **Book of Common Prayer**), offertory, hymn, and the blessing from the Anglican rite.

Third Order

In this order the compilers presented a modernized version of the Eucharistic Prayer found in the Middleburg edition of the **Genevan Service Book.**

After the communion hymn, the Words of Institution were read as a warrant, followed by an exhortation. In contrast to the exhortation in **A Manual for Ministers** which taught that the communion kept fresh in our hearts the memory of the Lord's sacrifice, this exhortation taught that the sacrament was instituted "for the perpetual remembrance and shewing forth of his sacrifice upon the cross". It called for worthy reception, and ended with words based upon the "Reformed Sursum corda" found in Farel and Calvin. The Eucharistic Prayer was a free adaptation of that found in the Middleburg book which derives from John Knox. The last two paragraphs seem to have been based upon a part of Calvin's Strasbourg liturgy which was added to the Long Prayer when the Eucharist was celebrated. [79]

After the prayer came the fraction, with words of delivery from the Middleburg book. The Post-communion prayer was from this same source, and this neo-puritan order was concluded with the blessing from Hebrews 13:20-21.

Fourth Order.

After the communion hymn, the Words of Institution were read as a warrant. Then came a Eucharistic Prayer. The opening paragraph was based on the language of the Sursum corda and Preface, followed by a thanksgiving for creation and especially redemption, concluding with the Sanctus. The emphasis on redemption may have been suggested by the outline of the Eucharistic Prayer given in the **Westminster Directory**, for this latter was the source of the petition for consecration which followed the Sanctus in this prayer:

Westminster Directory	**A Book of Public Worship**
Earnestly to pray to God, the Father of all mercies, and God of all consolation, to vouchsafe his gracious presence, and the effectual working of his Spirit in us, and so to sanctifie these Elements both of Bread and Wine, and to blesse his own Ordinance, that we may receive by Faith the Body and Blood of Jesus Christ crucified for us, and so to feed upon him, that he may be one with us, and we with him, that he may live in us, and we in him, and to him, who hath loved us, and given himself for us.	O God our Father, grant unto us, we humbly beseech thee, thy gracious presence, and the powerful working of thy Spirit in us; and so sanctify these elements of bread and wine, and bless thine own ordinance, that we may receive by faith the body and blood of Jesus Christ, crucified for us, and so feed upon him, that he may be one with us, and we with him; and that he may live in us and we in him who loved us and gave himself for us.

This Eucharistic Prayer concluded with an oblation of the sacrifice of praise and thanksgiving. The fraction followed, and, as in the **Directory**, the administration of the bread was completed before the taking of the cup. After a Post-communion prayer, hymn and offering, the order concluded with the Peace.

A Shorter Order

This order was designed for those who had early communion services on such days as Easter Sunday. [**80**] It combined the service of Word and Sacrament, the service of the Word being abbreviated in content as compared with the five main orders for worship. The whole service followed closely the structure of the second shorter order found in **The Book of Common Order** 1940.

The service of Word consisted of Scripture sentences, Collect for Purity, confession and absolution, three short lessons (Isaiah 53:1-6; 2 Cor. 5:14-21 and St. John 6:47-58 were suggested, the first and last being also recommended in the Scottish book), and the sermon.

After the communion hymn, the order proceeded with the Institution Narrative, sentences of scripture (those of the first communion order), and the Eucharistic Prayer. The latter seems to have been a composite prayer gathered from several sources. The first paragraph echoes phraseology in the Eucharistic Prayer of the second short order in the Scottish book (page 146), and the second paragraph, the second part of the Post-sanctus in the first order in the Scottish book. After the Sanctus came a petition for consecration which echoes both that of the **Westminster Directory** and part of Baxter's **Reformed Liturgy**. After the oblation of praise and thanksgiving, the prayer continued with a series of intercessions, echoing those in the Eucharistic Prayer of the first shorter order of the Scottish book (page 128), in imitation of the memento of the classical anaphoras: for the church, for all people, relatives and friends, the sick, suffering and bereaved, and thanksgiving for the faithful departed. These made up for the omission of intercessions in the service of the Word.

After the Eucharistic Prayer came the Lord's Prayer, fraction and administration of bread, taking the cup and administration of the wine, and a Post-communion prayer from the Scottish book. After the offertory and the final hymn came either the Grace or the blessing from the Prayer Book communion service.

It is useful to summarize the main liturgical principles which underlie the Eucharistic liturgy in **A Book of Public Worship:**

1. Word and Sacrament properly belong together.

2. The service of Word should not be constructed on the lines of a choir office, namely, Anglican Matins and Evensong, but on the pattern of ante-communion. As such it had its own structure--confession, lections, sermon and intercessions.

3. The sacrament also has a particular underlying structure--thanksgiving, fraction and communion.

4. The thanksgiving, or Eucharistic Prayer, may follow the pattern of the classical anaphoras with Sursum corda, preface and sanctus; it may even have the Words of Institution within it; but it always contains thanksgiving for the mighty acts of God, a petition for consecration, and an element of oblation.

5. The Eucharist is not just an occasion for Christians to remember Christ. Here Christ comes to his people, and what he promises, that they receive in eating of the broken bread and the wine poured out.

Prayers and Services for Christian Festivals 1951

This liturgical work was prepared as a companion volume to **A Book of Public Worship**, and fulfilled a hope expressed in the Introduction of that book, "We have in mind a book of services for use on the great festivals of the Christian Year and other occasions of the Church's life, together with some services of a more experimental nature". [**81**] It was compiled by James M. Todd, then minister at Great Yarmouth, and who had been responsible for much of the drafting of the 1948 book. [**82**] This supplementary book was divided into three parts; Part II contained three short orders for the Lord's Supper, for Christmas, Easter and Whitsunday, all designed for early celebrations. As with the short order in the 1948 book, each of these orders combined Word and Sacrament. The layout of the orders was as follows:

Call to worship
Hymn
Collect for purity
Confession
Collect
Old Testament lesson
Epistle
Gospel
Sermon (or intercessions)
Intercessions for: (or sermon)
  the Church
  Commonwealth, Empire, King and those in authority,
  the sick, poor, persecuted and bereaved, and the
  communion of saints
Te Deum or hymn
Offerings
Institution Narrative
Taking and setting apart the elements
Eucharistic Prayer

Lord's Prayer
Fraction
Administration
Post-communion thanksgiving
Hymn
Blessing

In addition to the variable lections and collect, the forms of confession, the post-communion prayer and the blessing also varied from order to order. For example, the Christmas order used the shorter commandments and a three-fold kyrie for a confession; that of Easter used an abbreviated form of the Roman Confiteor and absolution, with kyries; that of Whitsunday used material from Psalm 51.

In these orders, Todd appears to have accepted Dix's view of a definite four action shape. The offertory was removed from its 1948 position after the communion to a place before the Institution Narrative. After the Narrative had been read, the minister--following the layout in **The Book of Common Order** 1940--took and set aside the elements of bread and wine:

> And now, in the name of the Lord Jesus Christ, who instituted this Sacrament of his body and blood, we take these elements of bread and wine (here the Minister lays hands on the bread and the cup) and set them apart for the holy use to which he appointed them; and as he gave thanks and blessed, let us present to God our prayers and thanksgivings.

In the order for Easter, the Scottish wording was given verbatim. It should be noted that the "taking" which is emphasized in the Scottish rite pre-dated Dix's **The Shape of the Liturgy**. The Scottish practice had not been adopted in the 1948 book, and it seems likely that Dix's work was the stimulus that accounted for its adoption here.

Only one Eucharistic Prayer was used throughout, differing only in the Preface which took the form of a Proper preface, with material from the Propers of the **Book of Common Prayer** and **The Book of Common Order**. The prayer followed very closely that of the first order of the Scottish liturgy, including the Benedictus qui venit after the Sanctus. Whereas the Scottish prayer's post-sanctus picked up on the word "holy" in the Sanctus, Todd, following the 1928 **Book of Common Prayer** and the United Church of Canada's **The Book of Common Order**, used the word "glory". After the fraction, the bread was distributed before the taking of the cup.

This book not only supplemented that of 1948, but also

reinforced the principles of the first book.

A Book of Services and Prayers 1959

During the preparation of **A Book of Public Worship** by members of the Church Order Group, a committee of the Congregational Union had asked to see the work with a view to publishing it. However, after seeing it, without giving reasons, they declined to assist with its publication, and this work was finally carried out by the Oxford University Press. [83] It would appear that the Committee of the Congregational Union in question was not prepared to encourage the replacement of **A Manual for Ministers** by this publication. However, the appearance of **A Book of Services and Prayers** in 1959, published by the Independent Press, witnessed to the success of the 1948 book and its principles of worship in replacing the 1936 book as a standard for the pattern of Congregtional worship.

A Book of Services and Prayers was the work of a Committee appointed by the Congregational Union. Under the Chairmanship of Dr. W. Gordon Robinson, President of the Lancashire Independent College, Manchester, the Committee comprised the Reverends, D. H. F. Leatherland, H. Bickley, D. E. Bowen, Dr. J. Trevor Davies, Dr. C. S. Duthie, Dr. John Marsh, J. S. Perkins, G. Phillips, J. M. Phillips, J. M. Todd, R. A. Wakely, and Miss Joyce Rutherford. Both Marsh and Todd had been responsible for the 1948 book, though Todd resigned from the Committee before the 1959 work was completed.

The 1959 book provided two orders for Morning worship, and gave the outline for three others; there were two orders for Evening worship. The orders for Morning worship steered a course between Ante-communion and the pattern of the Anglican Morning Prayer. On the whole the Calvinist tradition was followed, with a Call to worship, confession, lections and intercessions, though the outline for the fourth order allowed for responses--the versicles and responses of the Anglican choir office. Furthermore, it was only in the fifth order that the sermon followed the lections; in all the others it followed the intercessions at the end of the service, as in the Anglican practice of Matins, intercessions and sermon. A table of lessons was provided which followed the liturgical calendar, but provided only for an Old Testament and New Testament lesson, and not the Eucharistic readings of Old Testament, Epistle and Gospel. However, also included was the lectionary of the Church of South India which did provide these three lessons.

In the section of the sacraments, two orders for the communion were given in which the principles and theology of the 1948 book were endorsed. The first order was a complete order of Word and Sacrament:

Scripture sentences
Collect for purity
Hymn
Confession of sins
Assurance of pardon
Prayer for grace
Old Testament lesson
Psalm or canticle
New Testament lesson (with rubrical provision for a reading from the epistles and other books in addition to a Gospel reading).
Hymn
Intercession
Notices
Hymn
Sermon
Offering
Prayer of Dedication
Hymn
Scripture sentences (Invitation)
Prayer
Communion hymn
Words of Institution
Eucharistic Prayer
Lord's Prayer
Fraction
Distribution
Peace
Post-communion prayer
Hymn
Blessing

The committee had conceded that the principle of Word and Sacrament together was correct. However, unlike the 1948 compilers, those of this book showed very little interest in their Puritan liturgical heritage. Much of the material in this order was taken directly from **The Book of Common Order** 1940 and Todd's **Prayers and Services for Christian Festivals.**

As in the Scottish rite, the service opened with three scripture sentences and the collect for purity; of these three--Psalm 116:11-13a, 1 Cor. 5:7a, and Psalm 136:1--only the latter differed from the Scottish rite which had Psalm 34:8.

The confession was based on Psalm 51, used in the first order of Morning worship in the 1948 book, and in Todd's communion order for Whitsunday (though also in 1920 and 1936, but not an identical composition). The prayer for grace was taken from the Scottish book. The Eucharist itself showed the same influences and sources:

> The Gracious words: **Book of Common Order** and first communion order of 1948.
>
> Prayer of the Veil: **Book of Common Order**.
>
> Institution Narrative with introductory formula: **Book of Common Order** and Todd.
>
> Taking of the bread and wine: Todd.
>
> Eucharistic Prayer: Todd, minus proper preface.
>
> Fraction: **Book of Common Order** and 1948.
>
> Peace: **Book of Common Order**.
>
> Post-communion prayer: **Book of Common Order** as adapted in the first order for communion, 1948.

This first communion order was not, then, a new composition, but presented material from the Scottish book and the two previous Neo-orthodox books as a norm for the denomination.

The second order for the Eucharist in this book gave only the sacrament itself, but presupposed that it would follow on from the normal Morning or Evening worship:

> The Service proceeds after the usual Order of Worship to the end of the Sermon. Then, if it has not been done already, the Offerings are received and presented.
>
> Sentences (Invitation)
> Prayer
> Communion hymn
> Words of Institution: Matthew 26:19-22, 26-29.
> Taking of bread and wine.
> Eucharistic Prayer
> Lord's Prayer
> Fraction and administration of bread.
> Giving of the wine to the deacons and administration.
> Post-communion prayer
> Hymn (and offering), Nunc dimittis or Gloria in excelsis.
> Grace

In this second order, the four actions shape was carefully followed. The Eucharistic Prayer did not open with the classical formula, but followed its themes with thanksgiving for redemption, the memorial of the Son's sacrifice, petition for sanctification of the elements by Word and Spirit, and oblation of worship and of self.

The Nunc dimittis may have been suggested by the Scottish liturgy, and the Gloria in excelsis by the **Book of Common Prayer**.

A Book of Services and Prayers 1969

The work of a small sub-committee under Dr. W. Gordon Robinson, this was a revised edition of the 1959 book, the principal difference being in the arrangement and the amount of material. This edition was smaller in content than the previous edition.

In the first order for communion three slight changes were made: the rubrics providing hymns before the intercessions and before the Words of Institution were omitted, and an alternative post-communion prayer from the Malabar liturgy was provided. [**84**] No change was made in the second order.

In these four Neo-orthodox books, Congregationalists were presented with Eucharistic liturgies which represented a return to the principles and patterns of both the Reformed and classical traditions. Although the 1948 book had attempted to revive the Genevan and the **Directory** forms of the Eucharistic Prayer, the tendency in subsequent books was to follow the classical anaphoras; this was usually the West Syrian type as reflected in **The Book of Common Order** 1940, with Sursum corda, Preface, Sanctus, anamnesis and epiklesis. However, with one exception all the orders followed the Reformed tradition in placing the Words of Institution as a warrant before the Eucharistic Prayer. The use of the anamnesis from the Scottish liturgy represented the Eucharist as a memorial pleading the eternal sacrifice of Christ, and thus conceding that some sacrificial language to describe the Eucharist is legitimate and desirable. The epiklesis also affirmed that Christ was present in the Eucharistic action, and was received by the communicant; the service was not just a pious reflection on the historic Jesus. However, the epiklesis was carefully constructed to present Calvin's teaching of the presence by faith and the working of the Holy Spirit; the elements were sanctified, not transmuted. Following the teaching of Calvin and the liturgical tradition of à Lasco, Middleburg, and the **Directory**, the fraction formed a distinct action within the liturgy; A. J. B. Higgins's estimation of its significance had not been influential. Compared with the orders contained in the Congregational Union books of 1920 and 1936, these books represented a liturgical and theological revolution; liturgical history of the early and the Reformation periods, together with orthodox Reformed theology, were for the first time taken seriously.

NOTES

1. For the term "Genevan" see, J. W. Grant, **Free Churchmanship in England 1870–1940**, 325ff. For the debt to Barth, D. Jenkins, **The Nature of Catholicity**, London 1942, 15; J. S. Whale, **Victor and Victim**, Cambridge 1960, 1, 16.

2. Editorial in CQ, 10 (1932), 2; for a shrill attack on Barthianism, C. J. Cadoux, **The Case for Evangelical Modernism**, London 1938, 40–54.

3. N. Micklem, **What is the Faith?** London 1936, 13.

4. Ibid., 153.

5. F. W. Dillistone observes the influence of Barth on Dodd's change of direction from psychology and general religious experience to the Gospel itself. **C. H. Dodd, Interpreter of the New Testament**, London 1977, 134.

6. W. D. Davies, **Paul and Rabbinic Judaism**, London 1948.

7. J. S. Whale, **The Protestant Tradition**, Cambridge 1955; A. G. Matthews, **Calamy Revised**, London 1934; **Walker Revised**, London 1948; **The Savoy Declaration of Faith and Order, 1658**, London 1959; B. L. Manning, **Essays in Orthodox Dissent**, London 1937; Daniel Jenkins, **The Nature of Catholicity; Congregationalism: A Re-Statement**, London 1954.

8. R. Tudur Jones, **Congregationalism in England 1662–1963**, 455.

9. N. Micklem, "The Sacraments" in **Christian Worship**, Oxford 1936, 243; R. Abba, **Principles of Christian Worship**, Oxford 1957, 138–139.

10. D. Jenkins, **The Nature of Catholicity**, 96.

11. J. S. Whale, **Christian Doctrine**, Cambridge 1941, 159.

12. "The Views of the Congregational Church" in **The Ministry and the Sacraments**, ed. R. Dunkerley, 1937, 214; N. Micklem, "The Sacraments", 245; J. S. Whale, **Christian Doctrine**, 154.

13. N. Micklem, ibid., 244.

14. J. S. Whale, **Christian Doctrine**, 153; "The Views of the Congregational Church", 218.

15. N. Micklem, "The Sacraments", 246; E. R. Micklem, **Our Approach to God**, London 1934, 53-54.

16. C. H. Dodd, "The Sacrament of the Lord's Supper in the New Testament", in **Christian Worship**, ed. N. Micklem, 78.

17. Ibid., 76.

18. Ibid., 78.

19. W. D. Davies, **Paul and Rabbinic Judaism**, 247.

20. Ibid., 248.

21. Ibid., 249.

22. Ibid., 251.

23. Ibid.

24. Ibid., 252.

25. A. J. B. Higgins, **The Lord's Supper in the New Testament**, London 1952, Higgins was subsequently ordained in the Church of England.

26. J. Jeremias, **The Eucharistic Words of Jesus**, E.T., Oxford 1955, 159ff.

27. G. Dix, **The Shape of the Liturgy**, 243-255.

28. J. S. Whale, **Victor and Victim**, 45.

29. Ibid., 137-138.

30. R. S. Paul, **The Atonement and the Sacraments**, London 1961, 369.

31. C. H. Dodd, "The Sacrament of the Lord's Supper in the New Testament", 76.

32. C. H. Dodd, **The Apostolic Preaching**, 234-235.

33. Ibid.

34. N. Micklem, "The Sacraments", 252.

35. N. Micklem, ibid., 245, 254; E. R. Micklem, op.cit., 261; R. Abba, op.cit., 177; R. S. Paul, op.cit., 373; J. S. Whale, "The Views of the Congregational Church", 218.

36. A. J. B. Higgins, op.cit., 51.

37. Ibid.

38. Ibid., 53.

39. Ibid., 54.

40. **Institutes**, 4.17.32.

41. See Chapter 2, 115ff.

42. B. M. Peake, "The Reform of Divine Worship", in CQ, 11 (1933), 433-437.

43. For a personal admission of this debt, J. M. Todd, "Tradition and Change: Worship in the United Reformed Church", in Liturgical Review 5:1 (1975), 1-18, p. 1.

44. W. D. Maxwell, **The Liturgical Portions of the Genevan Service Book**, 17-39; **An Outline of Christian Worship.** 111. 126.

45. **The Liturgical Portions**, 33; **An Outline**, 112-119.

46. **The Liturgical Portions**, 134; **An Outline**, 26-71, p. 59; **Concerning Worship**, Oxford 1948, 19.

47. J. S. Whale, "Calvin" in **Christian Worship**, where Whale admits his indebtedness to Maxwell.

48. Ibid., 168, 170-171.

49. E. R. Micklem, op.cit., 260; D. Jenkins, **The Nature of Catholicity**, 96, 143; R. Abba, op.cit., passim.

50. H. Davies, **Worship and Theology in England 1900-1965**, 45.

51. G. A. Michell, **Landmarks in Liturgy**, London 1961. It will be recalled that William Perkins had taught that the Eucharist was a four-fold action; Baxter had taught a three-fold action. See above.

52. Supra, note 34.

53. N. Micklem, **Congregationalism To-day**, London 1937, 30.

54. **A Book of Public Worship**, vii.

55. Ibid., viii.

56. Ibid., xii.

57. Ibid., xi.

58. Ibid., xiii.

59. The Report of the Commission on the Sacraments of Baptism and the Lord's Supper, 1936, in CYB, 1937, 116. When the production of **A Book of Public Worship** was first discussed in 1938 the possibility of a single order of Word and Sacrament was rejected as going too far, and would result in many ministers rejecting it out of hand. J. M. Todd, art.cit., 6.

60. **A Book of Public Worship,** xiii-xiv.

61. This rubric varied in the precise wording.

62. D. Jenkins, **The Nature of Catholicity,** 143; Cf. R. Abba, op.cit., 56-57.

63. J. M. Barkley, **The Worship of the Reformed Church,** London 1966, 49.

64. W. D. Maxwell, Review of **A Book of Public Worship,** in The Presbyter, 6 No. 4 (1948) 15-18.

65. E. R. Micklem, op.cit., 261, 263-264; R. S. Paul, op.cit., 373, 383; R. Abba, op.cit., 177, 182.

66. N. Micklem, "The Sacraments", 254.

67. E. R. Micklem, op.cit., 261.

68. J. S. Whale, **Christian Doctrine,** 160.

69. The text of the Eucharistic Prayer is printed in R. Abba, op.cit., 171ff.

70. For Luther, see Bryan D. Spinks, **Luther's Liturgical Criteria and His Reform of the Canon of the Mass,** Brancote 1982; Calvin, **Corpus Reformatorium,** 49, 485-6.

71. For an exception, see the Pfalz-Neuburg Order, 1543: "we bring before thy divine majesty these thy gifts of bread and wine".

72. Cosin, **Works,** Vol. 1, 31.

73. Ed. P. Edwall, E. Hayman and W. D. Maxwell, **Ways of Worship,** 1951, 33-34.

74. Ibid., 229, 239, 246-247.

75. **Intercommunion,** ed. D. Baillie and J. Marsh, 1952; T. F. Torrance,

"Eschatology and the Eucharist", 324, 326, 331; D. M. Baillie, **The Theology of the Sacraments,** 1957, 118.

76. **Ways of Worship,** 115-116.

77. C. H. Dodd, "The Sacrament of the Lord's Supper in the New Testament", 81-82.

78. J. S. Whale, **Victor and Victim,** 138-139.

79. Text in Bard Thompson, **Liturgies of the Western Church,** 202.

80. **A Book of Public Worship,** xiv.

81. Ibid., xxii.

82. Ibid., xxiii.

83. J. M. Todd, art.cit., 6.

84. This prayer had been included in "A Treasury of Prayers" in a separate section of the 1959 edition, 259.

Chapter Eleven

AN ECUMENICAL LITURGY: AN ORDER OF PUBLIC WORSHIP 1970

> We who have come together from all parts of the world and from virtually all the prominent traditions of the Church, have reached what is to us a remarkable consensus.
>
> Worship and the Oneness of Christ's Church (Report of Section IV of the Montreal WCC Conference 1963).

In 1964 the Congregational Union formed a "Liturgical Group", one of the purposes of which was to draw up a new order for the Eucharist for the use of the denomination. This Liturgical Group, subsequently to become the "Liturgical Committee" (1966) and the "Worship Committee" (1967) was responsible for the compilation of the last order of worship to be prepared by the denomination before the formation of the United Reformed Church in 1972. Although ready for publication in 1967, **An Order of Public Worship** was not published until 1970.

The 1970 Congregational Eucharistic order must be seen not only in direct succession to the previous Neo-orthodox books, but also in the wider context of ecumenical agreement on forms of worship. It was prepared at a time when the other major Churches in England, and indeed, throughout the Western world, were revising and re-writing their liturgies.

The Congregational Union had taken an active part in the Faith and Order Movement (subsequently to become the World Council of Churches) since its inception at the Edinburgh World Missionary Conference in 1910. [1] At the 1937 Edinburgh conference, a committee had been appointed to consider an important aspect of any attempts at co-operation and understanding between Churches, namely the traditions of worship in the various member Churches. Its report, delayed by the war, was published in 1951, entitled **Ways of Worship.** The report stated:

> In the course of this enquiry we have been struck by the extent to which a "liturgical movement" is to be found in Churches of widely differing traditions. [2]

The report continued:

> There is a widespread genuine unrest, a very definite feeling that worship ought to regain its central place in life, and that it can only do this if Churches return to the primitive patterns. To this end many Churches turn away from the habits and practices of their recent past in order to regain the purity and strength of worship as it was practised in their classic periods . . . But in one way or another there is a desire to recover the "original pattern".
>
> For this reason worshippers in Reformed Churches are rediscovering the liturgical principles and orders of service of the primitive Reformation, while members of all Churches, including the Roman Catholic, are studying afresh the worship of the early Church. [3]

This latter statement in the report adequately summed up the character of the Congregationalist Neo-orthodox books which themselves were both a product of and a contribution to the Liturgical Movement. However, the renewed interest in the forms of the early Church, taking all Churches back beyond the controversies of the Reformation, has resulted in a remarkable consensus of opinion on the structure and content of the Eucharistic liturgy. This may be illustrated by reference to the Anglican Communion and the Roman Catholic Church.

A sub-committee report of the 1958 Anglican Lambeth Conference suggested modifications or additions to the communion service in the 1662 **Book of Common Prayer** for the further recovery of elements of the worship of the primitive church. [4] It suggested that, in the Ministry of the Word, an Old Testament lesson should be included, together with psalmody, that the sermon should follow the readings, and that the "People's Prayers" should be restored. It also suggested that the Kyries and Gloria in excelsis might be restored to this part of the service. For the actual Eucharist, it was suggested that the offertory should be more closely connected with the "Prayer of Consecration", and that the latter should not be confined to thanksgiving for Calvary, but should include all the principal "mighty works of God", especially the resurrection and ascension of our Lord and his return in glory. The consecration, it suggested, was by thanksgiving, eucharistia, and not by a formal recitation of a formula of consecration. On the delicate subject of Eucharistic Sacrifice, the sub-committee pointed to the growing agreement among Roman

Catholic and Protestant scholars on the approach to the question. It argued that although the sacrifice of Christ is once for all, it is not merely a past event, but an eternal truth. He unites us with himself, and we participate in his own sacrifice.

A further document, "The Pan-Anglican Document", stated that the Eucharistic rite has five parts: The Preparation, The Service of the Word of God, The Great Intercession, The Service of the Lord's Supper and The Dismissal. [5] Concerning "The Service of the Lord's Supper" the document maintained:

> This should include the placing of the gifts on the Lord's Table and the ancient form of Sursum corda. The consecration prayer should be in the form of a thanksgiving for creation and for God's mighty acts in Christ and in sending the Holy Spirit. There should be a recital of the words and acts of the Lord at the Last Supper and a prayer for the communicants. The Lord's Prayer makes a fitting ending to this prayer. The Breaking of the Bread follows, and the Communion of clergy and people.

The Eucharistic liturgy in the Roman Catholic Church which was practically "frozen" in the Missal of Pope Pius V in 1570, has undergone a complete revision, set in action by the Constitution on the Sacred Liturgy of the Vatican II council. In the light of the work of scholars of comparative liturgy, the Constitution suggested a streamlining of the mass. [6] The Mass, it maintained, consists of two intrinsically linked parts, the Liturgy of the Word and the Eucharistic liturgy. The rite was to be translated into the vernacular, and the doublets and later additions removed. An Old Testament lesson was restored, and the sermon was to be an integral part of the service. The Common Prayers or Intercessions were also to be restored.

In the Eucharist proper, the offertory prayers were modified, and as well as a revision of the traditional **Canon missae**, three new Eucharistic Prayers were authorized. One of the members of the sub-committee studying the structure of the Mass, Dom Cipriano Vagaggini, concluded that every anaphora should contain as well as the introductory dialogue and concluding doxology, a hymn of joyful thanksgiving for the works of salvation, the Institution Narrative, the anamnesis-oblation, the committing the sacrifice to God, and an epiklesis. [7]

There is here a remarkable degree of consensus between Roman Catholic and Anglican thinking on liturgical principles. The consensus was, however, ecumenical, as was expressed in the 1963 report of the World Council of Churches' Montreal conference:

Orders of Holy Communion
usually include the following elements:

a) A service of Word, containing:
   i. the reading and preaching of the Word,
   ii. intercession for the whole Church and the world.

b) A service of the Sacrament, having a shape determined by the actions of our Lord at the Last Supper:
   i. taking bread and wine to be used by God in this service,
   ii. blessing God for creation and redemption and invoking the Holy Spirit, or referring in some other way to the Holy Spirit, reciting the Words of Institution, whether before or within or after the prayer of thanksgiving, saying the Lord's Prayer,
   iii. breaking the bread,
   iv. giving the bread and the wine.

This list of liturgical items is not meant to exclude reference during the service to many other important theological themes such as the expression of contrition, the declaration of forgiveness of sins, the affirmation of faith in credal form, the celebration of the communion of saints, the announcement of the Lord's coming and the self-dedication of the faithful to God. [**8**]

As well as this wider ecumenical background, the work of the Congregational Liturgical Group was carried out at a time when the other major English Churches were also producing revised and new Eucharistic liturgies: The Church of England, Series 2 1967, and the draft of Series 3 1971; the Methodist **The Sunday Service** 1968; the Presbyterian Church of England's **The Presbyterian Service Book** 1968; and the Roman Catholic Missal of Pope Paul VI 1970. With growing ecumenical co-operation there was a considerable amount of cross-fertilization between the liturgical committees of the denominations. A member of the Presbyterian Church of England sat with the Congregational Group, and Congregationalists (J. M. Todd, J. Huxtable and W. S. Evans, all members of the Liturgical Group/Worship Committee) were among the members of the Joint Liturgical Group (JLG), an English ecumenical body which produced essays (1965), a calendar and lectionary (1967), a daily office (1968), services for Holy Week (1971) and more recently a statement on the structure of Christian initiation and the Eucharist (1972). It can be inferred, therefore, that the compilers of **An Order of Public Worship** took careful note of the character of revisions in other Churches.

It should also be added that most liturgical committees

took considerable interest in the structure and substance of the Eucharistic liturgy as recorded by Justin Martyr in his **First Apology** c. 150 A.D., and that found in the **Apostolic Tradition** attributed to Hippolytus c. 212 A.D.

The Liturgical Group first met in April 1964. Among the members of the Group, the chairman, J. M. Todd, was by now a veteran liturgiographer, [**9**] and John Huxtable had assisted with the 1948 book. Dr. J. K. Gregory had written a thesis on Eucharistic thought in Congregationalism; and Stuart Gibbons had studied early liturgy under the Anglican liturgiologist, A. H. Couratin.

At the meeting of 13th July 1965, it was proposed to draw up four orders for discussion, the task being given to Gibbons, Gregory, Todd and John Young. The Minutes of the Liturgical Group reveal the following suggested principles:

1. The orders would have provision for an Old Testament lesson, an Epistle and Gospel. [**10**]

2. Each Eucharistic Prayer would contain an epiklesis. [**11**]

3. One Eucharistic Prayer would end with the Sanctus. [**12**] The Minutes also disclose that J. M. Todd was preparing to write a Eucharistic Prayer which would lead up to the Sanctus, and then the Institution Narrative would be read as a warrant before the Eucharistic Prayer was resumed. [**13**] However, this idea was not put into effect.

The four orders [**14**] all had a similar structure, though the precise sequence of items differed from order to order, and some material was optional. The ministry of the Word consisted of a call to worship, a prayer of praise or approach, a hymn or psalm, a confession and assurance of pardon, the collect for the day, an Old Testament lesson, an epistle and gospel, the sermon and the intercessions as bidding prayers or in litany form.

The Eucharist proper commenced with an offertory of bread, wine and money. After an optional hymn came the Peace. Next came the Institution Narrative (if not in the Eucharistic Prayer), the Eucharistic Prayer, Lord's Prayer, the fraction, and the communion. The orders concluded with a short post-communion prayer, an optional hymn, the blessing and dismissal.

The orders conformed to the ecumenical consensus on the Eucharistic rite. Word and Sacrament were united in one service, and traditional elements such as the kyries and the Gloria in excelsis were used. All the Eucharistic Prayers began with the Sursum corda and contained the Sanctus, and those of the third and fourth orders contained the Institution Narrative. The Eucharistic Prayer of the fourth order contained no epiklesis of the Holy Spirit, and it ended with the Sanctus in place of or as a doxology.

The four orders were in fact never published. The reason was that in 1966 the Congregational Union of England and Wales was in the process of becoming the Congregational Church in England and Wales. This process involved more than just a change of name. The member Churches now covenanted together to form a Church, and this implied that the principle of the congregation itself being paramount had somewhat receded. Some members of the new Church were slightly suspicious that the denomination was abandoning Congregationalism, and moving nearer to the more authoritarian Presbyterian system of Church government. Such were the sensitivities in some quarters that the Executive Committee of the new Church took the view that to publish a new order of worship so soon might be taken by some as implying liturgical uniformity, and arouse hostile suspicion. The four orders were thus referred back to the Liturgical Group, with instructions to try to conflate them to produce one experimental order.

The Group, which had by now become the Liturgical Committee, was not encouraged in its task by the comments received on a Liturgical Report which had been circulated to the Congregational Churches. Views on the Report included:

> The members of the committee are looking over their shoulder either
> a) at the Presbyterians,
> b) at the Anglicans
> c) at Rome "just round the corner". [**15**]

and,

> In general we do not feel that there is need for guidance in liturgical practice. This comment would apply particularly to the suggestion that the Group proposes to publish complete Orders of Worship for the Sunday Services. This is contrary to our traditions. Much of the life of the Congregational Church comes from the fact that its worship does not follow any set pattern. [**16**]

The Report also raised the question of the frequency of communion. Here replies included:

> Congregationalists are historically Zwinglian. [**17**]

and,

> Congregationalists are akin to the Quakers. [**18**]

The remarks indicated that many Congregationalists (like the rank and file members of most denominations) had little knowledge of ecumenism or of the historic origin of their own Church. The "Genevan" school had left many areas of Congregational life unpenetrated.

On account of the request of the Executive Committee, and in the light of comments upon the Liturgical Group Report, the original plan for the order of worship was revised, using a scheme based upon the Sunday Service of Worship of the French Reformed Church. In this liturgy the normal Sunday worship was the Eucharist, and the order was divided into four parts, each part consisting of several alternative prayers and forms. The Worship Committee as they were by now called, increased their original four orders to six, and rearranged the material to give one order of Word and Eucharist with a number (up to six) of variables for each item.

The Oxford University Press was asked permission to include some prayers from **A Book of Public Worship** 1948 in the new order, and when granting this they requested that they might publish the new rite. The finished work was sent to them in 1967, but publishing was delayed, and **An Order of Public Worship** did not appear until 1970. This delay by the publishers caused considerable disappointment to the compilers, for they realized that by the time the order actually appeared it was out of date, both in its retention of the "thee" and "thou" forms of address, and by its inability to use the agreed ICET texts.

In the 1970 order normal Congregational worship was presented as a unity of Word and Sacrament. What the previous Neo-orthodox books had asserted was here made perfectly plain; the structure of this order was the Eucharist without division. In the "Notes on the Service", concerning the position of an Invitation to communion, the committee hoped that

> . . . it should clearly encourage the Congregation to regard the service as a whole, and remain together even though some do not share in the bread and wine.

On paper, at least, it represented the recovery of the unity of Word and Sacrament envisaged by Calvin.

Reference has already been made to the cross-fertilization that occurred between liturgical committees of the different denominations in England. The overall ecumenical character of the 1970 order becomes apparent when compared with other modern English revisions: the Church of England's Series 2 1967 and Draft Series 3 1971; the Methodist **Sunday Service** 1968; the Roman Catholic **Ordo Missae** 1969; and the Presbyterian Church of England **Presbyterian Service Book** 1968. Of these, the Presbyterian book was by far the most conservative revision.

Comparative Chart of the Orders

1970 Order	Ordo Missae	Presbyterian 1968
Call to worship		
Hymn or Psalm	Antiphon or Hymn	Psalm 43:3-5
		Call to Prayer: Ps. 126:12-14
Prayer of Approach, or		Prayer of Adoration, or
	Salutation	
	Confession	
	Absolution	
	Kyries	
Gloria in excelsis	Gloria in excelsis	Gloria in excelsis
		Collect for Purity
Confession		Confession
Assurance of Pardon		Assurance of Pardon
Collect of the Day	Collect of the Day	Collect
Old Testament	Old Testament	Old Testament
(Psalm, canticle or Hymn)	(Psalm)	Metrical or prose psalm
Epistle	Epistle	
		New Testament
(Psalm, canticle or Hymn)	Gradual	Creed
Gospel	Gospel	

(Chart continued page 204)

Methodist 1968	Series II	Series III (Draft)
Hymn or Psalm	Psalm or Hymn	Hymn, Canticle or Psalm
		Sentence
Prayer of Adoration		
		Salutation
(Decalogue)	Collect for Purity	Collect for Purity
Confession	Decalogue or Summary of the Law, or	
	Kyries	Kyries, or
Gloria in Excelsis	Gloria in Excelsis	Gloria in Excelsis
Collect of the Day	Collect of the Day	Collect of the Day
Old Testament	Old Testament	Old Testament
Hymn or Psalm	Psalm, canticle or Hymn	Silence: Psalm
Epistle	Epistle	Epistle
Hymn of Psalm	(Psalm, Canticle or Hymn)	Silence: (Canticle, Hymn or Psalm)
Gospel	Gospel	Gospel

(Chart continued page 205)

Comparative Chart of the Orders (cont.)

1970 Order	Ordo Missae	Presbyterian 1968
(Hymn)		Hymn
Sermon	Sermon	Sermon
Prayer		
	Creed	
Intercessions	Intercessions	Prayer for Church and World.
Presentation of Gifts. Hymn	Offertory Antiphon or Hymn	Offertory
		Invitation
		Prayer of the Veil
(Institution Narrative)		Institution Narrative
		Taking the Bread and Cup.
Peace		
Eucharistic Prayer	Eucharistic Prayer	Eucharistic Prayer
Lord's Prayer	Lord's Prayer	Lord's Prayer
	Peace	
Fraction	Fraction	Fraction
	Agnus Dei	Agnus Dei
Communion	Communion	Communion
		Peace
		Thanksgiving for communion, for the Church and for the Departed
Post communion	Post communion	
Hymn or Doxology		
Dismissal and Blessing	Blessing and Dismissal	Blessing
		Nunc Dimittis

Methodist 1968	Series II	Series III (Draft)
(Dismissal of Children)		
Sermon	Sermon	Sermon
(Collection)		
	Creed	Creed
Intercessions	Intercessions	Intercessions
Lord's Prayer	Confession	(Comfortable Words)
Hymn	Absolution	Confession
	Comfortable Words	Absolution
	Humble Access	Humble Access
Peace	Peace	Peace
Creed		
Offertory	Offertory. Hymn.	Hymn
Eucharistic Prayer	Eucharistic Prayer	Eucharistic Prayer
Fraction	Fraction	Fraction
	Agnus Dei	
	Lord's Prayer	Lord's Prayer
Prayer of Access		
Communion	Communion	Communion. Benedictus and Agnus Dei
		Sentence
Post Communion	Post Communion	Post Communion
Dismissal and Blessing	Dismissal and Blessing	Blessing and Dismissal

In structure, in the position of the Confession and Assurance of Pardon, and the use (in some instances) of the Words of Institution as a warrant, the 1970 order is identical to the Presbyterian; in all other features it stands closer to the Anglican and Roman Catholic rites.

In the Liturgy of the Word, the sermon was placed immediately after the reading of the lessons, and the intercessions between the sermon and offertory, thus in harmony with Calvin's rite and the structure found in the Anglican, Roman Catholic and 1968 Methodist rites. The liturgical calendar was followed, both in the provision for the collect of the day and in the lections. For the collect, the order referred to the JLG's **The Daily Office**, and the calendar and lessons (Old Testament, Epistle and Gospel) were those provided in the JLG's **The Calendar and Lectionary.** Six sets of Intercessions were provided, four of which were in litany or bidding prayer style. The first set of intercessions used phraseology similar to that found in those of Series 2, and the fifth set was based on a form considered for, but later rejected from, the same Anglican rite. [**19**]

The midway point between Word and Sacrament was marked by the "Presentation of Gifts":

> Then the people's gifts of money are collected.
>
> The bread and wine and money are then brought to the Lord's Table; or, if the bread and wine have been placed on the Table already, they are uncovered; and then the minister may say one of these prayers:

If there was to be no Eucharist, the money was collected and presented, a hymn sung, and the service closed with the dismissal and blessing. If the Eucharist was in fact to follow, then at this point the bread and wine were also presented or uncovered. This seems to represent an acceptance of the first of Dix's four-action shape as Anglican practice had interpreted it, namely, by connecting it with the "offertory" of money. In the Congregational books of 1951 (J. M. Todd) and 1959, the taking of the bread and wine as a deliberate action came after the Institution Narrative and immediately before the Eucharistic Prayer, following Scottish practice and giving better expression to the four-action shape. In the 1970 rite the "taking" (or uncovering) is separated from the Eucharistic Prayer by a hymn, the optional Institution Narrative and the Peace. The compilers seem to have had their eyes on Justin Martyr and the **Apostolic Tradition** at this point. But in both these, the sequence was the Peace, bringing, or taking, bread and wine, and the Eucharistic Prayer, as adopted in Series 2 and Series 3. [**20**] It would seem that the compilers rearranged the patristic sequence to allow the "Presentation of Gifts" to be the midway point of the service.

Any one of six "offertory" prayers could accompany the "Presentation of Gifts". Each prayer spoke of the gifts as being brought, laid before, given or offered, to God, seemingly to imply that the money, bread and wine (and just money when there was no Eucharist) are offered to God. This is partly explained in the notes to the order which explained that this action is a response to the Word. This seems rather a strange explanation, if, as the Genevans asserted, the Sacrament is merely the Word in action, for the bread and wine are no more gifts to God than is the opening of the Bible to read a lesson; we are commanded to hear the Word and to "Do this". However, it would seem from the prayers that the compilers were expressing the symbolism that the bread and wine are chosen from among the gifts God has given us, and are offered to him as a symbol of the offering of ourselves, of our possessions, and of the whole of material creation.

A rubric gave a wide latitude regarding the recital of the Words of Institution:

> The Words of the institution of the Lord's Supper are then read; but they may be omitted here if they are to be included in the prayer of thanksgiving (as in prayers III, V and VI) or if they are to be said at the breaking of the bread.

This rubric preserved the traditional Reformed practice of using the narrative as a warrant, but at the same time three prayers which contained the narrative, thus recognizing the legitimacy of the form of the classical anaphora, and of the Roman Catholic, Anglican and Methodist practice. In the Neo-orthodox books this latter practice had been provided for only in the second order of the 1948 book.

In the "Notes on the Service" the Peace was explained thus:

> It was an ancient Christian custom (revived in the Church of South India today) for the Congregation to greet each other at this point with the "kiss" or handclasp of "peace". We have provided sentences by which the minister can express the fact that we offer our thanksgiving to God at peace with each other and with him.

This was not an entirely new feature, for the 1959 book, in imitation of the Scottish **Book of Common Order**, had provided for the declaration of Peace after the communion.

The 1970 order provided six Eucharistic Prayers. All commenced with the Sursum corda, and all contained the Sanctus;

each had a Preface and included thanksgiving for creation (except V) and the work of redemption. Prayers III, V and VI contained an Institution Narrative, and all had petitions of varying types for consecration. Prayer III had proper Prefaces for Christmas, Easter and Pentecost.

A fascinating feature of Prayers IV, V and VI was that they all ended in the Sanctus. This feature can be traced to two factors, one academic and the other practical or pastoral.

The first factor is the influence of English liturgical scholarship, following the hypothesis of the Anglican liturgiologist, Professor E. C. Ratcliff, that this was the original ending of the anaphora in the **Apostolic Tradition.** [21] This is not totally unrelated to the fact that one of the committee, Stuart Gibbons, had studied under A. H. Couratin, himself a friend of Ratcliff and his successor as lecturer in liturgy in the University of Oxford. Couratin accepted and supported Ratcliff's hypothesis, [22] and their combined influence is to be seen in the Eucharistic Prayer in the Church of England Series 2, which was composed to allow a later transposition of the Sanctus to the end. [23]

A hint of this influence was to be seen in a paper which Gibbons read to the Church Order Group, c. 1960, entitled The Eucharistic Prayer. Gibbons observed that in Exodus 24, the making of the Covenant, half the blood of the sacrifice was thrown on the altar, and half on the congregation; the people were joined to God by the symbolism of the blood which was a sharing of life. After this the Elders were able to ascend the mountain, and they beheld God, ate and drank. Christ's death, the new covenant, has admitted Christians to eat and drink in the presence of the Holy God. The Words of Institution contain a promise:

> This act of worship, this thank-offering of bread and wine, in this relationship of utter dependence and gratitude, is regarded by God as my body and my blood. From you, this is enough, in God's gracious design, to admit you poor, imperfect worshippers, into his sight, to stand in his presence. [24]

Gibbons had already pointed out that when Isaiah was admitted to the presence of God, he heard the Sanctus; in the book of Revelation, the Church is admitted to God's presence and joins in the Sanctus. The inference must be that the Sanctus would form a fitting conclusion to the Eucharistic Prayer. [25] During the early 1960's Gibbons was already using a Eucharistic Prayer which terminated with the Sanctus, and he successfully persuaded the Committee that they should adopt this pattern for some of the prayers. He himself explains:

> It seemed to me that Ratcliff has made a good case for the hypothesis that this was the position in which the Sanctus had come into liturgical use, but that as a hypothesis it provided no basis for an argument from history. However, I felt that the theological argument for a final Sanctus is weighty if the biblical associations of the Sanctus are given due emphasis. Isaiah's reaction to finding himself a spectator of the heavenly worship is that he is not fit to be there, and he has to be cleansed before he can serve. In Revelation 5, the joining of all creation to sing the glory of God follows the celebration of the death of the Lamb whose blood has ransomed men for God. The point that we can only participate in the worship of heaven because Christ has died for us, seems to be given its proper emphasis when the Sanctus follows the anamnesis or making present/effective to us of the sacrifice of Christ. The inclusion of a final Sanctus in three out of six prayers suggests that the committee was persuaded of the weight of this argument, but equally unwilling to break with tradition. [26]

A second factor was of a more pragmatic nature. Dr. J. K. Gregory had also experimented with closing the Eucharistic Prayer with the Sanctus. The reason was that in **Congregational Praise**, the Sursum corda, Preface (Prayer Book) and Sanctus were provided for minister and people. The people say together the words leading up to the Sanctus, "Therefore with Angels" etc. A problem arose as to when the people should sit; furthermore, the congregation would have no idea when the minister would conclude the Eucharistic Prayer. It seemed a good idea to Gregory for the Eucharistic Prayer to follow the first part of the Preface, and concluding with "Therefore with Angels" etc., in which the people could join, and from which they would know that the Prayer was coming to its conclusion. Thus for pragmatic reasons there was support for Gibbon's argument that some of the prayers should end with the Sanctus. [27]

With the exception of Prayer VI--which will be considered separately--and the experimentation with the Sanctus, all the prayers followed roughly the West Syrian pattern--dialogue, thanksgiving (Sanctus), thanksgiving (Institution Narrative), anamnesis-oblation, epiklesis and doxology.

Prayer I was based upon that of Draft order 2. Prayer II, composed by J. M. Todd, was based upon the confession of faith in the Scheme of Union of the then proposed United Reformed Church, and the concluding paragraph was taken from the French Reformed Liturgy, adapted from the **Didache**. [28] Prayer III which contained Proper Prefaces for Christmas, Easter and Pentecost, and was the first part of the Eucharistic Prayer in Draft order 3, won the recognition of the Anglo-Catholic party of the Church of England, [29] and Prayer IV (based on Draft order 1) drew upon the old favorite, the main order of the 1940 Scottish **Book of Common Order**. Prayer V, following the vogue of most Churches, was based upon the anaphora of **Apostolic Tradition;** it was based upon material from the Post-sanctus of the prayer in Draft order 3.

Each of the Eucharistic Prayers had varying forms of the anamnesis-oblation, representing the different emphases in the eucharistic thinking of the Committee: in I the bread and the cup are said to be the thank-offering of the people, and in II are "taken" to "make the remembrance which he willed us to make"; in III they are offered as "this bread of eternal life and this cup of everlasting salvation" before the petition that by the sanctification of the Holy Spirit they may "be for us the body and blood of our Lord Jesus Christ"; in IV, we "recall his perfect sacrifice and, with this bread and cup, make the remembrance of him which he willed us to make"; and Prayer V, following the **Apostolic Tradition**, offers "thee this bread and cup".

The first five Prayers also all contained an invocation of the Holy Spirit; I and II merely requested that through the Spirit, or by the Spirit, a true communion would be made; III and IV asked for sanctification of "us and these thy gifts of bread and wine"; Prayer V follows **Apostolic Tradition**, interpreting the corrupt text of the epiklesis as a petition for the Spirit to come upon the Church. [30]

Prayer VI (Draft order 4) was the composition of the Rev. Stuart Gibbons. It is considered separately here on account of its structure, and because the Rev. S. Gibbons kindly supplied some interesting information on its history.

This Prayer was based upon a Eucharistic Prayer used by Stuart Gibbons during the 1960's at Wombourn. This latter had many features in common with the **Apostolic Tradition** and the Roman **Canon missae**, and was therefore "Western" in structure, and not West Syrian. It contained Proper Prefaces for Advent, Christmas, Epiphany, Easter, Pentecost and Harvest, as well as three common Prefaces. We give the text with the common Preface which underlies Prayer VI:

(Sursum corda)

It is truly meet and right, our duty and our salvation, at all times and in all places to give thanks unto thee, O Lord, Holy Father, Almighty Everlasting God, through thy most dearly beloved Son, Jesus Christ our Lord.

Whom thou hast appointed heir of all things;
Through whom thou didst also create the world;
Who being not ashamed to call us his brethren, himself partook of the same nature, that through death he might destroy him who had the power of death;

Who for the joy that was set before him endured the cross, despising the shame, and through the eternal spirit offered himself without blemish to thee, for all time a single sacrifice for sin;

Who being our High Priest, exalted above the heavens and crowned with glory and honour, has opened for us a new and living way into thy sanctuary, to offer thee acceptable worship with reverence and awe.

We therefore set before thee this bread and this cup, the thank-offering of thy people. Do thou of thy mercy approve and accept them, that they may be for us the body and blood of Jesus Christ our Lord:

Who on the night in which he was delivered up took bread, and when he had given thanks to thee his God and Father, broke it and said: "This is my body which is for you; do this in remembrance of me".

In the same way also he took the cup after supper, saying: "This cup is the new covenant in my blood; do this as often as you drink it, in remembrance of me".

Wherefore we thy humble servants by thy mercies O Father, present ourselves with the obedience of our lives, to offer to thy most glorious majesty of thine own gifts this pure, holy and acceptable sacrifice, the remembrance of his blessed passion, his mighty resurrection and his glorious ascension; and we bless thee that thou hast washed us from our sins and anointed us with thy Holy Spirit, making us worthy to stand before thee and serve thee as a royal priest hood:

We beseech thee to accept this our sacrifice of praise before thy throne on high, at the hand of thy beloved Son our great High Priest, and mercifully to admit us to the company of thy saints, where with angels and archangels and all the company of heaven, we now laud and magnify thy glorious name, evermore praising thee and saying:

Holy, holy, holy, Lord God of Hosts,
Heaven and earth are full of thy glory:
Glory be to thee, O Lord most High. AMEN

We have already observed that Gibbons accepted Ratcliff's hypothesis regarding the original ending of the **Apostolic Tradition**, which is adopted here. But there are certain other features in this prayer which suggest that Gibbons had accepted some other convictions which were held by Ratcliff and Couratin.

Ratcliff had a high regard for the anaphora in **Apostolic Tradition**, though he accepted Dix's estimation that the epiklesis in the Latin Verona text was an interpolation. [31] The thanksgiving and the offering of the bread and wine are in agreement with the Roman tradition alluded to by Justin Martyr and Irenaeus: the eucharistic bread may be compared with the oblation of flour in Leviticus 14; the eucharistic bread and cup are the "pure sacrifice" of Malachi 1; they are also, by Christ's command, for the anamnesis of the incarnation and passion. [32]

Regarding the Roman **Canon missae**, Ratcliff argued that if the Sanctus and the Intercessions were removed, being interpolations, then the sequence Vere dignum et iustum est . . . tibi gratias agere . . . Te igitur . . . supplices rogamus . . . uti accepta habeas . . . haec dona preserves for us the same Eucharistic sacrifice as conceived by Irenaeus; the bread and wine are offered as a thank-offering for creation, as the first-fruits, as a thank-offering for redemption, and as a thank-offering which Christians offer to the Father through the hands of Christ. [33] Furthermore, the Western tradition, as represented by Cyprian, regarded the Words of Institution as of great importance; by means of the Narrative, the Church's actio in the Eucharist is identified with, and becomes, the actio of Christ at the Institution; through the agency of the celebrant pronouncing the Dominical words, Christ continues to consecrate, offer and to command as he did at the Supper. [34]

Elsewhere Ratcliff argued that the epiklesis found in the Eastern anaphoras is a late novelty interpolated into, or unto, the Eucharistic Prayer; he himself showed preference for the more "simple" petition of the Quam oblationem. [35] A. H. Couratin has supported most of these views. [36]

This provides the background to the Eucharistic Prayer compiled by Stuart Gibbons. It opens with the Vere dignum, giving thanks for creation and, like **Apostolic Tradition**, particularly for redemption. It then develops into something very similar to the Quam oblationem, including the words adscriptam and acceptabilem, and then into the Narrative. The anamnesis echoes that of **Apostolic Tradition** and the Roman Unde et memores, and it terminates with the Sanctus. There is no epiklesis.

This Eucharistic Prayer formed the basis of that presented by Gibbons to the Liturgical Group. According to the Minutes, the use of the word "approve" was criticized, and also the omission of an epiklesis. [37] Furthermore, Gibbons was used to a weekly celebration of the Eucharist, whereas the members of the Group, although approving in theory, were concerned with providing a Prayer for a denomination which still had only a monthly celebration, and therefore the seasonal prefaces were discarded. The Prayer was redrafted from the Post-preface:

> We praise, we bless, we glorify thee, O God our Father, through Jesus Christ our Lord: grant for his sake that our thank-offering of bread and wine may be for us his body and his blood:
>
> Who on the night in which he was delivered up took bread, and when he had given thanks to thee his God and Father, broke it and said: "This is my body which is for you; do this in remembrance of me".
>
> In the same way also he took the cup after supper, saying: "This cup is the new covenant in my blood; do this, as often as you drink it, in remembrance of me".
>
> Wherefore, O Lord, we offer unto thee of thine own gifts this bread and this cup, to set forth the remembrance of/his forgiving death, his resurrection in glory, and his everlasting reign (OR . . . his death for our salvation, his resurrection from the dead and his heavenly reign until his coming again). We bless thee that thou hast washed us from our sins and anointed us with thy Holy Spirit, and hast called us to serve thee as a royal priesthood. Grant that in Christ we may be made a living sacrifice acceptable to thee, and sharing his body and blood may be strengthened for obedience and joyful service.
>
> Mercifully accept our sacrifice of praise before thy throne on high, at the hand of Christ our great High Priest. Unite us by thy Holy Spirit with all thy saints on earth and all the company of heaven, to laud and magnify thy glorious name, evermore praising thee and saying:

(SANCTUS)

This formed the basis of Prayer VI.

The Prayer has a carefully worked out idea of Eucharistic sacrifice, expressing that Christ is himself involved in the eucharistic sacrifice not only as victim but as High Priest of the royal priesthood, the Church. In a Paper read to the Committee, in reference to Exodus 24:8 and Jeremiah 31:31-34, he argued:

> Against this background it is surely possible to state with some confidence at least part of what was in our Lord's mind in giving the cup. His words were meant to establish his impending death as a sacrifice which would not only be the full expression of his own obedience but would fulfil the function of the original covenant sacrifice in inaugurating the new covenant foretold by Jeremiah. If this is so, the Last Supper is crucial not only as indicating our Lord's own estimate of the significance of his death, but also as establishing that death as the ground of all Christian obedience. The eucharistic cup symbolises for Christians their participation in the death, and therefore the obedience of Christ. . . . .
>
> The New Testament differs from the old in seeing obedience as the achievement not of man in response to God, but of God himself, as man in the person of Jesus Christ, and in man in the person of the Holy Spirit. Like faith, obedience is a gift. The achievement of Christian obedience is therefore not a matter of striving to emulate Christ, but of union with him and receptivity to his will imparted by his Spirit. But the obedience of the people of God is as much the object of the New Covenant as it was of the old.
>
> The purpose of Christian worship would seem to be to secure within the worshipping community the realization of true obedience, that is the coincidence between worship expressed in liturgical action and worship expressed in the whole of life. This coincidence, which was not realized within the terms of the Old Covenant, is claimed by the New Testament to have been uniquely realized in Christ, and to be capable of realization in Christians through the gifts of Christ imparted by his Spirit. But without the anamnesis or becoming present of Christ, Christians will not be brought to the unique and only sufficient starting-point for contemporary obedience. . . . it is suggested that our Lord's words concerning the eucharistic cup point the only way to the obedience to which he is the key and which it is the Church's business to offer. [38]

This explains the term "we offer"; it is as Augustine's dictum: "in that which she (the Church) offers (Christ's sacrifice), she herself is offered". [39] Sacrifice is here conceived in terms similar to the Irenaean tradition.

There is no invocation of the Spirit upon the elements--despite the criticism of the Liturgical Group--but a form of Quam oblationem before the Narrative. Gibbons explains:

> The relation of the eucharistic elements to the thanksgiving of the congregation, seems to me best expressed in terms of a eucharistic offering, consecrated by thanksgiving for the Gospel (along the lines of 1 Tim. iv 4-5), rather than by some special operation of the Holy Spirit. I have held the view that an epiclesis of the Holy Spirit either on the elements or on the congregation at the eucharist, obscures the theological understanding of the eucharistic action. For if there is an epiclesis on the elements themselves (and in the New Testament the Holy Spirit is surely poured out on people rather than on things) this obscures the truth that they are consecrated by thanksgiving for the sacrifice of Christ which they symbolise, while an epiclesis on the congregation seems to suggest that the Spirit has not been fully active already in the response to the Gospel which the congregation have made in giving thanks. [**40**]

Following **Apostolic Tradition** and the Unde et memores--and indeed most of the classical anaphoras--Gibbons used an anamnesis which interpreted "Do this in remembrance" as including a formal offering of the bread and cup; we have indicated the thinking behind Gibbon's idea of Eucharistic sacrifice. However, the same phraseology is used in Prayer III and Prayer V. This has particular ecumenical implications.

In the original draft of the Anglican Series 2 this phraseology from the **Apostolic Tradition** was used, but after dissension by the Evangelical party--presumably seeing in it the sacrifice of the mass--it was deleted. [**41**] Avoiding the phraseology also caused some ambiguity in the anamnesis in the Methodist **Sunday Service** 1968. [**42**] The phraseology is to be found in the Roman Catholic Eucharistic Prayers.

The formal offering of the bread and the cup in three Prayers in the 1970 order does not represent an acceptance of the Roman Catholic doctrine of the sacrifice of the mass, nor does it represent a specific doctrine of Eucharistic sacrifice being put forward as the norm for the denomination. (In fact, as we have noted, they each have a different emphasis.) What it does indicate is that in 1967 the Committee accepted that the phraseology was used in liturgical texts which antedate the medieval doctrines of transubstantiation and sacrifice, and therefore it expresses legitimate ideas of the early church. Unless the denomination was to call in question the catholicity of the early church, and therefore it own catholicity, the same phraseology was accepted as quite legitimate within the Calvinist tradition. The phraseology occurring in the three Prayers indicates that through liturgical scholarship, this form of the anamnesis is no longer regarded as a decisive factor between Congregationalists and Catholicism. [43] In this context it is interesting to note a statement upon the Eucharistic offering in the Liturgical Group Report of 1965:

> When, in our worship today, we take bread and wine and repeat the words and actions he used in the upper room our offering of all that we have and are is united to his perfect offering of himself. Here is the fulness of worship we need to offer and which the Gospel requires from the faithful and obedient people of God. [44]

After the Eucharistic Prayer came the Lord's Prayer and fraction or fraction and then the Lord's Prayer. For the fraction, either the Institution Narrative could be read, or 1 Cor. 10:16-17, though the bread-saying preceded the cup-saying. 1 Cor. 10:16-17 was also used at the fraction in Series 2.

Four sets of words of administration were given, including, strangely, the "Zwinglian" words of the 1552 **Book of Common Prayer**. After the communion came a short post-communion thanksgiving, a hymn or doxology, and finally--as in the Roman Catholic Mass, Series 2 and Series 3, and the Methodist 1968 rite--a short dismissal and benediction.

In the 1970 **An Order of Public Worship** ecumenical co-operation is abundantly clear, and the denomination was provided with a Eucharistic liturgy which, although faithfully preserving features of the Reformed tradition, harmonized wherever possible with the revised rites of other traditions. In the six Eucharistic Prayers, forms were provided which Reformed, Anglican (Catholic and Evangelical) and Roman Catholic could have taken upon their lips. Shorn of doctrinal and ceremonial polemics, some of the features of the liturgical tradition promoted by Dr. Orchard were accepted as legitimate, though not exclusively so. Liturgical scholarship was in this order given due recognition.

It is to be regretted that the Oxford University Press delayed the publication until 1970, highlighting the archaic language. Furthermore, with the coming into being of the United Reformed Church, a new joint liturgy was needed. Both these factors have meant that the 1970 order has had an unjustified short life, and its influence has been minimal. [45] It represented an important contribution to the ecumenical debate on the Eucharistic liturgy.

NOTES

1. For Congregational involvement in ecumenism, see R. Tudur Jones, **Congregationalism in England 1662-1962,** 362-366; 426-428; J. W. Grant, **Free Churchmanship in England 1870-1940,** 314ff.

2. **Ways of Worship,** ed. P. Edwall, E. Hayman, W. D. Maxwell, 1951, 16.

3. Ibid., 21.

4. **The Lambeth Conference 1958,** London and Greenwich, Connecticut, 1958, 2.78-2.85.

5. "The Structure and Contents of the Eucharistic Liturgy", 1965, in ed. C. O. Buchanan, **Modern Anglican Liturgies 1958-1968,** Oxford 1968, 31-32.

6. **Constitution on the Sacred Liturgy,** E.T. 1967, paras. 47-56.

7. Cipriano Vagaggini, **The Canon of the Mass and Liturgical Reform,** E.T. London 1967, 90-91.

8. Worship and the Oneness of Christ's Church. Report of Section IV of the Montreal Conference in SL 2 (1963), 243-255, p. 248.

9. This word is used by C. O. Buchanan in **Modern Anglican Liturgies 1958-1968** to describe those who write and compose liturgical texts. Although it has been criticized as being "non-existent", it fittingly describes the work of the Rev. J. M. Todd for Congregational liturgy.

10. Congregational Union of England and Wales. Liturgical Group, Minutes, 15th November, 1965, 2.

11. Ibid.

12. C.U.E.W. Liturgical Group Minutes, 6th May 1966, 1.

13. C.U.E.W. Liturgical Group Minutes, 15th November 1965; letter to the writer from the Rev. J. M. Todd, 13th June 1972.

14. I am grateful to the Rev. W. S. Evans for supplying me with copies of these orders. At the time of writing my M.Th. essay on this rite, I understood that these orders had not been kept.

15. Summary of Comments from the Churches on the Liturgical Report. Made by M. T. Shepherd (Cyclostyled); C.U.E.W. Liturgical Group Report 1965.

16. Ibid.

17. Ibid.

18. Ibid.

19. According to J. M. Todd in a private conversation.

20. It should be noted that in the Anglican rites Series 1 and 3, a short prayer accompanies the taking of the bread and wine, or "Offertory", a feature which is absent in Justin Martyr and the **Apostolic Tradition.**

21. E. C. Ratcliff, "The Sanctus and the Pattern of the Early Anaphora", in JEH 1 (1950), 29-36; 125-134.

22. A. H. Couratin, "The Sanctus and the Pattern of the Early Anaphora: a note on the Roman Sanctus", in JEH 2 (1951), 19-23; "The Sacrifice of Praise" in Theology 58 (1955), 285-291; "Liturgy" in **The Pelican Guide to Modern Theology**, ed. R. P. C. Hanson, Vol. 2, 1969, 148, note 26; 152.

23. C. O. Buchanan, MAL, 122; W. Jardine Grisbrooke, "Series II: The new Communion service of the Church of England examined", in SL 7 (1970), 2-36, pp. 19-21.

24. S. Gibbons, The Eucharistic Prayer, (Cyclostyled), 6.

25. In the Paper, Gibbons claimed that he was not arbitrarily imposing on the Eucharist a pattern from obscure OT texts: "For we have found in common with better scholars than ourselves, and under their guidance, that the early history of the eucharistic prayer . . . presuppose(s) such a notion of worship as we have outlined" (5). We may infer that this refers to Ratcliff and Couratin. Gibbons's Paper echoes the themes of Couratin's "The Sacrifice of Praise", op.cit.

26. Letter to the writer, 7th June, 1974.

27. A private conversation with Dr. Gregory, July 1976.

28. Joint Committee for conversations between the Congregational Church in England and Wales and the Presbyterian Church of England, **The Scheme of Union**, 1970, 23.

29. Letter from the President of the Church Union, the Rev. D. Carter, in the possession of J. M. Todd.

30. The difficulties here are well known: G. Dix, **The Apostolic Tradition** (1937) 1968, 75-79; C. C. Richardson, "The So-called Epiclesis in Hippolytus" in Harvard Theological Review 40 (1947), 101-108; B. Botte, "L'Epiclèse de l'Ana-

phore d'Hippolyte" in Recherches De Theologie Ancienne et Medievale 14 (1947), 241-251; E. C. Ratcliff, art.cit.

31. E. C. Ratcliff, "The Sanctus and the Pattern of the Early Anaphora". For Ratcliff's views, see Bryan D. Spinks, "The Cleansed Leper's Thankoffering Before the Lord: Edward Craddock Ratcliff and the Pattern of the Early Anaphora", in Bryan D. Spinks (ed.) **The Sacrifice of Praise,** Rome 1981, 159-178.

32. Ibid.; Justin Martyr, **Dialogue with Trypho** 41, 117.

33. E. C. Ratcliff, "Christian Worship and Liturgy", in K. E. Kirk, **The Study of Theology,** 1939, 443; E. C. Ratcliff and A. H. Couratin, "The Early Roman Canon Missae" in JEH 20 (1969). Cf. Irenaeus, **Adversus Haereses** IV.21.5; 29.5.

34. E. C. Ratcliff, "The Institution Narrative of the Roman Canon Missae: Its Beginnings and Early Background", in Studia Patristica, II, Berlin, 1957, 81. Cf. Cyprian, **Epistle** 63.

35. E. C. Ratcliff, "A Note on the Anaphoras described in the Liturgical Homilies of Narsai" in **Biblical and Patristic Studies in memory of Robert Pierce Casey.** ed. Birdsall and Thompson, Freiburg 1963, 235-249, esp. 239ff.

36. A. H. Couratin, "Thanksgiving and Thankoffering" in SL 3 (1964), 53-57; "Liturgy" in **The Pelican Guide to Modern Theology** Vol. 2, 148, 152-155, 178-179, 194-195.

37. C.U.E.W. Liturgical Group Minutes, 15th November 1965.

38. S. Gibbons, Christian Worship as the Primary Expression of Christian Obedience. (Cyclostyled).

39. **De Civitate Dei,** 10.6.

40. Letter to the writer, 7th June 1974.

41. C. O. Buchanan, **The New Communion Service--Reasons for Dissent,** London 1966; C. O. Buchanan and R. T. Beckworth, "This bread and this cup: An Evangelical Rejoinder" in Theology 70 (1967), 265-271.

42. A. H. Couratin, "The Methodist Sunday Service" in CQR 2 (1969), 31-38, p. 36.

43. The same would seem to be true of some Lutherans; Ottfried Jordahn, "The Ecumenical Significance of the New Eucharistic Prayers of the Roman Liturgy" in SL 11 (1976), 101-117. It is strange that in a report form of worship drawn up in South Africa by Anglicans, Methodists, Congregationalists and Presbyterians, it was again the Anglican Evangelicals and not the Reformed Churchmen who dissented from the formal offering of the bread and cup. C. O. Buchanan, **Further Anglican Liturgies 1968-1975,** Bramcote, 1975, 200-201.

44. C.U.E.W. **Liturgical Group Report,** 1965, 16.

45. Of an original printing of 3,000 copies, in November 1976, 1,250 remained in stock with the publisher. The writer has spoken with several former Congregational (now URC) ministers who were not aware of its existence!

Chapter Twelve

CONTEMPORARY PRAYERS FOR PUBLIC WORSHIP 1967, AND SOME UNPUBLISHED LOCAL RITES 1965-1973

An Order of Public Worship was the work of the official Worship Committee of the Congregational Church, and took shape under the guidance of J. M. Todd. It sought to apply to a Congregationalist situation the best principles of comparative liturgy in traditional (i.e. largely Elizabethan and Jacobean) language. In the Preface the Committee expressed welcome for "experiments which are being made to express the Church's prayer and praise in contemporary terms". One important venture of this nature was **Contemporary Prayers for Public Worship** 1967, an unofficial publication by a group of Congregationalists. Edited by Caryl Micklem, it was the work of Anthony Coates, John Gregory, William Sewell, David Stapleton, Roger Tomes, Brian Wren and Caryl Micklem; two of this group were also members of the offical Worship Committee.

Contemporary Prayers was compiled principally to urge upon people that it was possible to compose an ordinary public service in modern English which was neither too colloquial nor too "gimmicky"; its use of modern English was sufficient to convince the compilers that they were not duplicating the work of the Worship Committee. [1] But the concern of the compilers was not simply that of modern English:

> It is more than a matter of finding new clothes for perennial thoughts. The categories we all use in framing our prayers, the mental diagrams we have about what is happening when we pray, and about what we expect to happen as a result, are themselves in question. If, for example, one wishes to express in modern terms the petition, "We beseech thee to hear us, O Lord", one has not only to deal with the "thee" and the "O" and find a modern equivalent for "beseech": one has also to consider whether the suppliant-to-potentate type of relationship presupposed by "beseech" (in any language) has still any significance for western democratic man,

> and, if so, whether that significance is any longer theologically defensible in the context of prayer. Even the asking God to "hear" us is questionable, not so much because it is anthropomorphic (the language of prayer is bound to be that), but because it suggests the possibility, surely inadmissible, that God might not be as ready to hear as we to pray. [2]

The thorny problem of hermeneutics was raised here. The book was not intended as a fixed liturgy:

> We mean to encourage on-the-spot experimentation, not to provide a substitute for it. It will often happen, however, that a minister will be able to prepare one "contemporary" prayer or group of prayers for a service, but not the rest. We hope this book will provide him with material (which he can adapt to his own style), and at the same time stimulate him to extend the range of his own experiments. [3]

The collection was divided into three parts: Material for General Use; Sacraments and Ordinances; and Prayers for the Christian Year. As in **Let us Pray** and **A Manual for Ministers,** the prayers in Part I were grouped together under headings of "Opening Prayers", "Thanksgiving" and "Confession", from which a service could be compiled. Part II contained the "Order for the Lord's Supper".

The Order for the Lord's Supper merely provided the Eucharistic Prayer, "A" or "B", the fraction, delivery and a Post-communion prayer. It presupposed that a service of "Praise and prayer, reading and preaching" would precede as a matter of course, and these were to be found in Part I. Five additional Eucharistic Prayers were included in "Additional Material for the Lord's Supper".

Since the Order for the Lord's Supper commenced at the Eucharistic Prayer, this appeared to give a three-fold action of thanksgiving, fraction and communion. Possible the Post-communion thanksgiving might be construed as a fourth action; however, since the order was not meant to be followed rigidly, but was to encourage experimentation and adaptation, it probably indicates nothing more than that the compilers wished to provide only what was absolutely necessary. The preparation of the elements was provided for, not in rubric but by presupposition in three prayers in Part I, "Offering of the Collection" where in numbers 13-15, "At the Lord's Supper", God is presented with bread, wine and money; we give the second of these (No. 14):

> Lord God,
> We bring to you the ordinary things of life--
> food and drink and money--
> and in bringing them we bring ourselves.
> Take us and our gifts of money
> to do your work in the world.
> Take this food and drink
> from our tables to your table
> and feed us with your love.
> Through Jesus Christ our Lord.

Thus, as in the 1970 order, the offertory included the offering of bread and wine to God for his use to feed us spiritually.

Eucharistic Prayer "A" in the Order for the Lord's Supper had the Sursum corda--Sanctus in the traditional **Book of Common Prayer** language; only in the post-sanctus was modern language employed. It contained a short thanksgiving for creation, a longer one for redemption (the work of Christ), an anamnesis and epiklesis. The last two of these read thus:

> We therefore set before you this bread and this cup, as the thankoffering of your people; and we thank you that in your fatherly mercy, by our Lord's provision, and with the help of the Holy Spirit, it may be a means by which we remember his holy sacrifice and share his body and blood.

To set before God a thank-offering is to offer him the bread and the cup, and this would seem to be a modernized version of the phraseology of Hippolytus. However, the epiklesis could hardly be described as such in the traditional sense; there was no calling upon God or the Holy Spirit (but see above concerning the validity of such language raised by the Preface), but thanksgiving that the Spirit is involved in the Eucharistic action. It did justice to Calvin's teaching, but can hardly be described as a modernization of the developed epiklesis of the classical rites.

Eucharistic Prayer "B" was a collective attempt to express concisely in modern terms the meaning of adoration, anamnesis and epiklesis of the classical liturgies. [4] It was more "streamlined" than "A". [5] Once again it is the anamnesis and epiklesis which pose certain questions:

> Remembering these things, we celebrate once again the supper of the Lord. We pray that despite our sins and doubts the Holy Spirit may transform what we are doing, so that as we eat the bread and drink the wine we may share in the eternal life of Christ.

"Remembering these things" referred back to the thanksgiving for the work of Christ, which included "he is always present through the Holy Spirit". However, it hardly does justice to the biblical concept of anamnesis which most scholars are agreed underlies the meaning at the Supper. [6] The astute critic might also question whether in the epiklesis a "translation" has been made, or the substitution of a modern doctrine, though without doubt the transformation of the action is implied in the classical anaphora. This Eucharistic Prayer ended with the Sanctus, showing the parallel thinking between the compilers and the official Worship Committee. [7]

The fraction followed the Eucharistic Prayer, and rubrics allowed for the distribution of the bread before the words over the cup and its administration. Four sets of words of administration were provided.

The post-communion prayer was a thanksgiving with petition for the Spirit to help make the communicants' lives a memorial to Christ.

The five additional Eucharistic Prayers were the efforts of individuals as passed through the crucible of the collective mind of the group. [8] They may be briefly summarized.

(1) This prayer was purely a "eucharistia", having no reference to the Supper. It thanked God "the controller of the process of creation, and matchless and tireless director of operations for our rescue and rehabilitation", for his mighty deeds in the Old Testament, and in and through Christ; it was a eucharistia for the deeds of the Father.

(2) A note explained that the anamnesis of this prayer was based on the paragraph "Christian awareness of God" in the Congregational Union of England and Wales 1964 draft of "A Declaration of Faith". [9] In fact, anamnesis here seemed to refer to the thanksgiving or the remembering of God's mighty works rather than the technical anamnesis. There was no petition for consecration, nor any reference to the Spirit in connection with the communion.

(3) Like Richard Baxter's Eucharistic Prayer, this consisted of three paragraphs addressed to the Father, the Son and the Spirit respectively. The work of the Spirit included thanks "because you use the bread and wine, so that they may become for us the body and blood of Christ". The latter wording is reminiscent of the Roman Quam oblationem, but the prayer, like "A", presupposed the action of the Spirit without any explicit request. The Prayer could end in an ascription of glory or the Sanctus.

(4) Consisting of several paragraphs with the congregational response "Our praise will never end", this prayer also had three alternative thanksgivings for redemption. The anamnesis included a reference to the Institution Narrative, and asked

As we eat and drink together
we ask that by the Holy Spirit's power
Christ who died for us may live in us
so that we may live for him.

This prayer also ended with the Sanctus.

(5) The thanksgiving here was for life and access to God through Christ. It incorporated part of the Institution Narrative, and referring to Christ's sacrifice, and his action at the Supper, asked God to "blend your action with ours so that we may be united with Christ". Again, this prayer ended with the Sanctus.

In this collection, the compilers accepted the traditional outline of the West Syrian anaphora, and also incorporated experimentation with the Sanctus. It will be a debatable point as to how successful the compilers were in modernizing the anaphora and its concepts, especially in the anamnesis and epiklesis. However, they did what no other modern English revision had done, which was to grapple with the question of hermeneutics. If it had been possible to combine this collection with **An Order of Public Worship,** the combined impact should have provided an exciting liturgical catalyst for all English speaking churches; few other compilations have been as adventurous as these two Congregational books.

Some Unpublished local rites, 1965-1973

The cost of printing books is such that few congregations can afford to publish their own service books, as was possible in the 1920's and 1930's. Duplicated forms have taken their place. A few local rites have come into our possession, and we consider them very briefly in this chapter.

1. Holy Communion, Bishop's Stortford Congregational Church 1965.

This order was compiled by Dr. J. K. Gregory for use in his own Church; Dr. Gregory was a member of the Worship Committee which produced the 1970 order, and of the group which compiled **Contemporary Prayers.** This particular order was cyclostyled so that the congregation had copies and could participate in the responses:

Praise
Biddings
Confession together
Assurance of Pardon
First Lesson
Psalm
Second Lesson
Confession of Faith
Words of Institution
Offering of Gifts
Salutation
Prayer of the Veil
Romans 12:1
Sursum corda, Eucharistic Prayer with congregational responses, ending in the Sanctus.
Lord's Prayer
Sentences
The Sharing
An Act of Praise
Silence
Biddings.

The overall structure was one of Word and Sacrament, though there was no mention of a sermon. As in many of the official and semi-official rites we have considered, the confession came before the ministry of the Word, and the Word consisted of lessons (rather than an explicit Epistle and Gospel) and psalmody. A simple confession of faith was included in imitation of the creed found in most traditional rites:

> The Lord our God is one Lord: the Father Almighty, maker of all things: the Lord Christ Jesus who died for our sins, who now reigns with the Father: the Lord Holy Ghost, promise of Christ, who helps our infirmities: Believing in God, we believe in His Church, in the Holy Scripture, and in Eternal Life. Amen.

The Prayer of the Veil was altered to ask that the worshippers might come towards God's presence "through the sacrifice of Jesus", and that God would accept "our gift" and renew the covenant.

The use of Romans 12:1, and the Eucharistic Prayer with people's responses and ending with the Sanctus is reminiscent of that of St. Mark's-in-the-Bouwerie, New York. [10]

> M: It is truly meet and right, and our bounden duty and our salvation, at all times and in all places to give thanks unto thee O Lord, Holy Father, Almighty Everlasting God: Who hast made the heavens and the earth,

and wonderful are thy works: who hast made man in thine own image, and holdest our soul in life: Who giveth wine to make glad the heart of man, and bread to strengthen his heart: whose mercies are new every morning.

P: Bless the Lord, O my soul
And forget not all his benefits.

M: We give thanks, O Father, for Jesus Christ our Lord: The Word made flesh, who went about doing good: Who hadst the words of eternal life, and came that men might have life: who for the joy that was set before him, endured the cross despising the shame, and now is set down at thy right hand.

P: Thy dying O Christ we remember
Thy rising O Christ we acclaim
Thy reign O Christ we acknowledge
Thy coming O Christ we look for.

M: Wherefore, O God, being unable of our own goodness to offer thee a sacrifice holy and acceptable to thee, we offer thee this remembrance of our Lord's most holy sacrifice, which he hath granted and willed us to make, saying, This do in remembrance of me. And we ask, both that our Doing may truly praise thee, in showing forth thy great goodness to us men: and also that thy Holy Spirit being with us, the bread which we break and the cup of blessing which we bless may be to us a sharing in the fulness of Jesus Christ our Lord.

P: Come Holy Spirit: Bless what we do: Take the things of Christ and show them unto us.

M: Thus we adore thee, Heavenly Father, that Christ may abide in us, and we in Him: that our life be hid(?) with Him in thee: to be made perfect in one, and to bring forth much fruit. And with angels and archangels, with all the company of heaven, we laud and magnify thy glorious name, evermore praising thee and saying

P: Holy -

The Prayer incorporated the Eastern-type of Anamnesis acclamations, and a very simple but effective epiklesis was found on the lips of the congregation in addition to the petition by the minister. The Eucharistic action, "this remembrance", was offered to God, again indicating that such terminology was not in conflict with Congregational thinking.

Some biddings to thankfulness, intercession and discipleship came after the communion. No blessing was provided in the text of this service.

2. The Liturgy, Congregational Church, Ormskirk Street, St. Helens.

This rite was compiled by the Rev. Wynford Evans, and was an adaptation of the Taizé rite for a parish situation. All the material is taken from the Taizé rite, mainly that for weekdays, with some from the Sunday rite, and the proper preface for Maundy Thursday. The outline was as follows:

Invocation
Confession
Collect for Day
Hymn
Old Testament Lesson
Chant
Epistle
Gospel
Hymn
Sermon
Profession of Faith
Intercessions
Offertory Hymn
Versicles and Responses (Sursum corda - preface)
Sanctus
Prayers (Institution, Memorial, Invocation and conclusion)
Lord's Prayer
The Fraction
Agnus Dei
Prayer for Peace
The Invitation
Communion (after each line of parishioners had received, they were dismissed with "Go in peace")
Prayer of Thanksgiving
Post communion hymn
The Blessing

The Rev. W. Evans has commented:

> I was concerned, not only to involve a fairly large number of people, but I was intent that both sexes should play their part and that the age range was faithfully reflected in the participants. Since it was a local arrangement there is no indication that the Psalm was sung

by a youth group and that the content of the intercessions, though the form was prescribed, i.e. The Church, The State, The Nation and All sorts of conditions of men, were left to those who were invited to offer particular intercessions. [11]

3. A Reformed Order of Service, Little Baddow Congregational Church.

At a Church Meeting held on September 28th, 1969 it was agreed that alterations should be made in the order of Morning Worship, and on Sunday October 26th 1969 an order of worship drawn up by the minister, the Rev. John Geyer, M.A. [12] was introduced. This order was in fact an outline for worship, but it was based upon "the pattern of classical reformed tradition". The outline was as follows: [13]

Biddings	Scripture Sentences through which God calls us to worship.
Prayer	Praise for God's work in Creation. Confession, appropriate to the Fall of Man
Assurance of Pardon	
Hymn	
Old Testament Lesson	Preparation for the coming of Christ.
Children's Address	
Hymn	
Children leave to attend Junior Church	
Epistle	The Apostles' witness to Christ.
Gospel	The Saviour speaks.
Sermon	The Spirit interprets the Word of Scripture that has been read, and makes it contemporary.
Hymn	
Notices, Offering Dedication	The offering of ourselves joined with the sacrifice of Christ.
Blessing	
Hymn	
Prayers of Intercession and Thanksgiving	The joining of our prayers with those of Christ.

Lord's Prayer	Thanksgiving for all the works of God, and especially for redemption.
COMMUNION of Bread and Wine	The Word become flesh; the Communion of Saints.
Hymn	
Benediction	

Appended notes explained that the Children's Address does not belong to traditional Reformed worship, and that in recent practice there was frequently only one reading from the New Testament. Communion was once a month, and the blessing after the notices, offering and dedication, was only used when there was a communion, allowing non-communicants to withdraw. When there was no communion, the rest of the service was followed, being an Ante-communion. In this practice, as in the structure of the rite, Calvin and Knox were very much the criteria.

4. An Order for the Lord's Supper, Paddington Chapel 1971.

This cyclostyled order was prepared by the minister of Paddington Chapel, the Reverend W. E. C. Sewell, who also assisted in the compilation of **Contemporary Prayers.** Compiled for use on Maundy Thursday, it was an adaptation of the liturgy prepared at the ONE conference at Swanwick, 1970, which attempted to bring together Protestant and the radical Catholic traditions. [**14**]

Opening hymn
Grace
Confession (in the form of biddings)
Assurance of Pardon
Scripture readings
Sermon
Intercessions
The Offering (place on Table beside the bread and wine)
Sursum corda, Eucharistic Prayer, with congregational parts, ending in the Sanctus
Hymn
Peace
Communion
Hymn
Blessing

The grace with salutation is the opening of the Roman Catholic rite, and the confession constructed with biddings is probably based upon that in St. Mark's-in-the-Bouwerie. The intercessions incorporated the song Kum-ba-ya.

The offering included some prayers, being based upon those in the Roman Catholic rite which in turn are based upon Jewish Berakoth. Like Dr. Gregory's Eucharistic Prayer, this order divided the Prayer between minister and people, having thanksgiving for creation and for Christ, the Institution Narrative, an Epiklesis, a petition for unity, and concluded in the Sanctus. The Epiklesis is of interest:

> Send your Holy Spirit among us
> that this bread and this wine
> may become for us the body and blood
> of your Son,
> the promise of eternal life.

It is similar to that found in the Roman Catholic rite, Eucharistic Prayer II, though in this Congregational Prayer, God is asked to send his Spirit upon the people, not upon the elements, and so ably expresses Calvin's teaching within the traditional form of the epiklesis.

The use of Kum-ba-ya indicates the occasional nature of this rite, and it would hardly stand regular use. However, a very similar order entitled "An Order for the Lord's Supper or EUCHARIST according to the Reformed Tradition" was produced for more general use. The main difference in this second order was the inclusion of a more traditional form of intercession (being intercession V of the 1970 **An Order of Public Worship**, with slight amendments) and the omission of the offertory prayers.

William Sewell has explained these two rites as an attempt to bring home to the Reformed tradition, where it rightly belongs, the thing which post-Vatican II Catholic liturgy has attempted to do much more vigorously, namely to show that the Eucharist is something which the whole congregation does corporately. [15]

5. Easter Morning Communion Service, Enderby United Reformed Church 1973.

Composed for the former Congregational Church at Enderby by the minister, the Reverend A. C. White, M.A., this cyclostyled service was for the early morning Easter Eucharist.

The order was divided into three parts: The Approach; The Gospel; and The Communion. The Approach consisted of an opening versicle and response, hymn, the Easter Anthem (Prayer Book) as versicles and responses, and prayer for forgiveness. The Gospel consisted of a reading from Matthew 28:1-10, the sermon, intercessions and a hymn. The Communion began with the Eucharistic Prayer with Sursum corda, Sanctus, and was followed by the Lord's Prayer. After the communion came a hymn, with a short dismissal and the blessing. The Eucharistic Prayer seems to have been based upon that of the **Book of Common Prayer** from the Sursum corda, preface and proper preface, and the Sanctus. These were provided on the cyclostyled sheet. After this the remainder of the prayer was "ad lib" with thanksgiving for creation and redemption, for the resurrection, the work of the Holy Spirit, the life of the Church militant and triumphant, and a prayer that by the work of the Holy Spirit the worshippers might in sharing the elements, share in the life of Christ himself. **[16]**

The order was in traditional language, and in general was a precis of the Eucharistic rite found in the post-1948 Congregational books.

6. Integrated Service with Communion. The Holy in the Common. United Reformed Church, Aberdeen Road, Croydon 1973.

This service was compiled for use in the former Congregational Church, Aberdeen Road, Croydon, by the late minister, the Reverend A. B. Clark, and his wife, Mrs. P. M. Clark. It was a thematic service, and not intended for regular worship. It was a service of Word and Sacrament, based upon the theme of "The Holy in the Common", and was inspired by the works of Alan Watts and de Chardin. The outline of the service was as follows:

Opening verse
Hymn
Prayer and Lord's Prayer
Notices and Offering
Hymn
Reading of Script: The Holy and the common in Hebrew Religion
Hymn
Reading of Script: The Holy and the common in the development of the Hebrew nation
Reading from Isaiah
Hymn
Reading of Script: The Holy and the common in the life of Jesus
Luke 4:14-19
Hymn
Reading of Script: The Holy and the common in communion
Prayer
Partaking of the bread and wine
Meditation

Silent Prayer
Hymn. Communion Offering
Benediction

The service has some points worth noting. The traditional sermon was replaced by the various scripts which supplemented the readings from Scripture. However, although the service combined Word and Sacrament, there seems to have been no reference to either the traditional Reformed rite, nor the classical rites. This is illustrated by the "Eucharistic" Prayer, where there was no Sursum corda or Sanctus:

> Father, we offer to you praise and thanksgiving for all life in your world and for the privilege of being alive in it in such times as this. We thank you for your trust in us to work with you to build your kingdom in the earth. You cannot do without us, and we cannot act without your guidance and inspiration. Give us the strength to resist greed and selfishness, pride and contempt and to work humbly for the good of our fellow men. Help us truly to see the Holy in the common and to work to bring in the day when man shall toil for the common good, when commerce shall be fair, all work shall be prayer, when men shall again rejoice in the things that their hands have made. In the name of your carpenter son we ask this. Amen.

The Prayer shows complete independence of the traditional forms and their themes, there being no mention here of the elements or for a true communion. The theme of "The Holy and the Common" itself suggests that there might be a tendency towards immanentism, and this is true of this Prayer; there is a stress on man's part in building the Kingdom of God, reminiscent of the theme of the "New Theology", and the statement that God "cannot do without us" appears to contradict completely the 1967 Congregational Church in England and Wales **A Declaration of Faith**, that God "needs nothing other than himself to be what he is". The words which accompanied the communion regarded the Eucharist as symbolic of Christ giving himself for men, and as an act of loving fellowship and dedication for service, themes which echo the orders of **A Manual for Ministers.** Certainly there seems to be no trace of the influence of the post-1948 books in this thematic rite.

No conclusions of much weight can be drawn from these six orders considered here, for it would be erroneous to suggest that they are in any way representative. We may simply conclude that: in orders 1, 2, 4 and 5 the influence of modern liturgical thought is quite evident. However, since the compilers of 1,

2 and 4 were also concerned with the compilation of **An Order of Public Worship** 1970, it is to be expected that their own rites should not be dissimilar to those of the 1970 order. With order 3 we find a deliberate attempt to resurrect the Reformed pattern of worship, and the structure adopted does not preclude the use of classical material such as a Eucharistic Prayer with Sursum corda and Sanctus; Word and Sacrament has been restored as the norm for worship. In order 6, allowing for its occasional character, the impression given that the type of un-historical and un-liturgical thinking which produced **A Manual for Ministers** still persists, despite the "Genevan" revival and the Ecumenical consensus on liturgy.

NOTES

1. Letter to the writer from the Rev. Caryl Micklem, 26th May 1972.

2. **Contemporary Prayers,** 11-12.

3. Ibid., 8.

4. Letter cited.

5. Ibid.

6. E.g., Anglican-Roman Catholic Agreement on the Eucharist, 1971.

7. Micklem and Gregory were members of both Committees.

8. Letter cited.

9. The final text of "A Declaration of Faith" is to be found in **Christian Confidence**, S.P.C.K., Theological Collections, 14.

10. Text in J. A. T. Robinson, **But that I can't believe!** 1967. This was based upon Dr. H. Boone Porter's reworking of Hippolytus. See Robinson, 108-112. The year was 1965. For Dr. Gregory's motive for following the pattern of a prayer with the Sanctus at the end, see Chapter 17.

11. Letter to the writer, 7th December 1976.

12. The Rev. Geyer is in fact a distinguished Hebrew scholar.

13. A Reformed Order of Service, including the sermon which accompanied its introduction, are available in printed form.

14. Letter to the writer 23rd July 1975.

15. Letter cited.

16. Letter to the writer, August 1975.

Chapter Thirteen

A UNITED REFORMED EUCHARIST

The United Reformed Church celebrates the gospel sacrament of the Lord's Supper.

The Faith of the United Reformed Church, in **The Scheme of Union,** p. 23.

Since the first series of joint talks in 1933, the Congregational Churches and the Presbyterian Church of England had had an extremely close relationship. In 1951 both denominations had approved a statement in which they "do hereby declare before God and the world, that sharing a common faith and inheriting together the traditions of Reformed Churchmanship, they do now enter into a new and solemn relationship with one another, covenanting together to take counsel with one another in all matters of common concern". [1] The frequent consultations and practical collaboration which resulted from this statement paved the way for the union of the two denominations; in 1972 the United Reformed Church came into being.

Not all of the Churches of the Congregational Church in England and Wales entered the new United Reformed Church. A minority who wished to continue with a form of independent church polity formed the Congregational Federation. Thus both the United Reformed Church and the Congregational Federation can claim to be the direct successors of the Congregational Church in England and Wales.

The Congregational Federation has taken no steps to produce a new liturgical compilation for the use of its federated congregations; the 1969 edition of **A Book of Services and Prayers** and the 1970 **An Order of Public Worship** remain the last liturgical orders which may be said to have any direct connection with the Federation.

On the other hand, the United Reformed Church has produced a new Eucharistic rite, which, like the **Westminster Directory** of 1645, brings together both Congregational and Presbyterian liturgical traditions. Since most of the drafting of this new rite was placed in the experienced hands of the Reverend J. M. Todd, the United Reformed Church order has a good claim as the direct successor to all major Congregational orders since 1948.

At the first meeting of the United Reformed Church General Assembly in May 1973, it was recommended:

> the Assembly instructs the Doctrine and Worship Committee to prepare material for inclusion in a Service Book for use in the United Reformed Church, and to consider the preparation of services for congregational use. [2]

The Doctrine and Worship Committee, under the Chairmanship of the distinguished hymnologist, Dr. Erik Routley, had in fact been engaged in the preparation of a Eucharistic liturgy of Word and Sacrament since 1972. The final form was published under the title of **Book of Order for Worship**, 1974.

As in many other spheres of church life, the Congregationalists and the Presbyterians had co-operated in matters liturgical for some years before the 1972 union. There had been cross-representation on the committees responsible for the 1970 **An Order of Public Worship** and the 1968 **The Presbyterian Service Book.** Added to this, the Congregational Worship Committee and the Presbyterian Committee on Public Worship and Aids to Devotion had co-operated in the publication of Symposia of worship papers resulting from the 1968 Uppsala World Council of Church Report on worship. [3] As might be expected, a new Eucharistic liturgy would to some extent be based upon the last orders approved for use within the respective denominations, the 1970 Congregational order, and the 1968 Presbyterian book.

The ecumenical character of the 1970 **An Order of Public Worship** has already been considered at some length. In comparison, the 1968 Presbyterian book, which was a complete book of services, was an extremely conservative work. It was a mild revision of the previous Presbyterian book of 1948, and had taken ten years to complete. Draft services had been presented to the Committee and these had been revised several times before being presented in batches to the Presbyterian General Assembly. By 1968 much of the earlier material was already out of date. The Committee convener, the Reverend Norman Leak, has commented:

> What had once seemed improvements on earlier services now appeared, to those still left on the committee, disappointingly out-of-date. True there were two services with the "you" form of address to God, but the remainder, whilst less wordy and archaic, still were formal and traditional. . . Now we had little pride in it and watched its emergence with relief rather than gratification. [4]

Leak's comment applies particularly well to the main communion order. It was the main communion order of the 1948 book with only minor revisions, and the latter had in turn been compiled under the long and influential shadow of the sister Church, the Church of Scotland. Appearing in 1968, it showed few signs of either the ecumenical consensus on Eucharistic liturgy or of contemporary liturgical scholarship. However, the remarks of the convener indicate that the committee was well aware of this fact, and the conservative nature of the Presbyterian rite meant that it took a secondary place in the formulation of the new United Reformed Church order.

However, the new order was not simply to be the 1970 Congregational order with a few concessions to the Presbyterians; two other factors played an important part in determining the shape of the new Eucharist.

(1) Both denominations were members of the JLG, and in 1972 the Group had produced **Initiation and Eucharist,** being some short essays on the structure of the baptismal and Eucharistic rites. Since the JLG represented Churches with differing rites, the document could be no more than a statement of what all the member Churches had in common. Nevertheless, it did make certain significant points, and proposed an outline for the Eucharistic liturgy.

The JLG document queried the four action shape argued by Dix. It noted that the seven-fold action of the Eucharist in the New Testament (which becomes nine-fold if the sayings of the interpretative words are included) as preserved by the Baptists and the Churches of Christ was rather artificial since the Lord's Supper is not a repetition of the Last Supper. Equally, Dix's four-fold action might be queried as artificial; from a theological perspective

> the basic action is seen to be twofold. "He blessed (or gave thanks) . . . and gave". The "taking" is a necessary if solemn prelude to the "blessing". The "breaking" is a necessary practical prelude to the "giving"--which is itself in order that a sharing may take place. <u>It is therefore Thanksgiving and Communion that constitute the essential pillars of the eucharist.</u> [5]

It is worth noting here that the JLG document endorsed the view of A. J. B. Higgins that the fraction was not an important symbolic action of the Supper. [6]

According to the JLG, there was no mandatory position for the Words of Institution; they may be read as a warrant, as part of the Eucharistic Prayer, or before the communion itself. The basic elements and progression of the Eucharistic Prayer are:

> the proclamation and recital of the mighty acts of God in creation and redemption
> the anamnesis (memorial) with the bread and wine of the crucified and risen Lord "until he come"
> the petition that, by the power of the Holy Spirit, what we do may be united to the perfect sacrifice of Christ and so accepted by God that in communion with our Lord we may receive the benefits of his passion and victory. [7]

While acknowledging ample room for diversity of "use", the JLG proposed a possible basic pattern:

> Act of Praise and Adoration
> Act of Confession and Assurance of Pardon (this element may come here or after the Intercession)
> Collect (this element may come after the Sermon)
> Scripture Readings (OT and NT with psalmody if desired)
> Sermon
> Hymn of Response (or Collect)
> Intercession
> Presentation (with hymn/psalm if desired)
> The Taking
> The Thanksgiving (controlled by the Narrative of Institution)
> Sursum corda
> Recital of the Mighty Acts of God and Sanctus
> Anamnesis
> Petition
> The Fraction
> The Communion
> Hymn/Prayer
> The Dismissal [8]

The Lord's Prayer could be used in a number of places.

Since both Congregationalists and Presbyterians were represented in the drawing up of this statement, it provided them with an agreed pattern for procedure, one which had an English ecumenical basis. J. M. Todd in commenting upon the 1974 United Reformed Church order has said:

> A comparison between what is said in that report (JLG **Initiation and Eucharist**) about "The Structure of the Eucharist" and the Order we have prepared will show how closely the two are in agreement. It could be said that we have clothed the bare bones of the structure outlined by the JLG with flesh and blood, and so made an outline into a liturgy. [9]

(2) A second factor which helped to determine the 1974 order was the question of language. The 1970 Congregational order had been compiled in language which tried to avoid archaisms, but which had retained "thee" and "thy" in addressing God. The appearance of **Contemporary Prayers for Public Worship** 1967 had indicated that some Congregationalists were in favor of modern language throughout the service. The Presbyterian book had used the "you" form of address for God in two services, but the Eucharist was in the traditional thee/thou language. However, other Churches were beginning to adopt modern English for liturgical worship. The Methodist Sunday Service had printed two forms of service, one in traditional language and the other in modern English. The Roman Catholic Church in English speaking countries adopted modern English, and a body known as the International Committee on English in the Liturgy (ICEL) was set up to produce standard English texts. In Series 2 the Anglican Church retained traditional language, but in 1968 the Church of England Liturgical Commission produced **Modern Liturgical Texts**, indicating that future revision would be in contemporary English. In 1969 an international ecumenical body was formed to attempt to work out agreed forms for English liturgical texts, known as the International Consultation on English Texts (ICET). In 1970 this body published a set of agreed texts which included for the Eucharist and Salutation, Gloria in excelsis, Nicene Creed, Sursum corda, Sanctus and the Lord's Prayer.

The adoption of modern English in worship, and in particular the "you" form of address for God, has provoked debate in most Churches, and the United Reformed Church has been no exception. An interesting exchange took place between the Reverend C. E. B. Cranfield, Reader in Theology, University of Durham, and Caryl Micklem, a co-editor of **Contemporary Prayers for Public Worship**, in Outlook (the Magazine of the Presbyterian Church of England). [10] Cranfield pleaded for the retention of "Thou" in addressing God, on the grounds:

> first because the oneness of God is so absolutely fundamental to Christian theology that it is perverse not to use the unambiguous singular which our English language possesses, when addressing Him, and, secondly, because the second person singular is more adequate to express the intensely serious and personal nature of

> our relationship with God than is the polite plural--the phrase "I-thou relationship" surely expresses something which the words "I-you relationship" would not convey at all clearly." [11]

Micklem defended the use of the "you" form of address, being unconvinced that God is more reduced in stature by being talked to as one would talk to one's friend than he is by being treated as an antique. [12] The compilers of the new order did not wish to produce a text which would be out of date, nor one which, because of its language, some sections of the new Church would not use. They therefore adopted the Methodist solution, providing two texts within one service:

> Within a single order of worship we have printed prayers and other texts in more traditional and in more contemporary language in parallel columns, the traditional on the left and the contemporary on the right of each page. We anticipate that it will be the contemporary version that will increasingly be used, but there are still many ministers and congregations who prefer the older form. . . The more traditional material was drawn mainly from the **Presbyterian Service Book** (1968) and from the Congregational **Order of Public Worship** (1970). The contemporary material was newly written, apart from ecumenical texts like the Gloria in excelsis and the Sanctus, where the ICET text has been used, and one short quotation in the eucharistic prayer from **Contemporary Prayers for Public Worship.** [13]

The United Reformed Eucharist consisted, then, of two texts, one in traditional language using material from the 1970 and 1968 orders (cited as Trad. text) and a second new composition in modern English using the ICET texts (cited as Mod. text). The underlying structure of the rite was that set out by the JLG.

Most of the drafting of the 1974 order was the work of J. M. Todd; [14] the drafts were subsequently revised in the light of comments from the Doctrine and Worship Committee--particularly after a meeting at Cambridge, 9-11 January 1973--and from members of the JLG, in particular Canon R. C. D. Jasper, Chairman of the Church of England Liturgical Commission and Secretary of JLG, and Neville Clark and Stephen Winward, Baptist members of JLG. [15]

An explanation of the various parts of the order was given in a series of notes preceding the service; a further valuable analysis has been given in an article by J. M. Todd. [16]

The service of the Word, entitled "The Word and the Prayers" begins with Scripture Sentences as a call to worship, as in the 1970 order. These may be seasonal or related to the theme of the day. The Prayer of Approach may be said before or after the first hymn or psalm, and the Confession and Assurance of Pardon remain at the beginning as in 1970, 1968 and as in the Roman Catholic Mass. Both the Gloria in excelsis and the Collect of the day retain their 1970 position. The Calendar and Lectionary was that of the JLG, though a New Testament reading (1968) may replace the Epistle and Gospel (1970).

In the Trad. text, the Collect for Purity occurs in 1970 and 1968, the Confession is based on that of 1968, the Assurance of Pardon from 1970, nos. 2 and 5. The Intercessions are the second set provided in 1970. The Intercessions in the Mod. text are similar to those found in the Anglican Series 3 Eucharist, with suggested topics followed by a summary petition. In both texts the Intercessions could be read as one continuous prayer, or in bidding prayer style with versicle and response after each section. In the January 1973 Draft, the following Litany had also been provided:

In peace let us pray to the Lord.

For the peace that he gives
and for the renewal of our life in Christ
let us pray to the Lord:
Lord hear our prayer. (and so after each bidding)

For the peace of the whole world
and for the unity of the Church and of mankind

For all ministers and members of the Church
and for their faithfulness in witness and service

For the nations, their rulers and peoples,
and for justice and goodwill among men

For all who exercise influence and authority
that our government may be righteous and our liberties preserved

For the welfare of this town, of our neighbours
and of the communities to which we belong

For all who spend themselves in the service of others
that they may be faithful and compassionate

For the sick and the suffering
that they may be comforted and healed

For the hungry, the homeless and the unemployed
that their need may be met

For the dying and the bereaved
that they may find peace in Christ

For our families and our friends
that they may be kept in safety and in joy

For ourselves and for all men
that with all who have served Christ and are now at rest
we may share the life of his kingdom

Help, save and have mercy upon us, Lord our God;
through Jesus Christ our Lord. Amen.

The second part of the rite was entitled "The Thanksgiving and The Communion", suggested by the JLG report.

The section from the Invitation and the Gracious Words to the taking of the bread and wine seems to have been influenced by the 1968 order, and the usage found in previous Congregational orders rather than the 1970 order.

1970	1974	1968
		Offertory
	Invitation and Gracious Words	Invitation and Gracious Words
	Peace	
		Prayer of the Veil
Presentation of gifts	Offertory. Hymn	
Hymn		
(Words of Institution)	Words of Institution	Words of Institution
Peace		
	Taking the bread and wine	Taking the bread and wine
Thanksgiving	Thanksgiving	Thanksgiving

Compared with the 1970 rite, the Peace has been brought back to a position before the Offertory, as in Justin Martyr and Hippolytus, and the Anglican Series 2 and Series 3.

In the January 1973 Draft the Peace was much fuller:

The Peace

The minister says:

> The Lord says to us: If, when you are bringing your gift to the altar, you suddenly remember that your brother has a grievance against you, leave your gift where it is before the altar. First go and make your peace with your brother, and only then come back and offer your gift.

Then the minister says:

> The peace of the Lord be with you all.

and all may respond by saying, each to his neighbour:

> The peace of the Lord.
>
> and a handclasp may be given.

From the comments made on the Draft, and from conversation about it, the question was raised whether or not the handclasp might cause some embarrassment. [12] In the 1974 order the Peace was merely given verbally by the minister, without the long scripture sentence:

> The Peace
>
> The minister says: The peace of the Lord Jesus Christ be with you all.

It is governed by the introductory notes where it suggested that it may be passed amongst the congregation by a handclasp.

The rite distinguished between the uncovering or preparing of the bread and wine at the offertory, and "The Taking of the Bread and Wine" before the Eucharistic Prayer. This apparent duplication has been queried in a review of the rite by Stuart Gibbons:

> . . . in the sense required by the institution narrative the elements have already been "taken" for the purposes of the sacrament when they were placed on the table. Is not the offertory the corporate ritual by which they are taken into the eucharistic action? For it is the Church corporately which follows the example of its Lord. [18]

In defence Todd has explained:

> We distinguish between the Offertory, when the elements are laid on the Table, or uncovered if they have been placed there before the service begins, and the Taking

> of the Bread and Wine. At the offertory all is made ready for the actions which follow. Then, as the Lord Jesus took bread and gave thanks, the minister either takes the bread and the cup into his hands or simply touches them to indicate that we are following the example of Christ with this bread and this cup. The minister says: "in the name of the Lord Jesus Christ, and following his example, we take this bread and this cup, and give thanks to God". The JLG Report on the structure of the Eucharist distinguished between "Presentation" and "Taking":
>
>> The Church "provides", and often the people's representatives "bring", so that the president may "take" and set apart the bread and wine. (**Initiation and Eucharist**, p. 25.) [**19**]

Indeed, the JLG outline suggests "Presentation" followed immediately by "The Taking" and explains "this complex action" as the hinge from Word to Supper; on the one hand the gifts of money as well as bread and wine are a response to the Word proclaimed; on the other hand, what is brought and set apart makes the Supper possible. [**20**] Yet at the same time JLG asserts that theologically, this is not part of the basic Eucharistic action. [**21**]

The same distinction between the bringing of the bread and wine and the taking is found in the Anglican Series 3 rite. There, the collection of alms is optional, suggesting that it need not take place at every service, or could take place at another point in the service. The term "Offertory" is avoided, the section being entitled "The Taking of the Bread and Wine". The bread and wine are brought to the table, and an extract from 1 Chron. 29 may be read. Then the President is directed to take the bread and wine before starting the Eucharistic Prayer. The Liturgical Commission explained:

> We have therefore provided a heading and rubric for a "taking" before the Thanksgiving begins; and we have distinguished this from the preparing of the table. At this point of "taking" we suggest that the president should hold the vessels containing the elements above the table to mark the beginning of the sacramental action proper. [**22**]

This arrangement was an attempt to remove the confusion between the offertory of money and the taking of the bread and wine. It has been defended on the ground that the preparation for the passover (the bringing the bread and wine) is quite distinct from Jesus' taking the bread and wine at the Supper. [**23**] Others have argued that the taking or preparing the bread and wine is purely functional; the important "taking" is after the thanksgiving and before the fraction. [24] However, since apart from the optional extract from 1 Chron. 29, nothing is said at the bringing of the bread and wine or at the taking, and since they follow one another, the distinction which is made is hardly prominent, or likely to be noticed.

The same cannot be said for the United Reformed rite. The term "offertory" is used for the collection of alms and for the uncovering or preparation of the bread and wine. Two Offertory prayers from the 1970 order were included which present the gifts to God. Once again this raises the question of whether God wishes for any other presentation as a response to his Word than ourselves? Furthermore, since we do not commence the service of the Word by offering to God the gifts of paper and print which he might like to use for his Word, there seems little justification for such prominence given here to the gifts of bread and wine, and money. Again, the apparent duplication of preparing and the taking is made more prominent by the intervening Institution Narrative, and the fact that the "taking" is accompanied by words, suggesting that, contrary to the JLG statement, it has a theological significance. The result is a five-fold shape: Preparing, Taking, Thanksgiving, Fraction (which involves another "taking") and the Communion. This section could be made tidier if the order reverted to former Congregational practice of placing the "offertory" of money after the communion, immediately before the dismissal and blessing. The preparation of the bread and wine could then immediately precede the Eucharistic Prayer. When only a service of the Word was celebrated, the order would be:

Intercessions
Offertory. Hymn
Dismissal and blessing

When the full Eucharist was celebrated,

Gracious Words
Peace
Institution Narrative
The Taking
Eucharistic Prayer
Fraction
Communion
Offertory. Hymn
Dismissal and blessing

At the taking of the bread and wine
the minister says:

> In the name of the Lord Jesus Christ, and following his example, we take this bread and this cup, and give thanks to God.

In the January 1973 Draft the minister was directed to take the bread and the cup into his hands. This was criticized by Caryl Micklem as detracting from the actions of taking at the fraction; at most the minister should touch them. [25] The rubric was removed from the final order, though a note before the service suggested that the minister take the elements or touch them, "to indicate that we are following the example of Christ with <u>this</u> bread and <u>this</u> cup".

Between the Offertory and the Taking of the bread and wine, the Committee, maintaining both Congregational and Presbyterian practice, placed the Institution Narrative to be read as a warrant. A rubric allowed it to be postponed until the fraction.

In the 1970 Congregational order three Eucharistic Prayers out of the six provided had contained the Institution Narrative, and thus the order had allowed three positions for it: as a warrant, within the Eucharistic Prayer, and/or at the fraction. The notes at the beginning of the 1974 order reiterated the 1970 position:

> There should be unfailing use of the narrative of the institution when the Lord's Supper is celebrated. It may be read as a warrant before the eucharistic prayer, and/or used at the breaking of the bread; or it may be included within the eucharistic prayer.

Although this note allowed for the use of the narrative within the Eucharistic Prayer, neither of the two provided contained it. As Stuart Gibbons has pointed out:

> It is inconsistent that the notes permit the institution narrative to be "read as a warrant before the eucharistic prayer, and/or used at the breaking of the bread, or included within the eucharistic prayer" (before the anamnesis or "doing-in-remembrance) - but in the prayer itself only the "before" and "after" positions have been indicated. Consequently, few will include the narrative within the prayer, in association with the anamnesis which logically flows from it. Yet this central point of reference for the eucharistic action did form part of the prayer in the ancient liturgies, and remains there in the revised liturgies of most traditions today. [26]

In the January 1973 Draft a third Eucharistic Prayer had been provided which did include the narrative, thus providing an ecumenical link with other traditions. It is surprising, therefore, that this prayer did not find a place in the final order. A reason for its omission has been given by J. M. Todd:

> In the notes preceding the Order we have referred to the possibility of including it (i.e. the narrative) in the prayer. We had hoped that it would have been possible to print in an appendix a canon prepared for ecumenical use and acceptable to all the Churches, including the Roman Catholic, on which the Joint Liturgical Group was known to be working. This text was not available in time; but we allowed the note to stand. [27]

In view of the earlier Draft, we may conclude that the third Eucharistic Prayer was removed, the intention being to replace it with the ecumenically agreed prayer. This would answer Gibbon's criticism. However, one wonders why the original prayer was not allowed to stand until the JLG Eucharistic Prayer was available; and how will the latter now be incorporated into the United Reformed Church order? In fact, there appears to be a clear preference for the traditional Reformed position for the narrative; the Doctrine and Worship Committee reported to the General Assembly,

> a distinctive feature of Reformed Church Liturgies has in the past been the placing of the Narrative of Institution before the Eucharistic part of the service as a "Warrant". Some modern liturgies in Britain have put these words within the Thanksgiving Prayer. The Committee would offer the guidance that there should be liberty to vary practice, but that normally the Narrative of Institution should either retain its place before the Thanksgiving Prayer as a Warrant, or be used after the prayer at the Breaking of the Bread. In any case, there should be unfailing use of the Narrative of Institution. [28]

We may compare this statement with words of Todd:

> Our preference is for the Narrative to be read as a warrant: that is the Reformed tradition, and we think it is a good one. Consecration is by the Word and prayer (indeed by the whole sacramental action) and the Narrative is Word rather than prayer. Now that there is widespread agreement among the Churches that it is not a consecration formula its use as a warrant is acceptable to many whose tradition has been to include it in the prayer. [29]

Certainly the JLG report stated, there is no compelling theological reason for the narrative to be within the prayer. But since other major English Churches--Anglican, Roman Catholic and Methodist--

do include it within the Eucharistic Prayer, it would have been more ecumenical, and less denominational, to have included a Eucharistic Prayer with the narrative. As Gibbons suggested, the provision for only the traditional Reformed usage will mean that few will bother to insert the narrative into the prayer, and members of other Churches will also be discouraged from using the rite. [**30**]

This narrative provided, 1 Cor. 11:23-26 was that of the RSV; the NEB "memorial" in verses 24 and 25 was thought to suggest a war memorial or plaque on a wall rather than an act of remembrance in the biblical sense of making something in the past effective in the present. [**31**]

The two Eucharistic Prayers provided, one in traditional language, and one in modern language, had the structure of Dialogue, Thanksgiving, Proper Preface, Sanctus, Benedictus, Anamnesis, Epiklesis, Oblation of praise and Doxology. The third Eucharistic Prayer which featured in the January 1973 Draft, and which began at the Post-sanctus, was as follows:

Lord God,
by what we do here
in remembrance of Christ
we celebrate
  his life and ministry
  his death and resurrection;
we declare
  that he is Lord of all;
and we prepare for
  his coming in his kingdom.

We do what he did
on the night in which he was betrayed.
He took bread
and gave thanks.
He broke the bread
and gave it to his disciples,
  saying,
"This is my body which is for you:
do this in remembrance of me".

In the same way
he took the cup
  saying,
"This cup is the new covenant in my blood;
do this as often as you drink it,
in remembrance of me".

We pray that
through your Holy Spirit
this bread may be for us
 the body of Christ
and this wine
 the blood of Christ.

Accept our sacrifice of praise;
and as we eat and drink
what you provide
unite us to Christ
as one body in him
and give us strength
to serve you in the world.

And to you,
one holy and eternal God,
Father, Son and Holy Spirit,
we give praise and glory,
now and for ever. Amen.

Apart from the eccentricity here of what appears to be the anamnesis preceding the Institution Narrative, [32] it followed the vaguely "West-Syrian" pattern of the final texts. The experimentation with the Sanctus, and the "Western" pattern of prayer found in the 1970 order was abandoned.

The thanksgiving included creation and redemption, with eight seasonal special thanksgivings: Advent, Christmas, Epiphany, Lent Passiontide, Easter, Ascension and Pentecost. In the mod. text, the ICET Sursum corda, Sanctus, and Benedictus were used, though the Committee were not entirely happy with the ICET Sanctus which attaches "Lord" to the three-fold "Holy" to produce "Holy, Holy, Holy Lord". [33] The Benedictus was absent in the earlier January 1973 Draft.

A doctrine of Eucharistic sacrifice and presence is clearly expressed in the statement of faith of the United Reformed Church:

> When in obedience to the Lord's command his people show forth his sacrifice on the cross by the bread broken and the wine outpoured for them to eat and drink, he himself, risen and ascended, is present and gives himself to them for their spiritual nourishment and growth in grace. United with him and with the whole Church on earth and in heaven, his people gathered at his table present their sacrifice of thanksgiving and renew the offering of themselves, and rejoice in the promise of his coming in glory. [34]

It is this doctrine, we may presume, which the anamnesis and epiklesis attempt to express:

Holy Father
we do this in remembrance
of Christ
we celebrate his perfect
sacrifice on the Cross
and his glorious resurrection
and ascension;
and as we look for the coming
of his Kingdom,
we set before thee
this bread and this wine
as the thank-offering
of thy people.

We pray thee
to sanctify with thy Spirit
both us and these thy gifts
that they may be for us
the body and blood of Christ
and that we, receiving them
in faith and with thanksgiving,
may be united in thy Church
and strengthened for thy service.

Lord God,
accept our sacrifice of praise;
and by thy power and love
make us and all things new;
through Jesus Christ our Lord
to whom with thee, the Father
and the Holy Spirit, one God
be glory for ever and ever. AMEN

Holy Lord God,
by what we do here in remembrance
of Christ
we celebrate his perfect
sacrifice on the Cross,
and his glorious resurrection
and ascension;
we declare that he is Lord of all;

and we prepare for his coming
in his Kingdom

We pray that
through your Holy Spirit
this bread may be for us
the body of Christ
and this wine
the blood of Christ.

Accept our sacrifice of praise
and as we eat and drink
at his command
unite us to Christ
as one body in him
and give us strength
to serve you in the world.

And to you
one holy and eternal God,
Father, Son and Holy Spirit,
we give praise and glory
now and for ever. AMEN

A rather different text for these prayers was given in the January 1973 Draft, the text being similar in each prayer apart from "you" or "thee" (we give the mod. text):

Holy Father in remembrance of
the life and ministry,
the death and victory
of our Saviour Christ,
and looking for the coming of his kingdom,
we set before you
this bread and this wine
as the thank-offering of your people;

and we ask you
to sanctify with your Spirit
both us and these your gifts
that they may be for us
the body and the blood of Christ;
and that we, receiving them
in faith and with thanksgiving,
may be united in the life of your Church
and strengthened for the service of your kingdom.

Lord God,
accept our sacrifice of praise;
and by your power and love
make us and all things new;
through Jesus Christ our Lord,
who, we praise with you, the Father,
and the Holy Spirit, one God,
now and always. Amen.

It will be seen that the Trad. text has retained most of the Draft text, but the Mod. text has used practically the entire proposed third Eucharistic Prayer, minus the Institution Narrative. The Trad. text has also made use of the term "celebrate" from the same source. However, the final form of the anamnesis should perhaps be compared with that in the Anglican Series 3:

> Therefore, heavenly Father, with this bread and this cup we do this in remembrance of him: we celebrate and proclaim his perfect sacrifice made once for all upon the cross, his resurrection from the dead, and his ascension into heaven; and we look for his coming in glory. Accept through him, our great high priest, this our sacrifice of thanks and praise;

In a previous chapter it has been noted that in Series 2 it was originally proposed to include the words from the **Apostolic Tradition**, "we offer thee this bread and cup", but on account of Evangelical dissent, it was replaced by a formula which made "the memorial" of the passion, resurrection and ascension. Many felt that "memorial" did not do justice to the biblical meaning of "remembrance" and its relation to the concept of sacrifice. In Series 3 a new anamnesis was worked out by C. O. Buchanan, K. Ross and R. C. D. Jasper, acceptable to all parties, and capable of several interpretations. The term "offer" in connection with the elements was avoided; "celebrate"--which Cyprian used as an equivalent to "offer"--and "proclaim" the perfect sacrifice does justice to an active and objective sense of "remembrance", and "our sacrifice of praise and thanksgiving" may mean the Eucharistic action, or simply verbal praise. [**35**]

The 1970 Congregational order had had various forms of anamnesis, including the use of the term "offer" in connection with the bread and wine. The 1968 Presbyterian order had followed the Scottish rite which "pleading his eternal sacrifice", "set before" God the elements. Clearly both traditions expressed some concept of Eucharistic Sacrifice. [36]

In the 1974 order the term "offer" was not utilized, nor was the eternal sacrifice pleaded. It would appear that Series 3 stimulated the use of "celebrate" which was used in both texts. In place of "eternal sacrifice", "perfect sacrifice" was used as in Series 3. J. M. Todd has explained:

> We have preferred "perfect sacrifice" to "eternal sacrifice" used in the Book of Common Order ("pleading his eternal sacrifice") as being more scriptural and, we venture to think, theologically more defensible. Christ offered a perfect sacrifice on the Cross once for all: that is what we celebrate. It has eternal significance; but it is more accurately described as a "perfect" than as an "eternal" sacrifice. [37]

In the Trad. text the anamnesis included

> we set before thee this bread and wine as the thank-offering of thy people.

This formula occurs in Eucharistic Prayer I of the 1970 order, and in Eucharistic Prayer "A" in **Contemporary Prayers for Public Worship.** To set the bread and wine before God as a thank-offering is in fact to offer him the bread and cup.

The Mod. text was less specific; by what is done, the perfect sacrifice is celebrated; later the text stated that we eat and drink at his command; but the action was not formally offered to God. However, according to Todd:

> Whether we speak of setting bread and wine before God as our thank-offering or of eating and drinking at his command--and of course we do both--we are expressing our sharing in that sacrificial action by which we are united to Christ in his perfect self-offering to the Father. [38]

Both texts followed Series 3 in offering the "sacrifice of praise", though in both the phrase is separated from the anamnesis by the epiklesis. Todd has explained the meaning of this phrase as:

> our recalling before him with thanksgiving and joy the once-for-all sacrifice of Christ which can never be repeated but which continually prevails to take away sin, to make us and all things new and to reconcile the world to God. [**39**]

Since this recalling includes the setting apart of bread and wine, these are included in the sacrifice of praise.

The emphasis of the epiklesis differs in the two texts. The Trad. text, following Prayers III and IV of 1970, and not too dissimilar from that in 1968, prayed for sanctification of the elements and the communicants, "that they (the bread and wine) may be for us the body and blood of Christ". The Mod. text, as in Prayer II of 1970, simply prayed "through the Holy Spirit"; petition for the sanctification of the elements or of the people was not specified, but rather that through the Spirit a true communion might be had. Both Eucharistic Prayers ended with a Doxology.

The Lord's Prayer could follow the Eucharistic Prayer, though it could also be used earlier in the rite, before the Lections. The Mod. text provided the ICET version as altered by the General Synod of the Church of England for Series 3. Since the members of JLG did not wish to have more than one modern text of the Lord's Prayer in use in England i.e., the original ICET version and Series 3 version, it recommended that the form adopted in Series 3 should be adopted by member Churches, and this recommendation has been followed in this rite. [**40**]

At the fraction the Words of Institution, with directions for taking the bread and the cup, could be used, as in the Congregational orders of 1951 and 1959, and the Presbyterian book, or, as in the 1970 order, words from 1 Cor. 10:16 may be used. In the January 1973 Draft a fuller version of 1 Cor. 10:16 had been given, but some felt that it was a difficult passage to digest, and suggested modifications. [**41**] The use of 1 Cor. 10:16 gives rather less emphasis to the fraction than the elaborate taking with the recital of the Institution Narrative, and suggests that the JLG observation on the theological significance of the fraction has been noted.

The two sets of words of administration were taken from the 1968 order and the third set of the 1970 order. The notes suggested that the bread and wine should be passed through the congregation so that each person serves his neighbor.

The Post-communion closely resembled that found in the Anglican Series 3, being a short thanksgiving with self-oblation and prayer for service in the world. The notes at the beginning of the rite allow for congregational acclamations to precede or follow the Post-communion prayer:

> Christ has died
> Christ is risen,
> In Christ shall all be made alive.
>
> Blessing and honour and glory and power
> be to our God for ever and ever. Amen.

Congregational acclamations are a feature found in many of the Eastern anaphoras, coming after the Institution Narrative as a response to "Do this in remembrance of me", introducing the anamnesis of the anaphora. Acclamations of this kind have been incorporated into the 1970 Roman Catholic Mass, Series 3 and the Methodist **Sunday Service**, and the United Reformed Church seems to have borrowed these particular acclamations from the draft order of Series 3. However, since the Eucharistic Prayers of the 1974 order did not contain the Institution Narrative, it was impossible for them to occur in their traditional place. The committee suggested therefore that this "congregational anamnesis" might come after the actual act of communion. As in the 1970 order, the service ended with a hymn or doxology, and a short dismissal and blessing.

Although the 1974 order is based upon the ecumenical outline of JLG, in some instances it appears to be far more conservative and less ecumenical than the 1970 Congregational order. This is especially so in the treatment of the Eucharistic Prayer. There seems to have been a conscious effort to retain and promote the traditional Reformed position of the Institution Narrative as a warrant before the Prayer. There also seems to have been a rather fundamentalist approach to the JLG description of the Eucharistic Prayer as thanksgiving, anamnesis and epiklesis, resulting in "West-Syrian" patterned prayers. It should be noted that a different structure exists in the East Syrian, Egyptian, Roman, Gallican and Mozarabic rites, and there is no reason to exclude the neo-Genevan Prayers of the 1948 **Book of Public Worship**, nor the experimental type found in the 1970 order. The Western tradition was well represented in the experimental Prayers V and VI of 1970, and the Taizé Eucharist provides an example of a Reformed Roman **Canon Missae**. The bold approach of the Congregational Worship Committee seems to have been abandoned in this 1974 order. However, in fairness it must be stated, the compilers had the task of not only preserving the gains made in the 1970 Congregational order, but also of up-dating the more conservative Presbyterian rite; this latter task had restricted any bold experimentation.

The 1973 General Assembly of the United Reformed

Church authorized, in addition to a Service Book, the production of a Hymn Book Supplement. [42] This latter was to include traditional hymns not found in **Congregational Praise** or the **Church Hymnary** (3rd edition), hymns found in other supplements which were becoming popular in the two uniting denominations, and new material. As well as hymns, it was to provide canticles and a musical setting for some parts of the Eucharistic liturgy. The supplement, entitled **New Church Praise,** was to be prepared for May 1975. As well as hymns, the new supplement contained an order for the Eucharist. Entitled Order of Worship for the Lord's Supper, the rite was basically that of the Mod. text of the 1974 **Book of Order for Worship,** though with some variations. Here we give the outline noting new material:

Call to Worship
Scriptural Sentences, as versicles and responses (2nd and 3rd of 1974 "General" sentences).
Prayer of Approach - Series 3 Collect for Purity as well as the modern prayer of 1974
Hymn or Psalm
Confession of Sin
Assurance of Pardon (both 1974 versions)
NEW- The Kyries (threefold) may be said
Gloria in excelsis
Prayer for Grace (Collect) here or after the sermon
(Omission of the Lord's Prayer)
O.T. and/or N.T. Reading
Psalm, Canticle, Hymn or Anthem
N.T. Reading, or Epistle and Gospel
Hymn
Sermon
Hymn
Prayers for the Church and the World

The Invitation and gracious Words
NEW- The Peace, with congregational response, "Peace be with you"
Offertory
Offertory Prayer
Hymn
Institution Narrative
The Taking of the Bread and Wine
The Thanksgiving
Lord's Prayer
Fraction
Administration
NEW- Acclamation
Prayer after Communion
Hymn or Doxology
Dismissal and Blessing

The wording of rubrics was slightly altered, and the Acclamations were now placed within the text of the order of service. Musical settings for the Gloria in excelsis, Sanctus and Benedictus, and the Acclamations by Dr. Erik Routley were provided in the supplement.

It will be recalled that in May 1973 the General Assembly had instructed the Doctrine and Worship Committee to prepare material for inclusion in the service book, and "to consider the preparation of services for congregational use". [43] Todd took this to imply a book which members of the congregation would have in their hands. [44] The problem here is that Congregationalists and Presbyterians have not been accustomed to having a liturgy in their hands, for this would imply uniformity and rigidity in liturgy. The only book the congregation has had has been a hymn book. Since this 1975 rite appears in a hymn book which by its nature is designed to be in the hands of the congregation, it goes some way to meeting the request of the General Assembly for a service for congregational use.

In 1980 this Eucharistic rite was incorporated with other services into **A Book of Services.** This book, which provides a liturgical norm for the denomination, presents the Eucharist as the normal pattern of Sunday worship. The modern rite, as contained in the 1975 **New Church Praise** was reproduced with very few alterations. The most notable innovation, which makes the rite both modern and ecumenical, was the inclusion of two additional Eucharistic Prayers. The first of these was the Eucharistic Prayer of the JLG published in 1978, and based in part on the Te Deum. [45] The other prayer was from the Table Prayers of the Dutch Roman Catholic Priest and Poet, Huub Oosterhuis. [46]

This United Reformed Church Eucharistic order, reaching its definitive form in **A Book of Services** 1980, is the first Eucharistic liturgy compiled jointly by English Congregationalists and Presbyterians since the **Westminster Directory** of 1645. We conclude our consideration of this rite with the words of its chief architect, the late J. M. Todd:

> We don't regard this order as a final form; nor do we intend that it should be followed slavishly or used invariably. We prize the heritage of liberty into which we have entered. We believe it to be an abiding principle of Reformed Church worship that the minister should never be so confined to any form of prayer that he is not at liberty to follow the leading of the Holy Spirit. But we hope that our worship will always be orderly and in obedience to the Gospel. There are dangers in freedom; there are dangers in fixity of form too. What

we have tried to do is to provide our Church with the text of a service which does justice to the traditions which we have inherited, which takes into account the new liturgical insights by which all branches of the Church are being enriched, and which will enable our congregations to worship God in freedom, with confidence and with joy. [**47**]

NOTES

1. Quoted in R. Tudur Jones, op.cit., 433.

2. The United Reformed Church, General Assembly 1973, Reports to Assembly, 25.

3. The Congregational Church in England and Wales, **About Worship**, 1971; Presbyterian Church of England, **Symposium on Worship**, 1971.

4. N. Leak, "Recent Developments in Public Worship and Aids to Devotion - Presbyterian Church of England", in LR 3 (1973), 26-31, p. 26.

5. The Joint Liturgical Group, **Initiation and Eucharist**, London, 1972, 25.

6. Supra, Chapter 10.

7. **Initiation and Eucharist**, 27.

8. Ibid., 30-31.

9. J. M. Todd, "Tradition and Change: Worship in the United Reformed Church", 7-8.

10. Outlook, January-February 1972, 8, and April 1972, 22-23. I am grateful to Charles Cranfield for drawing my attention to this.

11. Outlook, April 1972, 23.

12. Ibid.

13. J. M. Todd, art.cit., 8.

14. Minutes of URC Committee on Doctrine and Worship, 9th-11th January 1973, 14th June 1973.

15. Minutes of URC Committee on Doctrine and Worship, 9th-11th January 1973; letter to all members of the URC Doctrine and Worship Committee, from J. M. Todd, 24th April 1973.

16. Art.cit.

17. Letter to all members of the URC Doctrine and Worship Committee, 24th April 1973.

18. S. Gibbons, "Thee/you we praise", in Reform, June 1974, 21-22, p. 22. This was also the criticism of Stephen Winward, Letter to all members of the URC Doctrine and Worship Committee, 24th April 1973.

19. J. M. Todd, art.cit., 13-14.

20. **Initiation and Eucharist**, 25.

21. Ibid.

22. Church of England Liturgical Commission, **A Commentary on Holy Communion Series 3**, London 1971, 21.

23. G. J. Cuming, "Series 3 and 1662. A Structural Comparison" in ed. R. C. D. Jasper, **The Eucharist Today**, London 1974, 40-41.

24. R. T. Beckworth and J. E. Tiller, **The Service of Holy Communion and its Revision**, Abingdon 1972, 55-56.

25. Letter to all members of the URC Doctrine and Worship Committee, 24th April 1973.

26. S. Gibbons, art.cit., 22.

27. J. M. Todd, art.cit., 13.

28. Reports to Assembly (1973) 24.

29. J. M. Todd, art.cit., 13.

30. The absence of the narrative has a precedent in **Addai and Mari.** For other Churches adopting the Reformed tradition, see the Anglican Church of Chile, Experimental rite 1967, in C. O. Buchanan, **Modern Anglican Liturgies 1958-1968;** D. D. Billings, **Alternative Eucharistic Prayers** (Grove Booklet on Ministry and Worship, No. 16), Bramcote 1973. The Institution Narrative appears in the Eucharistic Prayer in the 1972 order of the Church of Scotland; George M. Henderson, "Brief Comments on **The Divine Service 1972**", in LR 4:1 (1974), 14-15.

31. Letter to all members of URC Doctrine and Worship Committee, 24th April 1973; Todd, art.cit., 13.

32. Apparently also found in the Church of Scotland **Divine Service** 1972, J. W. Frazer, "The Revised Orders of Holy Communion: Comparison and Comments" in LR 5:1 (1975) 41-48.

33. J. M. Todd, art.cit., 14.

34. **The Scheme of Union,** 23, par. 15. Joint Committee for Conversations between the Congregational Church in England and Wales and the Presbyterian Church of England.

35. For further discussion see, ed. R. C. D. Jasper, **The Eucharist Today.**

36. It has been pointed out above that it would be wrong to deduce that a particular doctrine of Eucharistic Sacrifice was implied.

37. J. M. Todd, art.cit., 14.

38. Ibid., 15.

39. Ibid.

40. Ibid., 15-16.

41. Letter to all members of the URC Doctrine and Worship Committee, 24th April 1973.

42. URC General Assembly 1973. Reports to Assembly, 23-24.

43. Ibid., 25.

44. J. M. Todd, art.cit., 7.

45. The Joint Liturgical Group, **The Daily Office Revised with other Prayers and Services,** London 1978, 11-13.

46. For a full discussion of the work of Oosterhuis, see John Barry Ryan, **The Eucharistic Prayer. A Study in Contemporary Liturgy,** New York 1974, Chapter 4; "Eucharistic Prayers for Contemporary Men and Women", Studia Liturgica 11 (1976), 186-206.

47. J. M. Todd, art.cit., 17-18. His words were written about the 1974 rite; he did not live to see the 1980 definitive text.

Chapter Fourteen

CONCLUDING OBSERVATIONS AND REMARKS

The primary task of this study has been to consider in some detail the Eucharistic liturgy in the English Independent Tradition as far as it can be discerned from printed rites produced for or by the denomination in the period 1645-1980. It is in fact a story of the tension between the demand for freedom in worship, and the search for an order that will keep that freedom in the faith without stifling it. The study has attempted to illustrate that there is an English Independent liturgical tradition. It is important that this tradition, as it continues either in the United Reformed Church, or in the Congregational Federation, accepts this tradition as its own. It is an over-simplification and a factual error to identify the Independent or Congregational tradition exclusively with the Separatists' insistence on free prayer and simple worship. The Separatist tradition is no more fully representative of Congregationalism than is the Eucharist of Dr. Orchard--yet both do belong to the tradition. The tradition has its roots in the Genevan rite, the Dutch Reformed rite, and the Anglican rite. Its first identifiable rite is the joint venture with the Presbyterians--the **Westminster Directory**. With the exception of the period 1658-1800, there has been a wide variety of Eucharistic rites used in the denomination.

As in the case of nearly all Western Churches, the influence of the Liturgical and Ecumenical Movements has resulted in the abandoning of much of the earlier tradition. This is nothing to lament; although Patristic fundamentalism is as bad as Reformation fundamentalism, it is right that where liturgical scholarship and theology demand it, denominational traditions should give way to catholic forms of worship. There is no virtue in perpetuating a "Separatist" or Genevan or Hunter pattern of worship, for this is pure liturgical archaism.

Other Churches have something to learn from the Independent Eucharistic tradition. The diversity of usage--even though not all usages are desirable--have much to teach the more traditional liturgical Churches where a single uniform Eucharistic rite has had to serve for house communions as well as more solemn types of celebration. It is surely significant that the "free" nature of the Separatist rites came into being in house churches. The provision of a liturgy with a basic structure serving as a directory is one which other Churches are slowly, and not without opposition, beginning to recognize as desirable. [1] Other Churches may also learn from the less desirable aspects of Congregational liturgical history. Mere copying from other sources--especially without careful scrutiny and criticism--does not generally produce a good living liturgy. Furthermore, for those who demand a liturgy which is "modern" and in harmony with modern culture, [2] the 1936 **A Manual for Ministers** serves as a somber warning; liturgical expression of passing dubious theology must be embarked upon with extreme caution.

The WCC **One Baptism, One Eucharist and a Mutually Recognized Ministry**, 1975, stated:

> The liturgical reform movement has brought the churches closer together in the manner of celebrating the Lord's Supper. However, liturgical diversity compatible with our common eucharistic faith should be recognized as a healthy and enriching fact. [3]

The question arises here as to the extent and definition of diversity. The Anglican Series 3 (and now Rite A), the Roman Catholic Mass, the Methodist **Sunday Service** and the United Reformed Church rites all have a great similarity, and yet at the same time show a diversity. The same cannot be said for the 1570 Missal, the rite in the 1662 Book of Common Prayer, and the rites of John Hunter. In the light of modern liturgical scholarship these latter are defective in terms of their plethora of late tradition which determines the shape (or lack of shape!) and content of the rite. It would be legitimate to conclude that where the old rites still persist, there unity is being consciously or unconsciously avoided; denominational traditions are given preference to an important step towards Christian unity. Perhaps one of the greatest problems of the United Reformed Church is how to make the 1974/1980 rite the normal rite of the denomination, not only officially, <u>but in reality</u>. The experience of the present writer is that local tradition is continued, and the recommended pattern of worship is ignored.

All the more recent rites of the Congregational tradition have stressed the unity of Word and Sacrament. However, the United Reformed custom of a monthly, or bi-monthly communion means that on most Sundays this unity is broken. The WCC Uppsala report on worship 1968 stated:

> We urge (a) that all Churches consider seriously the desirability of adopting the early Christian tradition of celebrating the Eucharist every Sunday; . . . [4]

This was repeated in **One Baptism, One Eucharist and a Mutually Recognized Ministry.** [5] In the papers of the Worship sub-committee of the Congregational Church, 1971, Stuart Gibbons read a paper pointing out that the weekly worship of the early Church was almost certainly the Eucharist. The Introduction to these papers noted:

> This may well be the hardest part of the Uppsala report for most Congregationalists to face squarely. For it asks them to think about something outside their long tradition of monthly Communion. We hope Churches will face it, however, if only because so many of our fellow Christians take it for granted that normal Sunday worship will be Eucharistic. [6]

For "Congregationalists" we can substitute "United Reformed Churchmen".

NOTES

1. See **The Book of Common Prayer of the Protestant Episcopal Church of the USA,** 1977.

2. E.g., J. L. Houlden, "Liturgy and her Companions: A Theological Appraisal", in **The Eucharist Today,** 168-176.

3. **One Baptism, One Eucharist and a Mutually Recognized Ministry,** Geneva 1975, para. 29, p. 27.

4. **Uppsala 68 Speaks,** 82.

5. Op.cit., para. 33, p. 27.

6. **About Worship,** 3.

APPENDIX

The themes of the Prayer after the Sermon of Petrus Datheen, and the Public Prayer before the Sermon in the **Directory**.

DATHEEN	THE DIRECTORY
1. We acknowledge and confess that we are not worthy to lift up our eyes to heaven . . . our sins witness against us.	1. To acknowledge our great Sinfulnesse . . . Original sin . . . Actual sins . . . we having broken all the commandments.
2. But . . . you have ordered us to invoke you in all distress . . . for the merit of our Lord Jesus Christ.	2. To bewaile our blindnesse of mind, hardness of heart, unbelief.
3. Besides the innumerable benefits . . . you have given us grace . . . we have deviated . . . we are guilty . . . we have sinned grievously.	3. To acknowledge and confess . . . we judge ourselves unworthy.
4. But . . . you are our God . . . maintain rather that work that you began in us by your mercy. (Like Israel) we have the covenant which you established in the hand of Jesus Christ our Mediator . . . a perfect sacrifice on the cross . . . look at the face of your anointed, and not at our sins, so that your wrath may be quenched by his Intercession.	4. Notwithstanding all of which, to draw near to the throne of grace . . . in the riches of that only one oblation, the satisfaction and intercession of the Lord Jesus Christ . . . through the same Mediator . . . supplicate for mercy.
5. . . . govern us with your Holy Spirit . . . renew us to a better life and bring forth in us true fruits of faith.	5. The Lord . . . vouchsafe to shed abroad his love in our hearts by the Holy Ghost . . . Pardon and reconciliation.
	6. with remission of sins through the blood of Christ, to pray for sanctification by his Spirit.

DATHEEN

6. . . . the doctrine of your holy Gospel, that it may be proclaimed and received . . . that the ignorant be turned.

7. send faithfull servants into your Harvest . . . Destroy false teachers.

8. all Christian congregations.

9. For the secular government, Roman Emperor, the King, and all other Kings and monarchs and Lords.

10. All who suffer persecution from the Pope or the Turk.

11. those in poverty, imprisonment, illness of body or temptation of the Spirit.

12. For protection and guidance. For strength against Temptation.

THE DIRECTORY

7. To pray for the propagation of the Gospel and kingdom of Christ . . . Jews . . . the fall of Antichrist . . . distressed churches abroad . . . cruel oppressions and blasphemies of the Turk.

8. To pray for all in authority . . . the Kings Majesty . . . Queen . . . Prince . . . Pastors and Teachers . . . Universities . . . the City . . . Congregation . . . averting the judgements . . . as famine pestilence the sword.

9. For Fellowship with God, and Grace; reverent use of the Ordinances.

10. For the Spirit of Grace . . . enjoy the fulness of those joys and pleasures which are at his right hand for evermore.

11. For the Minister . . . for his sermon . . . that those who hear may receive the word.

BIBLIOGRAPHY

UNPUBLISHED

The Seconde Parte of a Register, Morrice Collection A, B, C, Dr. William's Library.

Ms. Minutes of the Sessions of the Westminster Assembly of Divines by Adoniram Byfield, Dr. William's Library. Transcript of the original, Vol. 3.

Fetter Lane Independent Church. Church Book, c. 1782-1820. Dr. William's Library Ms.38.46.

Copy of the Church Book belonging to the Congregational Church at Denton, 1725-89 (made by Joseph Davey) Dr. William's Library Ms.76.17.

Copy of the records of the Congregational Church worshipping at the Quay Meeting, Woodbridge, 1651-1851 (made by Joseph Davey) Dr. William's Library Ms.76.5.

Dr. William's Library Ms. 209 (King's Weigh House Church):
Scrap Book 1905-1917.
Church Minutes 1916-1926.
Church Committee Meetings 1915-1925.

Congregational Union of England and Wales. Liturgical Group Minutes.
Liturgical Committee Minutes.

United Reformed Church Doctrine and Worship Committee. Minutes.

S. Gibbons, The Eucharistic Prayer (Cyclostyled)
Christian Worship as the Primary Expression of Christian Obedience (Cyclostyled)
Type-written Eucharistic Prayers.

M. T. Shepherd, Summary of the Comments from the Churches on the Liturgical Report. Cyclostyled).

Four Draft orders of the Liturgical Group, Congregational Church in England and Wales.

Letter to all members of the URC Doctrine and Worship Committee, 24th April 1973.

Note to members of the URC Doctrine and Worship Committee on the text of the Lord's Prayer.

January 1973 Draft of **Book of Order for Worship.**

Correspondence and taped interview with the Rev. John Phillips, Chairman of the Committee responsible for **A Manual for Ministers** 1936.

Correspondence with: The Revs. J. M. Todd, S. Gibbons, C. Micklem, Dr. J. K. Gregory, Dr. Erik Routley, W. S. Evans, W. E. C. Sewell, A. C. White, and Mrs. P. M. Clark.

J. K. Gregory, "The Understanding of the Lord's Supper among English Congregationalists 1850-1950", D.Phil. Thesis, University of Oxford, 1956.

E. P. Winter, "The Theory and Practice of the Lord's Supper, Among the Early Separatists, Independents and Baptists, From A.D. 1580 to A.D. 1700", B.Litt. Thesis, University of Oxford, 1953.

B. D. Spinks, "The Impact of the Liturgical Movement on Eucharistic Liturgy of the Congregational Church in England and Wales", Dissertation as part requirement of the M.Th., University of London, 1972.

PUBLISHED WORKS

Anonymous: **Account of the Doctrine and Discipline of Mr. Richard Davies of Rothwell in the County of Northampton, and those of his separation.** London, 1700.

A Biblical Service of Prayer for the House of the Lord, n.d., n.p.

The Book of Common Prayer Adapted for the Use of the Congregational Church Finchley Common. London, 1864.

The Book of Common Prayer and Administration of Baptism and the Lord's Supper, with other Services Prepared for use in the Evangelical Churches by ministers and members of the Established and Nonconformist Churches. London, 1867.

The Common Prayer-Book unmasked. London, 1660.

The Congregational Service Book. A Form of Public Worship designed for the use of the Independent and Other Nonconformist Bodies in Great Britain. London, 1847.

Forms Submitted for the use of Nonconformist Churches. London, 1870.

Liturgies for Divine Worship. London, 1879.

A Parte of a Register, Middleburg, 1593.

Public Prayer by an Independent Minister, London, 1869.

A Supply of Prayers for Ships of this Kingdom that want Ministers to pray with them: Agreeable to the Directory Established by Parliament. London, 1645.

R. Abba, **Principles of Christian Worship.** Oxford: Oxford University Press, 1957.

G. W. O. Addleshaw, **The High Church Tradition.** London: Faber and Faber, 1941.

William Ames, **The Marrow of Sacred Divinity,** London, 1642.
Conscience with the Power and Cases Thereof. Divided into 5 Books. London, 1643.

K. C. Anderson, **The New Theology.** London: Stockwell, 1907.

E. Arber, (ed.) **A Brief Discourse of the Troubles at Frankfort, 1554-1558 A.D.** London: E. Stock, 1908.

C. W. Baird, **A Chapter on Liturgies: Historical Sketches, with an Introduction and Appendix by Thomas Binney.** London, 1856.

J. M. Barkley, **The Worship of the Reformed Church.** London: Lutterworth Press, 1966.

J. G. Baum, (ed.) **La Manière et fasson** (G. Farel), Strasbourg, 1859.

R. Baxter, **Five Disputations of the Church Government and Worship.** London, 1659.

L. Bouyer, **Life and Liturgy.** ET London: Sheed and Ward, 1956.

W. Bradshawe, **English Puritanism,** London, 1605.

Y. Brilioth, **Eucharistic Faith and Practice Evangelical and Catholic,** ET A. G. Hebert, London: S.P.C.K., 1930.

C. O. Buchanan, **The New Communion Service--Reasons for Dissent,** London: Church Book Room Press, 1966.
Modern Anglican Liturgies 1958-1968, Oxford: Oxford University Press, 1968.
Further Anglican Liturgies 1968-1975, Bramcote: Grove Books, 1975.

L. Buchsenschutz, **Histoire des liturgies en langue allemande dans l'église de Strasbourg au XVI siécle,** Cahors, 1900.

R. Buick Knox, **Little Baddow United Reformed Church.** A History, n.p., 1976.

H. Bulcock, **Orders of Service for Free Church Use**, Prenton, n.d.
The Modern Churchman at Prayer. Some Orders of Worship, London: Union of Modern Free Churchmen, 1943.
A Re-stated Faith: Positive Values. London: Independent Press, 1934.
A Modern Churchman's Manual. London: Union of Modern Free Churchmen, 1941.

G. B. Burnet, **The Holy Communion in the Reformed Church of Scotland 1560-1960.** Edinburgh: Oliver and Boyd, 1960.

C. J. Cadoux, **Catholicism and Christianity.** London: Allen and Unwin, 1928.
The Case for Evangelical Modernism. London: Hodder and Stoughton, 1938.
The Historic Mission of Jesus. London: Lutterworth Press, 1941.
The Life of Jesus. London: Penguin, 1948.

R. J. Campbell, **The New Theology.** London: Chadman and Hall, 1907.

E. Cardwell, (ed.) **A History of Conferences and other Proceedings.** Oxford, 1841.

Leland H. Carlson, (ed.) **The Writings of John Greenwood 1587-1590.** London: Allen and Unwin, 1962.
The Writings of John Greenwood and Henry Barrow 1591-1593. London: Allen and Unwin, 1970.

S. W. Carruthers, **The Everyday Work of the Westminster Assembly.** Philadelphia: The Presbyterian Historical Societies of America and England, 1943.

S. Cave, **The Gospel of St. Paul,** London: Hodder and Stoughton, 1928.

E. D. Cecil, **Prayer and Praise,** Penge, 1914.

I. Chauncey, **The Divine Institution of Congregational Churches, Ministry and Ordinances.** London, 1697.

Christian Confidence. Theological Collections 14. London: S.P.C.K., 1970.

Church Service Society, **Euchologian.** Edinburgh, 1884.

Church of Scotland, **The Book of Common Order**, Oxford: Oxford University Press, 1940.

P. Collinson, **The Elizabethan Puritan Movement,** London: Cape, 1967.

G. W. Conder, **The Form of Morning and Evening Serice for the use of Free Churches.** Manchester, 1869.

Intelligent and True Worship: A Sermon Preached in the Congregational Church, Cheetham Hill, August 22nd. 1869. Preparatory to the Introduction of a Liturgical Service. Manchester, 1869.

Congregational Church in England and Wales, **An Order of Public Worship,** Oxford: Oxford University Press, 1970.

About Worship, n.p., 1971.

Congregational Union of England and Wales, **Conduct of Public Worship,** Congregational Union Tract Series, No. XIV. London, 1845.

Book of Congregational Worship, Edinburgh: Independent Press, 1920.

A Manual for Ministers. London: Independent Press, 1936.

A Book of Services and Prayers. London: Independent Press, 1959.

A Book of Services and Prayers. London: Independent Press, 1969.

Liturgical Group Report. n.p., 1965.

S. Cradock, **Knowledge and Practice together with the Supplement.** London, 1702.

G. J. Cumin, **A History of Anglican Liturgy.** London: Macmillan, 1969, [**1**] 1982 [**2**].

The Durham Book. Oxford: Durham University Publications, Oxford University Press, 1961.

R. W. Dale, **History of English Congregationalism.** edited and completed by A. W. W. Dale, London: Hodder and Stoughton, 1907.

W. F. Dankbaar, (ed.) **Marten Micron, De Christlicke Ordinancien der Nederlantscher Ghemeinten te Londen (1554).** Kerkhistorische Studien Deel VII. 's-Gravenhage: Martinus Nijhoff, 1956.

H. Davies, **The Worship of the English Puritans.** London: Dacre, 1948.

Worship and Theology in England 1850–1900. Princeton: Princeton University Press, 1962.

Worship and Theology in England 1900–1965. Princeton: Princeton University Press, 1962.

W. D. Davies, **Paul and Rabbinic Judaism.** London: S.P.C.K., 1948.

C. H. Davis, **Orders of Service for the Solemnization of Matrimony, The Baptism of Infants, The Burial of the Dead and The Ordinance of the Lord's Supper.** Isle of Wight, 1909.

F. W. Dillistone, **C. H. Dodd, Interpreter of the New Testament.** London: Hodder and Stoughton, 1977.

G. Dix, **The Apostolic Tradition.** London: S.P.C.K., 1937.
The Shape of the Liturgy. London: Dacre, 1945.

P. Doddridge, **The Correspondence and Diary of Philip Doddridge D.D.** ed. T. D. Humphreys, 5 Vols., London, 1831.

G. Donaldson, **The Making of the Scottish Prayer Book of 1637.** Edinburgh: Edinburgh University Press, 1954.

B. H. Draper, **Solemn Recollections, Before, At and After, the Celebration of the Lord's Supper.** Southampton, 1825.

R. Dunkerley, (ed.) **The Ministry and the Sacraments.** London: SCM, 1937.

Eden and Gethsemane. Addresses for Communion Services. Manchester: J. Robinson, 1903.

Hastings Eells, **Martin Bucer.** New Haven: Yale University Press, 1931.

T. J. Fawcett, (ed.) **The Liturgy of Comprehension, 1689.** AC Southend-on-Sea: Mayhew-McCrimmon, 1973.

C. H. Firth and R. S. Rait, (eds.) **Acts and Ordinances of the Interregnum 1642-1660.** 3 Vols., London: For the Statute Law Committee, 1911.

P. T. Forsyth, **The Church and the Sacraments.** London: Longmans, 1917.

French Protestant Industrial Mission, **Sunday Service of the French Reformed Church.** Translated by the British Committee of the French Protestant Industrial Mission, n.d., n.p.

W. H. Frere and C. E. Douglas, (eds.) **Puritan Manifestoes.** London: S.P.C.K., 1907.

A. E. Garvie, **Studies in the Inner Life of Jesus.** London: Hodder and Stoughton, 1907.
Studies of Paul and his Gospel. London: Hodder and Stoughton, 1911.
The Holy Catholic Church from the Congregational Point of View. London: Faith Press, 1920.

H. Gee and W. J. Hardy, **Documents illustrative of English Church History.** London, 1896.

J. F. Gerrard, **Notable Editions of the Prayer Book.** Wigan: Starr, 1949.

George Gillespie, **Notes of Debates and Proceedings of the Assembly of Divines and other Commissioners at Westminster, February 1644 to January 1645.** ed. D. Meek, 1846.

W. B. Glover, **Evangelical Nonconformists and Higher Criticism in the Nineteenth Century.** London: Independent Press, 1954.

T. Goodwin, et al., **An Apologeticall Naration.** London, 1643.

J. W. Grant, **Free Churchmanship in England 1870–1940.** London: Independent Press, (1955).

W. Jardine Grisbrooke, **Anglican Liturgies of the Seventeenth and Eighteenth Centuries,** AC London: S.P.C.K., 1958.

B. Gustafsson, **The Five Dissenting Brethren.** Lund: Gleerup, 1955.

H. D. M. A., **A Sober and Temperate Discourse Concerning the Interests of words in Prayer.** London, 1661.

Basil Hall, **John à Lasco 1499–1560. A Pole in Reformation England.** London: Dr. Williams's Trust, 1971.

C. Newman Hall, **Free Church Service Book.** London, 1867.
Newman Hall. An Autobiography. London, 1898.

R. Halley, **Lancashire: Its Puritanism and Nonconformity.** Second edition, London, 1872.
The Sacraments. Second edition, 2 Vols., London, 1844 and 1851.

Henry Hammond, **A View of the New Directory, and a Vindication of the Ancient Liturgie of the Church of England.** Oxford, 1646.

M. L. Harper, **The Communion Service.** London: Independent Press, 1926.

W. Harris, **The Nature of the Lord's Supper, and the Obligations to it, briefly consider'd; with a serious Exhortation to a due Attendance upon it: in four discourses preach'd at the Merchants Lecture at Salters-Hall, November and December, 1736.** London, 1737.

M. Henry, **The Communicant's Companion.** London, 1704.

J. H. Hexter, **Reappraisals in History.** London: Longmans, 1961.

C. Hill and E. Dell, **The Good Old Cause: the English Revolution of 1640–60: its causes, course and consequence.** Oxford: Lawrence and Wishart, 1950.

C. Hill, **Society and Puritanism in Pre-Revolutionary England.** London: Panther, 1969.

A. J. B. Higgins, **The Lord's Supper in the New Testament.** London: SCM, 1952.

E. Brooks Holified, **The Covenant Sealed: The Development of Puritan Sacramental Theology in Old and New England, 1570-1720.** New Haven and London: Yale University Press, 1974.

A. C. Honders, (ed.) **Valerandus Pollanus Liturgia Sacra (1551-1555).** Kerkhistorische Bijdragen 1, Leiden: E. J. Brill, 1970.

E. Paxton Hood, **Thomas Binney: His Mind, Life and Opinions.** London, 1874.

J. P. Hopps, **Prayers for Private Meditation and the Home.** Second edition. London, 1866.

C. S. Horne and T. H. Darlow, **Let us Pray.** Second edition. London, 1897.

R. F. Horton, **The Teaching of Jesus.** London, 1895.
The Growth of the New Testament. London: Congregational Union, 1913.

T. D. Humphreys, (ed.) **The Correspondence and Diary of Philip Doddridge D.D.** 5 Vols., London, 1831.

J. Hunter, **Devotional Services for Public Worship.** 3rd edition, Glasgow, 1886.
4th edition, Glasgow, 1890.
5th edition Glasgow, 1892.
6th edition, Glasgow, 1895.
7th edition Glasgow: Maclehose, 1901.
8th edition, (impression of 7th edition) London: Dent, 1903.
The Coming Church. London: Williams and Norgate, 1905.
A Plea for a Worshippful Church. London: Dent, 1903.

L. S. Hunter, **John Hunter D.D. A Life.** London: Hodder and Stoughton, 1921.

W. John F. Huxtable, et al., **A Book of Public Worship.** Oxford: Oxford University Press, 1948.

W. Huycke, **Geneva: The Forme of common praiers used in the churches of Geneva: The mynystracion of the sacramentes, of Baptisme and the Lordes supper: The vysitacion of the sycke: And the Catechisme of Geneva: made by master John Calvyne. In the ende are certaine other Godly prayers privately to be used: translated out of frenche into Englyshe.** London, 1550.

A. T. S. James, **A Cotswold Minister.** London: Independent Press, 1945.

R. C. D. Jasper, **Prayer Book Revision in England 1800-1900.** London: S.P.C.K., 1954.

(ed.) **The Renewal of Worship,** Essays by members of the Joint Liturgical Group, London: Oxford University Press.

D. T. Jenkins, **The Nature of Catholicity.** London: Faber, 1942.
Congregationalism: A Restatement. London: Faber, 1954.

Joint Committee for Conversations between the Congregational Church in England and Wales and the Presbyterian Church of England, **The Scheme of Union,** London, 1970.

Joint Liturgical Group, **The Daily Office.** London: S.P.C.K. and Epworth, 1968.
The Calendar and Lectionary. London: Oxford University Press, 1967.
Initiation and Eucharist. London: S.P.C.K., 1972.
The Daily Office Revised. London: S.P.C.K., 1978.

R. Tudur Jones, **Congregationalism in England 1662-1962.** London: Independent Press, 1962.

J. A. Jungmann, **The Mass of the Roman Rite.** 2 Vols., New York: Benziger, 1951-55.

Elaine Kaye, **The History of the King's Weigh House Church.** London: Allen and Unwin, 1968.

A. Kuyper, (ed.) **Joannis à Lasco Opera.** 2 Vols., Amsterdam, 1866.

D. Laing, (ed.) **The Letters and Journals of Robert Baillie A.M.** 3 Vols., Edinburgh, 1841.

The Lambeth Conference 1958. London and Greenwich, Connecticut: S.P.C.K. and Seabury Press, 1958.

F. Lenwood, **Jesus - Lord or Leader?** London: Constable, 1930.

J. Lightfoot, **The Journal of the Proceedings of the Assembly of Divines. From January 1st 1643 to December 31st 1644. And letters to and from Dr. Lightfoot.** ed. J. R. Pitman, **The Whole Works of the Rev. John Lightfoot D.D.** Vol. 13, London, 1824.

J. Lindeboom, **Austin Friars. History of the Dutch Reformed Church in London 1550-1950.** s'Gravenhage: Martin Nijhoff, 1950.

Little Baddow Congregational Church, **A Reformed Order of Service.** 1969.

P. Lorrimer, **John Knox and the Church of England.** London, 1875.

Donald Maclean, **London at Worship: 1689-1690.** Manchester: Aikman, 1928.

B. L. Manning, **Essays in Orthodox Dissent.** London: Independent Press, 1939.

R. Marchant, **The Puritans and the Church Courts in the Diocese of York 1560-1642.** London: Longmanns, 1960.

J. Martineau, **Common Prayer for Christian Worship.** London, 1861.

James Matheson, **Common Prayer without Liturgical Forms.** Address to the Nottinghamshire Association of Independent Ministers and Churches, Nottingham, 1873.

A. G. Matthews, (ed.) **The Savoy Declaration of Faith and Order.** London: Independent Press, 1959.

J. M. Maxwell, **Worship and Reformed Theology.** The Liturgical Lessons of Mercersburg, Pittsburgh, Pennsylvania: The Pickwick Press, 1976.

W. D. Maxwell, **The Liturgical Portions of the Genevan Service Book,** Edinburgh: Oliver and Boyd, 1931; London: Faith Press, 1965.
Concerning Worship, Oxford: Oxford University Press, 1948.

S. Mayor, **The Lord's Supper in Early English Dissent.** London: Epworth Press, 1972.

J. D. McClure, **Devotional Services for use in the Tiger Kloof Native Institution.** Vryburg, 1912.
(?), **Devotional Services for use in Mill Hill School Chapel.** 1895.

W. McMillan, **The Worship of the Scottish Reformed Church, 1550-1638.** London: James Clarke, 1931.

Caryl Micklem, et al., **Contemporary Prayers for Public Worship.** London: SCM, 1967.

E. R. Micklem, **Our Approach to God.** London: Hodder and Stoughton, 1934.

N. Micklem, (ed.) **Christian Worship.** Oxford: Oxford University Press, 1936.

N. Micklem, **What is the Faith?** London: Hodder and Stoughton, 1936.
Congregationalism Today. London: Hodder and Stoughton, 1937.
The Box and the Puppets, London: Bles, 1957.

A. F. Mitchell and J. Struthers, (eds.) **Minutes of the Sessions of the Westminster Assembly of Divines (November 1644 to March 1649),** 1874.

J. Mountain, **The Free Church Prayer Book.** London, 1897.

D. Neal, **A History of the Puritans.** 4 Vols., London, 1732-38.

S. Neill, **The Interpretation of the New Testament 1861-1961.** Oxford: Oxford University Press, 1964.

G. F. Nuttall, **Visible Saints.** Oxford: Blackwell, 1957.
The Holy Spirit in Puritan Faith and Experience. Oxford: Blackwell, 1946.

Richard Baxter. London: Nelson, 1965.

P. Nye, **Beames of Former Light.** London, 1660.

H. O. Old, **The Patristic Roots of Reformed Worship.** Zurich: Theologischer Verlag, 1975.

W. E. Orchard, **The Order of Divine Service.** London and Oxford: Oxford University Press, 1919 and 1926.
Service Book. c. 1911.
Foundations of Faith. 4 Vols., London: Allen and Unwin, 1924-27.
From Faith to Faith. London: Putman, 1933.
The New Catholicism and Other Sermons. London: Allen and Unwin, 1917.
"The Distribution of the Sacrament", c. 1919.

W. Orme, (ed.) **The Practical Works of the Rev. Richard Baxter.** London, 1830.
W. Orme, **The Ordinance of the Lord's Supper Illustrated.** London, 1826.

J. Orton, **Letters to Dissenting Ministers.** ed. S. Palmer, London, 1806, 2 Vols.

K. M. J. Ousey, **McClure of Mill Hill.** London: Hodder and Stoughton, 1927.

T. W. Packer, **The Transformation of Anglicanism 1643-1660.** Manchester: Manchester University Press, 1969.

S. Palmer, **The Nonconformist Catechism.** London, 1773.
A New Directory for Nonconformist Churches. London, 1812.

R. S. Paul, **The Atonement and the Sacraments.** London: Hodder and Stoughton, 1961.

J. S. Pearsall, **Public Worship.** London, 1867.

A. E. Peaston, **The Prayer Book Reform Movement in the XVIII th Century.** Oxford: Blackwell, 1940.
The Prayer Book Tradition in the Free Churches. London: James Clarke, 1964.
The Prayer Book Revisions of the Victorian Evangelicals. Dublin: S.P.C.K., 1963.

A. Peel and L. H. Carlson, (eds.) **The Writings of Robert Harrison and Robert Browne.** London: Allen and Unwin, 1953.

A. Peel, **The First Congregational Churches.** Cambridge: Cambridge University Press, 1920.
These Hundred Years. A History of the Congregational Union of England and Wales 1831-1931. London: Independent Press, 1931.
Christian Freedom. London: Independent Press, 1938.
Inevitable Congregationalism. London: Independent Press, 1937.

A. Peel, (ed.) **The Seconde Parte of a Register.** 2 Vols., Cambridge: Cambridge University Press, 1915.

The Phenix: or a Revival of Scarce and Valuable Pieces From the remotest Antiquity down to the present Times Being a Collection of Manuscripts and Printed Tracts, no where to be found but in the closets of the Curious. 2 Vols., London, 1707, 1708.

F. J. Powicke, **A Life of the Rev. Richard Baxter.** London: J. Cape, 1924.

The Reverend Richard Baxter under the Cross. London: J. Cape, 1927.

Robert Browne Pioneer of Modern Congregationalism. London: Congregational Union, 1910.

Vavasor Powell, **Common-Prayer-Book. No Divine Service.** Second edition, London, 1661.

Presbyterian Church of England, **The Presbyterian Service Book.** London, 1968.

Symposium on Worship. 1971.

Priests of St. Severin and St. Joseph, **What is the Liturgical Movement?** London: Burns and Oates, 1964.

F. Procter and W. H. Frere, **A New History of the Book of Common Prayer.** London: Macmillan, 1901.

J. Pye-Smith, **First Lines of Christian Theology.** Second edition, London, 1861.

M. Ramsey, et al., **The English Prayer Book 1549-1662.** AC London: S.P.C.K., 1966.

L. D. Reed, **The Lutheran Liturgy.** Philadelphia: Fortress, 1947, 1959.

E. Renan, **The Life of Jesus.** ET London, 1864.

Reports in the following CYB: 1917, 1919, 1920, 1935, 1936, 1937, 1938.

The Report of the Commission on the Sacraments of Baptism and the Lord's Supper. 1936, in CYB 1937, 94-119.

H. R. Reynolds, (ed.) **Ecclesia.** London, 1870.

E. Routley, **English Religious Dissent.** Cambridge: Cambridge University Press, 1960.

John Barry Ryan, **The Eucharistic Prayer.** A Study in Contemporary Liturgy. New York: Paulist Press, 1974.

G. H. Russell, **Intercession Services.** Matlock, 1923.

F. R. Salter, **Dissenters and Public Affairs in Mid-Victorian England.** London: Dr. Williams's Trust, 1967.

J. Seeley, **Ecce Homo.** London, 1866.

W. B. Selbie, **Freedom in the Faith.** London: Independent Press, 1944.
The Sacraments. London, 1928.

W. A. Shaw, **A History of the English Church During the Civil Wars and under the Commonwealth 1640-1660.** 2 Vols., London: Longmans, 1900.

Thomas Shephard, **A Treatise of Liturgies, Power of the Keyes, And of matter of the Visible Church.** London, 1653.

Shirley, **The Life and Times of Selina Countess of Huntingdon.** by a member of the Houses of Shirley and Hastings, 2 Vols., 1839.

M. A. Simpson, **John Knox and the Troubles Begun at Frankfurt.** West Linton, Tweedale, 1975.

M. Spencer, **The Social Function of the Church.** London: SCM, 1921.
Living Witnesses. London: Independent Press, 1939.

B. D. Spinks, **Luther's Liturgical Criteria and His Reform of the Canon of the Mass.** Grove Liturgical Study 30, Bramcote: Grove Books, 1982.

Anneliese Sprengler-Ruppenthal, **Mysterium und Riten nach der Londoner Kirchenordnung der Niederlander.** Köln: Bohlau Verlag, 1967.

J. H. Srawley, **The Liturgical Movement.** AC London: Mowbray, 1954.

C. Stirling, **The Protestant Prayer Book.** London, 1894.

John Stoughton, **Reminiscences of Congregationalism Fifty Years Ago.** London, 1881.

D. F. Strauss, **The Life of Jesus.** ET 2 Vols., London, 1879.

M. Sylvester, (ed.) **Reliquiae Baxteriannae.** London, 1696.

D. Thomas, **A Biblical Liturgy.** London, 1855.

Bard Thompson, **Liturgies of the Western Church.** New York: World Publishing Co., 1962.

J. M. Todd, **Prayers and Services for Christian Festivals.** Oxford: Oxford University Press, 1951.

P. Toon, **Hyper-Calvinism.** London: Orange Tree, 1967.
Puritans and Calvinism. Swengel, Pennsylvania: Reiner Publications, 1973.

L. J. Trinterud, **Elizabethan Puritanism.** New York: Oxford University Press, 1971.

E. Troeltsch, **Protestantisches Christentum und Kirche in der Neuzeit.** Die Kultur der Gegenwart, 1:IV,1,2. Halfte, 1922.

E. B. Underhill, **Fenstanton, Warboys and Hexham Records.** London, 1854.

United Reformed Church, General Assembly 1973, **Reports to Assembly.**
Book of Order for Worship. London, 1974.
New Church Praise. 1975.
A Book of Services, Edinburgh: The St. Andrew Press, 1980.

W. Urwick, **Nonconformity in Herts.** London, 1884.
Nonconformity in Worcester. London, 1897.

C. Vagaggini, **The Canon of the Mass and Liturgical Reform.** ET London: Chapman, 1967.

G. J. Van De Poll, **Martin Bucer's Liturgical Ideas.** Assen: Van Gorcum, 1954.

Vatican Council, The Second Ecumenical, **Constitution on the Sacred Liturgy,** 1964.

Richard Vines, **A Treatise of the Right Institution, Administration and Receiving of the Sacrament of the Lord's Supper delivered in XX Sermons at St. Lawrence Jewry.** London, 1657.

G. S. Wakefield, **Puritan Devotion. Its Place in the Development of Christian Piety.** London: Epworth Press, 1957.

W. Walker, **The Creeds and Platforms of Congregationalism.** New York, 1893; Reprint Boston: Pilgrim Press, 1960.

R. S. Wallace, **Calvin's Doctrine of the Word and Sacrament.** Edinburgh: Oliver and Boyd, 1953.

J. Warschauer, **The New Evangel.** London: James Clarke, 1907.

Thomas Watson, **A Body of Divinity** (1692). London: Banner of Truth Trust, 1970.

Isaac Watts, **A Guide to Prayer.** in **The Works of the Rev. Isaac Watts D.D.** 7 Vols., n.d. Vol. 4.

H. Webb, **The Ordinances of Christian Worship.** London, 1873.

Edwin Welch, **Two Calvinist Methodist Chapels 1743–1811.** Leicester: London Record Society, 1975.

J. S. Whale, **What is a Living Church?** London: Edinburgh House Press, 1937.
Christian Doctrine. Cambridge: Cambridge University Press, 1941.
The Protestant Tradition. Cambridge: Cambridge University Press, 1955.
Victor and Victim. Cambridge: Cambridge University Press, 1960.

B. R. White, **The English Separatist Tradition from the Marian Martyrs to the Pilgrim Fathers.** Oxford: Oxford University Press, 1971.

C. E. Whiting, **Studies in English Puritanism.** London: S.P.C.K., 1931.

T. Rhondda Williams, **The New Theology.** Bradford: P. Lund, 1907.

W. Hale White, **The Autobiography of Mark Rutherford.** London, 1881.

World Council of Churches, **Ways of Worship.** ed. P. Edwall, E. Haymen, and W. D. Maxwell, London: SCM, 1951.
Worship and the Oneness of Christ's Church. Report of Section IV of the Montreal Conference 1963.

H. J. Wotherspoon and G. W. Sprott, **The Liturgy of Compromise used in the English Congregations at Frankfort.** Edinburgh: Blackwood, 1905.

F. S. Young, **A Service Book for Use in Bishop's Stortford College.** London, 1925.

G. Yule, **The Independents in the English Civil War.** Cambridge: Cambridge University Press, 1958.

ARTICLES, ESSAYS, ETC.

Anonymous, "An Invitation to Communion" in Evangelical Magazine, N.S. 39 (1861) 862-867.
"Remarks on Ecclesiastical Architecture as applied to Nonconformist Chapels", CYB 1847.
"The Book of Common Prayer", in BQR 47 (1868), 69-128.
"Review of **A Form of Morning and Evening Service, for the use of Free Churches**" in BQR 50 (1869), 591-592.

E. L. Allen, "Adventure in Worship" in CQ 11 (1933), 429-433.

H. Allon, "The Worship of the Church" in **Ecclesia,** London, 1870.

F. H. Ballard, "Public Worship" in CQ 11 (1933), 424-429.

G. S. Barrett, "Congregational Worship" in CYB 1897, 83-89.

J. V. Bartlet, "The Eucharist in the Early Church" in **Mansfield College Essays.** London: Hodder and Stoughton, 1909.

C. O. Buchanan and R. T. Beckwith, "'This bread and this cup': An Evangelical Rejoinder" in Theology 70 (1967), 265-271.

(Bury Street) "From the Bury Street Records" in CHST 6 (1915), 333-342.

P. Collinson, "The Authorship of A Brieff Discours off the Troubles Begonne at Franckford" in JEH 9 (1958), 188-208.
"The Elizabethan Puritans and the Foreign Reformed Churches in London" in Proceedings of the Huguenot Society of London 20 (1958-64), 528-555.

E. R. Conder, "The Lord's Supper" in The Congregationalist 14 (1885), 169-179.
"More Thoughts concerning the Lord's Supper" in The Congregationalist 15 (1886), 128-135.

A. H. Couratin, "The Sanctus and the Pattern of the Early Anaphora: a note on the Roman Sanctus" in JEH 2 (1951), 19-23.
"The Sacrifice of Praise" in Theology 58 (1955), 285-291.
"Thanksgiving and Thankoffering" in SL 3 (1964), 53-57.
"The Tradition Received. 'We Offer this Bread and this Cup': 2" in Theology 69 (1966), 437-442.
"Liturgy" in **The Pelican Guide to Modern Theology.** ed. R. P. C. Hanson, Vol. 2, Harmondsworth: Penguin, 1969.
"The Methodist Sunday Service" in CQR 2 (1969), 31-38.
and the late E. C. Ratcliff, "The Early Roman Canon Missae" in JEH 20 (1969), 211-224.

H. J. Cowell, "Valerand Poullain. A Precursor of Congregationalism?" in CHST 12 (1933-36), 112-119.

T. G. Crippen, "Dr. Watts's Church-Book" in CHST 1 (1901), 26-38.

C. Bernard Crockett, "George Cokayne" in CHST 12 (1933-36), 225-235.

C. J. Cuming, "Two Fragments of a Lost Liturgy" in **Studies in Church History,** Vol. 3, Leiden: E. J. Brill, 1966, 247-253.

R. W. Dale, "A High-Church Scheme of Liturgical Revision" in The Congregationalist 6 (1877), 46-56.
"The Doctrine of the Real Presence and of the Lord's Supper" in ed. H. R. Reynolds, **Ecclesia,** London, 1870.

H. Davies, "Liturgical Reform in Nineteenth Century English Congregationalism" in CHST 17 (1954), 73-82.

C. H. Dodd, "Eucharistic Symbolism in the Fourth Gospel" in The Expositor 1911, 530-546.

J. W. Fraser, "The Revised Orders of Holy Communion: Comparison and Comments" in LR 5:1 (1975), 41-48.

S. Gibbons, "Thee/you we praise" in Reform, June, 1974, 21-22.

T. H. Gill, "Ulrich Zwingli" in The Congregationalist 5 (1876), 321-336.

W. Jardine Grisbrooke, " 'Series II': The new Communion Service of the Church of England examined" in SL 7 (1970), 2-36.

E. Grubb, "The Last Supper" in CQ 8 (1930), 57-63.

H. Hageman, "The Liturgical Origins of the Reformed Churches" in J. H. Bratt (ed.) **The Heritage of John Calvin.** Grand Rapids, Michigan: Eerdmans, 1973.

C. Newman Hall, Devotional Address, CYB 1853, 58.
Address to the Congregational Union, CYB 1867, 11.

George M. Henderson, "Brief Comments on the **Divine Service 1972**" in LR 4:1 (1974), 14-15.

E. G. Herbert, "The Congregational Character" in **Religious Republics.** London, 1867, 60-96.

J. Angell James, "The Sacraments" in Evangelical Magazine N.S. 20 (1842), 215-221.

Ottfried Jordahn, "The Ecumenical Significance of the New Eucharistic Prayers of the Roman Liturgy" in SL 11 (1976), 101-117.

N. Leak, "Recent Developments in Public Worship and Aids to Devotion - Presbyterian Church of England" in LR 3:2 (1973), 26-31.

R. Mackintosh, "The Living Church. Its Sacraments" in A. Peel (ed.), **International Congregational Council. Proceedings of the Fifth Council.** London, 1930.

J. Marsh, "The Eucharist, The Bible and Reform" in The Presbyter 4:2 (1946), 1-10.

A. D. Martin, "The Administration of the Communion Service" in CQ 10 (1932), 73-81.

W. D. Maxwell, Review of **A Book of Public Worship** in The Presbyter 6:4 (1948), 15-18.

J. D. McClure, "The Public Worship of God" in CYB, 1920.

N. Micklem, "The Reformed Worship in Great Britain" in The Presbyter 5:2 (1947), 17-20.

Ministerial Libraries. Dr. John Hunter's Library at the King's Weigh House, in The British Monthly, June 1904, 303-306.

G. F. Nuttall, Review of **A Book of Public Worship** in CQ 26 (1948), 366-367.

W. E. Orchard, The following articles in The King's Weigh House Monthly:
"Our Liturgy", February, 1927.
"The Meaning of the Mass", August, 1928.
"Our Offering of Christ's Sacrifice", December, 1928.
"The Real Presence", August, 1931.

B. M. Peake, "The Reform of Divine Worship" in CQ 11 (1933), 433-437.

E. J. Price, "The Eucharist in History and Experience" in CQ 5 (1927), 135-148.

E. C. Ratcliff, "The Savoy Conference" in G. F. Nuttall and O. Chadwick (eds.) **From Uniformity to Unity.** London: S.P.C.K., 1960.
"Christian Worship and Liturgy" in K. E. Kirk, **The Study of Theology.** London: Hodder and Stoughton, 1939.
"Puritan Alternatives to the Prayer Book" in **The English Prayer Book 1549-1662.** M. Ramsey et al., AC London: S.P.C.K., 1963, 56-81.
"The Sanctus and the Pattern of the Early Anaphora" in JEH 1 (1950), 29-36; 125-134.
"A Note on the Anaphoras described in the Liturgical Homilies of Narsai" in **Biblical and Patristic Studies in memory of Robert Pierce Casey.** eds. J. N. Birdsall and R. W. Thompson, Freiburg: Herder, 1963, 235-249.

J. G. Rogers, "Sacramentalism" in The Congregationalist 13 (1884), 980-989.
"Liturgical Forms" in CYB 1871.

G. H. Russell and C. Bentley Jutson, "Public Worship" in CQ 3 (1925), 456-467.

John Barry Ryan, "Eucharistic Prayers for Contemporary Men and Women" in SL 11 (1976), 186-206.

W. B. Selbie, "Free Church Worship" in CQ 11 (1933), 437-439.

F. Smith, "From Principle to Procedure. A study concerning Modes of Worship" in CQ 8 (1930), 481-484.

B. D. Spinks, "The Supply of Prayer for Ships: a forgotten Puritan Liturgy" in The Journal, United Reformed Church History Society, 1:5 (May, 1975), 139-149.
"A Precursor to Dr. W. E. Orchard's Divine Service?" in The Journal, United Reformed Church History Society, 2:3 (April, 1979), 73-75.
"The Cleansed Leper's Thankoffering Before the Lord: Edward Craddock Ratcliff and the Pattern of the Early Anaphora" in **The Sacrifice of Praise.** Studies on the Themes of Thanksgiving and Redemption in the central prayers of the Eucharistic and Baptismal Liturgies. In Honour of Arthur Hubert Couratin, ed. Bryan D. Spinks, Rome: Edizioni Liturgiche, 1981, 159-178.

J. M. Todd, "Tradition and Change: Worship in the United Reformed Church" in LR 5 (1975), 1-18.

K. W. Wadsworth, "An Eighteenth-Century Country Minister" in CHST 18 (1959), 111-124.

C. E. Watson, "Whitefield and Congregationalism" in CHST 8 (1920-1923), 171-180; 237-245.

Edward White, "The Comprehensive Theory" in CYB 1874.

W. H. Willans, "Attendance at Public Worship" in CYB 1874.

NEWSPAPERS

The English Independent 1867.

The Christian World: H. B. S. K., "A Quiet Communion Service", 25th September, 1890.

Anon., "Sacraments", 13th February, 1908, 10-11.

"At the Weigh House", 8th October, 1914, 9.

E. Shillito, "The Worship of the Free Churches", 13th, 20th and 27th September, 1917.

"Rev. B. Smith of Salem Church, Leeds", 24th September, 1925, 12.

A Re-Statement of Christian Thought. Letters to the editor, 9th February, 1933, 7.

A. E. Garvie, "The Valid Sacraments", 13th February, 1936, 8.

INDEX OF PRINCIPAL LITURGIES DISCUSSED